FIRE BOMBER INTO HELL

A Story of Survival in a Deadly Occupation

Linc W. Alexander

BookLocker.com, Inc.
2010

Also by Linc Alexander

Pilot's Notes for Fire Bombing

Revised – Pilot's Notes for Fire Bombing

Air Attack on Forest Fires

UFOs...Alien Thought Machines

Acknowledgements

Special thanks to Bob Fish, my mentor on this project. Bob is a Trustee for the aircraft carrier USS Hornet Museum in Alameda, CA. He created an exhibit on the "civilian reuse of Navy aircraft" after their military career was over, much of which is in the field of aerial firefighting. He is on the board of directors of the Associated Airtanker Pilots (AAF). He has written historical articles on the early history of Airtankers, and Bob is the author of **Hornet Plus Three,** the story of the 1969 recovery of Apollo 11. Bob supported my idea that this book should not only tell the story of the hazards of this business, but enlighten the public on the inside workings of fighting fires from the air. In our daily communications over the months of my final entries and proofing, Bob was tireless in his efforts in providing me with historical data, photographs, an initial proof-read and many other helpful contacts.

I wish to give thanks to the people who have assisted me by responding to my many requests for information and photographs. Thanks to Walt Darran, Jim Barnes, Tom Stein, Tim Daly, Tom Wilson, Ray Horton, Dennis Graham, Jerome Laval, Chris Jurasek, Cedric Soriano, Cyril Defever, Lee Monson, Bob Forbes, Clark Cook and Britt Gourley, the CEO of Aero Union for permission to use the cover photo.

Thanks to Jean Barbaud (France) who supplied his priceless caricatures of the bombers that I flew. The book would just not be the same without them.

Special thanks to my daughter Pamela. She took on the monumental task of an in-depth editing and proof-reading of the book, and to my grandson Ben who took on the final read.

Thanks to George Plawski for the photos and the suggestion that I include a number of items I had missed, including sinking my DC-6 in a mud hole.

I give thanks (but I'm not entirely sure how to do it) to my Guardian Angel, or the Fairy Siren as I sometimes called her, or whatever entity it was that decided to save me at the last second when I was so sure I was going to die. Nice to have you around.

And thanks to Monika for her loving encouragement and tolerance for my endless hours on the computer.

To the Fire Bomber pilots who risk their lives in the service of others.

Table of Contents

Preface

Hearing the phrase "the right stuff" causes most people to think about the US military test pilots who became astronauts at the dawn of the space age. It conjures up thoughts about daring men who constantly pushed the edge of an aircraft's flight envelope, going ever higher and faster, even to the edge of space. Character traits such as focus, passion and courage, immediately come to mind.

Yet there is clearly another group of pilots who, beginning in the 1950s, have also had the right stuff and for similar reasons. They are aerial firefighters, also known as Fire Bomber pilots. While most of these professionals earned their wings in the military, it is as civilians they fly their aircraft to the edge of its envelope, although lower, slower and through intensely hazardous skies.

Many North Americans are aware that government forest management agencies often use airplanes to fight wild-land fires. However, few know more than what's contained in the video coverage from an occasional TV news segment. Only a handful are privileged to understand what actually happens inside this industry, including the dangerous situations a pilot faces on almost every mission.

In this book, Linc Alexander shoehorns the reader into the cockpit beside him. Make sure your seat belt is fastened because Linc has captured not only the details but the emotions of being a Fire Bomber pilot. His 37-year career spans the majority of the aerial firefighting period, so he knows it as well as anyone possibly could. Linc masterfully weaves a wide range of technical, business and personal knowledge into a delightful, yet educational, primer on the history of firebombing. Along the way, the reader gets a first-hand look at the supreme highs of doing a job well, savings homes and lives from a raging wildfire, while tempered by the awful lows of losing good friends.

Growing up in Canada, Linc first tested his skills with the pioneering "borate bombers," little agricultural biplanes that flew from grass strips and dropped barely enough water to wet the ground. He then advanced to more powerful war-birds, such as the TBM Avenger, F7F Tigercat and A-26 Invader. He became educated in the ways of flying high-performance aircraft in the roiling, smoky skies found over giant firestorms. He finished his career as Captain of the venerable DC-6, often flying from towns in northwestern Canada that have names but don't appear on many maps.

When a pilot gets into a tight situation with a Fire Bomber, he must have a tight focus, wise instincts and fast reflexes, as there is no time to logically think oneself into a safe exit. Linc shares great insight into many of these moments, as well as other adventures he and his comrades managed to entwine themselves in.

Linc's contributions to the aerial firefighting community go far beyond his flight time over a fire. He helped various companies and government agencies test out new aircraft, such as the S-2F Tracker, and explored new techniques that helped improve operational safety.

And there are many pilots who owe their lives to Linc. Very early in his career, he started taking notes while flying on missions. He studied the way aircraft handled under various circumstances, whether wind and terrain conditions, aircraft speed and height, or payload drop configurations. In 1967, he wrote ***Pilot's Notes for Firebombing***, which provided valuable guidance for pilots. In 1972, he published ***Air Attack on Forest Fires,*** which became the world-wide, definitive manual on the techniques of Firebombing.

This book puts the exclamation mark on a great career – well done, Linc!

Bob Fish

Introduction

Fire Bomber into Hell was written for the reader who knows little more about the business of Fire Bombing than watching TV news clips of bombers in action next to the subdivisions of Los Angeles.

For nearly four decades, I was immersed in the North American forest firefighting juggernaut, a massive, ponderous machine encompassing fire trucks, airplanes, helicopters, boats and countless men and women. A fire sets it all in motion. I was fortunate to have entered into this business shortly after the bomber was introduced in California in 1955. I watched and was part of the progress of the Fire Bomber from its beginnings with primitive Stearman aircraft to the modern turboprop bombers of today. Fire Bombing has become a highly successful art.

This book is the inside story of the inner workings of this business. It details the development of a phenomenally successful method of initial air attack on newly-discovered fires called "One Strike." It describes the various bomber attack methods and how they are carried out.

Here, you will sit beside me in the cockpit to experience walls of fire never seen any other way, plummet down steep mountain sides and dive into the firestorm maelstroms we have all seen on TV.

The Fire Bomber does not take the high, smooth road of airliners. You will fly with me into lower levels of the atmosphere, the "boundary layer" of air that rages with turbulence, horizontal tornadoes called rotor winds, downdrafts and sudden tailwinds that can instantly rob an airplane of its ability to fly. Experience turbulence so severe that it has torn airliners and Fire Bombers apart!

The Fire Bombing actions detailed in this book are but a small part of my story played out over thirty-seven years of flying six different types of bombers in both the United States and Canada. Although this book is my own story, it is not unique; every Fire Bomber pilot sits in the same dangerous seat. We can all relate to "coming close" too many times. In truth, we enjoy what we do, but there are moments of terror when we know that we will die. This business has not been without its sacrifices. Fire Bombing is a dangerous occupation. It has taken, and will continue to take, the lives of those who dare to place themselves in harm's way.

Understand and feel what really goes on in Fire Bombing as you step inside this great adventure.

Linc W. Alexander

Chapter One
Permanently Flying at the Edges

When in doubt, hold on to your altitude.
No one has ever collided with the sky.
Fighter control to pilot

When I'm asked what kind of flying is involved in fire fighting with an airplane, I'm never quite sure how to answer that question. When I tell people I'm a Tanker Pilot, it's a euphemism for someone who's a few clowns short of a circus, someone who flies an airplane at low level loaded with retardant to drop on a fire in variable mountain air currents. They say: "What's that? Is that like dropping supplies by parachute down to men fighting the fire? Do you go over the fire and drop your water?"

Wouldn't it be nice if I could say, "Yes, that's how it is. We fly safely high above the mountains and drop from way up there. Then we go back for another load and keep doing that until the fire is out." What a delightful way to fly: deliver retardant from a tanker staying up high in our big, pig of a performing airplane. Big, heavy multi-engined aircraft were never designed for that kind of flying; they were built to carry cargo and passengers.

Of course, everybody knows that air tankers are cargo airplanes carrying fuel bladders for delivery to some remote mining site. In the stuff of movies, they're the Air Force tankers flying high in the middle of the sky delivering fuel to thirsty fighters on a ferry trip or topping off after a combat mission. Calling us Tanker Pilots and our airplanes Air Tankers opportunely takes the sting out of the job. Tankers are safe; they carry and dispense their load like any other cargo airplane. Tankers aren't bombers; conversion to a tanker is just another freight job for an airplane. The name suggests that we simply carry retardant from one place to another. No one in their right mind would take a heavy transport aircraft down among the peaks and downdrafts to drop their load close to the ground.

Should I be honest? Do I tell the truth and say that I'm engaged in a dangerous occupation that has killed dozens of my friends and on every trip there are a myriad of elements conspiring to do the same thing to me? Do I say that I would often fly my machine into a firestorm, or get smashed around the cockpit in turbulence so violent, I thought my airplane would come apart? Do I tell people that on some of my drops I'll be exceeding the performance limitations of my airplane? Is that clever, an adventure or just plain stupid?

Calling Fire Bombers "Air Tankers" is a disarming, innocuous term that makes the dangers go away. The forest services that contract these airplanes and pilots don't want to admit that Fire Bombing is a dangerous occupation. If they did, they would have to acknowledge the fact that the pilots continue to be grossly underpaid. Few have insurance or pension plans. Widows and families are just out of luck. Recognizing the occupation for what it is would necessitate a radical re-evaluation of pay, perks and pensions for these pilots: they would have to be paid for what they're worth.

Early in my Air Force flying career I read the words of a Royal Air Force Air Marshall: "Aviation in itself is not inherently dangerous. But to an even greater degree than the sea, it is terribly unforgiving of any carelessness, incapacity or neglect."

We know what the words mean: get serious if you're going to be a pilot or sailor, or you can get your butt into real trouble very quickly. The reality, however, is that these words — carelessness, incapacity, neglect and ignorance — are relative. On a gorgeous, calm, sunny day, a rookie pilot or sailor can go out and enjoy a flight or a cruise in ideal conditions and have a pleasant, safe day. He has no real hazards to contend with; the untested greenhorn goes merrily on his way. It's a very different story when the air is turbulent and stormy and the ocean is standing on edge. Suddenly all of the Air Marshall's admonitions about things we must not be come into play: safe flying or sailing becomes Survival-of-the-Fittest.

Everyone who wants to sail the ocean of air or water will have to be at least reasonably proficient and not be deliberately careless or neglectful. Professionalism also demands that we have the self knowledge and humility to know and keep certain of our human frailties in check: it takes effort to set an ego aside and follow the rules. Some adjuncts to the Air Marshall's words would encompass the very human pilots that we are:

On a calm day the air, just like the sea, is not inherently dangerous, but on a turbulent and stormy day it can be terribly unforgiving not only of any carelessness, incapacity and neglect but also of arrogance, overconfidence and inflated ego. We all make mistakes; in a single-pilot environment, we can only hope our mistakes are little ones. In a crew environment, we can hope that the captain wants crew input and his ego doesn't persuade him into thinking he's flying a one-man airplane.

I tested myself against the Air Marshall's admonitions every day of my flying career both in the RCAF and as a Fire Bomber Pilot. How did I stack up against these inviolate commands for staying alive in aviation? Safe flying demands the highest degree of flying knowledge, but equally importantly an understanding of one's strengths and weaknesses. "Know your and the airplane's limits" was the way it was put to us in the RCAF.

We take flying seriously, but we often describe our profession with black humour, or talk to each other as if we were a raging gang of simpletons (which many will agree we are). We have given ourselves some simple rules for safe flying, applicable to all pilots who can read:

Basic Flying Rules
1. Try to stay in the middle of the air.
2. Do not go near the edges of it.
3. The edges of the air can be recognized by the appearance of ground, buildings, sea, trees and interstellar space. It is much more difficult to fly in the edges.

It sounds silly to talk about flying in the middle of the air and avoiding the edges of it. Doesn't everybody do that? Everybody should, except those who are unbalanced enough to go to the edges every day.

Airline flying, like most other types of flying, is dedicated to flying in the middle of the air. After takeoff, airplanes climb to safe altitudes where the air is smooth and the edges are far away. The flight is pleasant and an army of controllers assures safe passage over land or sea to guide the flight to its destination. A vast array of beacons, radar and flight aids assure a safe approach leading to a safe landing. If we can define safe flying, this is it.

But why even bother to give one type of flying the definition of safe flying? Isn't all non-military flying supposed to be safe? Would we consider that there is a lack of sanity to anyone deliberately flying into unsafe conditions? Don't all sane and safe pilots avoid conditions that are hazardous to flight at best and that could be lethal at worst?

The avoidance of deadly meteorological hazards is for everybody else; their flying must be as safe as our current knowledge about flying safety permits. But the safety standards for others don't apply to the Fire Bomber. I have never once seen an action on a fire be called off because of turbulence. Bombing fires during the fall gales of the Santa Ana winds in California is an experience that is dreaded and never forgotten. At one particular action, turbulence twisted an airplane so severely it was rendered into a piece of junk. The pilot was lucky. He was able to fly it home. Actions are called off for restricted visibility, which makes sense, as well as for not being able to find the target, people don't want to run into each other. But turbulence and unpredictable winds are another matter. If we didn't fly in these conditions, we would rarely be dispatched to a fire.

Fire Bombing Protocol

In the world of Fire Bombing, we fly into unsafe conditions almost every day; it is simply expected. The roughest rides in moderate to severe turbulence happen to fairly light airplanes like the TBM

(Avenger), the F7F (Tigercat), or the S2-F (Tracker). I think of the many times where only my helmet saved me from being knocked unconscious when my head was smashed against the sides of the cockpit by the violent gyrations of my airplane. Severe turbulence throws an airplane around like a dog shaking a rag doll. Updrafts throw your head and shoulders down to snap against your shoulder harness and downdrafts lift the years of debris on the floor into your face. These violent up-and-down gyrations occur only split seconds apart. When you know you're in for an extremely rough ride, you haul down on the seat and shoulder harness straps tightly enough to mummify your lower body. You have to stay put in the seat to be able to reach the controls, otherwise your head would be smashing against the top of the canopy as well as the sides.

Everything that isn't fastened down flies around the cockpit, and the turbulence takes total control. You're not in charge of the airplane; you only hang on to the controls until it's over. I've heard loud, sharp cracks like the sound of a Karate Master smashing a stack of boards with his fist. Was that just the sound of the airplane flexing or did something break? Did structural bolts or rivets snap? Did I hear something crack like the wing spar or some other critical structure in the wing or fuselage? Many times have I wondered how the airplane stayed together. In the worst cases, airplanes are tumbled or cartwheeled or literally torn apart. Every bout of bone-jarring turbulence gave me a new respect for the strength and resilience of my airplane. That marvelous bird took me safely through it again. How could the airplane take these primordial beatings and not come apart?

Heavier airplanes like the DC-6, DC-7, CY-P4Y, FA-119C, L P2V and the C-130E are still thrown around the sky, but the wings soften the blows to the crew in the cabin. They flex and groan and disapprove of their beating with the same frightening sounds. Big wings carrying heavy loads just weren't meant for this kind of punishment. But what of all those terrifying noises? Will the airplane one day say, "I've taken all I can, my friend. My body is tired. I have suffered the final overstress and fatigue. Don't punish me anymore or I will die. If I die, I will take you too in my death."

Will all of those sharp cracks and bangs one day conspire to cause massive airframe or wing failure? The unfortunate and sad truth is it has happened to all too many Fire Bombers. The limits of their bombing overstresses and fatigue had expired. The airplanes and their crews had run out of time.

I really learned about flying in the Royal Canadian Air Force (RCAF). NATO was sufficiently impressed with the proficiency and professionalism of the RCAF to select it to train all of the NATO pilots with the exception of the Americans. We were good, our standards were exceptionally high and we turned out the best. I remember the bloodletting of my own pilot intake. Eighty-seven of us started boot camp but only five got our wings. Thereafter, years of instructing and mutual training with the best A-1 instructors taught me how to fly. I took flying seriously. I learned how to evaluate and safely and effectively fly any airplane to its limits. I learned about what all airplanes had in common as well as the differences. High-speed wings were vastly different than low-speed wings: each was to be treated with deserved respect. Every airplane configuration had its own special quirks and personality. I thoroughly "wrung out" every airplane I ever flew so we were cooperative partners in flight. I made sure that the airplane would never have a dirty trick to spring on me. I did not suffer from flying incapacity. I knew how to fly.

Flying the T-33, Royal Canadian Air Force.

But I was totally ignorant of the type of flying I was getting myself into when I began Fire Bombing. I was guilty of the indiscretion of "ignorance" before I even started. Rotor winds, wind shear, downdrafts, severe turbulence and downbursts were terms I had yet to become familiar with. Furthermore, I had not done any flying in the mountains. There was no comprehensive study of rotor winds around mountains; wind shear and downburst were terms still to be coined. There was no precedent to follow, for no aircraft routinely operated in a close mountain environment.

I discovered what mountain air currents would do to me as I experienced them. I flew blindly into dangerous conditions completely unprepared. I learned by experience, the toughest taskmaster, where the test came before the lesson. The new occupation of Fire Bombing would necessitate writing a manual on what to do in treacherous mountain air currents, and little did I know I would have to write it.

The early pilots would make all of the mistakes, and for years learned everything the hard way. Tragically, even in spite of what we know today, the fatalities continue.

No one knew the demands of the job would be so severe as to cause massive structural failure of aircraft wings. Airplanes were shedding wings. Was it the fault of the pilot or the aircraft? No one knew Fire Bombing aircraft fatigued 5.7 times more quickly than normal-category aircraft. There was no firefighting manual for pilots. There was no firefighting manual for Fire Control Officers. No one even suspected that we needed them.

I entered this business in its infancy. I was eager and innocent and little did I suspect I would get so many surprises about what Fire Bombing in the mountains held for me. Flying was my passion and I was a quick learner. Happily, every "close shave" was a lesson I never forgot. Yet, in spite of my flying professionalism, studied approach to every aspect of bombing, allowance for the capricious nature of mountain winds and execution of my bombing runs only after meticulous planning for any eventuality, on a number of occasions I experienced what I never thought could happen to me: I was out of control in an aircraft plunging toward the trees and only seconds away from certain death.

Chapter Two
The Deadly Winds of the Boundary Layer

Flying isn't dangerous. Crashing is what's dangerous. Anonymous

On March 5, 1966, a Boeing 707 designated as Flight 911 (Speedbird 911) and operated by British Overseas Airways Corporation took off from Tokyo International Airport to depart southbound on an IFR flight plan with Hong Kong as its destination. The crew asked for a visual departure procedure which would allow them to climb westbound near Mount Fuji to give the passengers a ringside seat view of the magnificent, snow-capped mountain. At an altitude of sixteen thousand feet, well above the mountain's 12,388 foot peak, the airplane encountered an invisible monster that would devour it in a matter of seconds.

Rotor Wind

A Herculean demon shook the aircraft like a giant predator shaking its helpless prey to numb its mind and body, preparing it for death. The vertical stabilizer attachment to the fuselage was ripped away first, a club in the monster's fist to smash away the left horizontal stabilizer. A violent, sharp twist to the left would destroy the ventral fin and tear all four engines away from the wings. But the leviathan wasn't finished: invisible teeth tore the fuselage into pieces and to be sure of his kill, he ripped away the outer starboard wing. His predatory instinct was satisfied, the kill assured. He had dispensed one more interloper daring to fly into his space. All 113 passengers and eleven crew members died.

Shortly after the accident, a Navy A-4 Skyhawk was sent up to search for the wreckage. When it neared the mountain, the predator was waiting. It smashed its fist into the Skyhawk: accelerometers on the fighter registered plus nine and minus four g-forces. The airplane was cartwheeled and tumbled in all directions and the pilot lost control. But the A-4 was a tough little bird; the pilot and the A-4 survived. They escaped the monster's grasp, but that invisible killer is always alive and waiting – somewhere.

A strong wind blowing over the top of a mountain or a mountain range can set up vortices on the leeward side that are the equivalent of a horizontal tornado. These rotary vortices can occur above and below the height of the mountain. It tore Flight 911 to pieces even when the crew thought they should be at a safe altitude, well above the mountain. This turbulent air takes many forms: eddies, vortices, upflow and downflow, and these currents can be aligned in any directional plane. The winds don't really have to be that strong to set up very dangerous conditions: twenty knots can make life hazardous for airplanes in the wrong place. The doubling of wind speed increases pressure forces and increases turbulence by a factor of four. Downdrafts can considerably exceed the climbing performance of most aircraft. The rotary currents can be sudden and violent. They can throw an aircraft completely out of control or, worse, they can tear the wings off.

Lee side turbulence, and its ever-present danger, is a fact of life in the mountains of California. Meteorology texts tell it exactly how it is:

> *Pre-conditions for these streaming or trailing rotors are a stable layer and a wind vector component across the barrier exceeding twenty knots. As the vortices stream downwind, severe turbulence may be encountered at or below the hilltop level and for some distance downstream.*

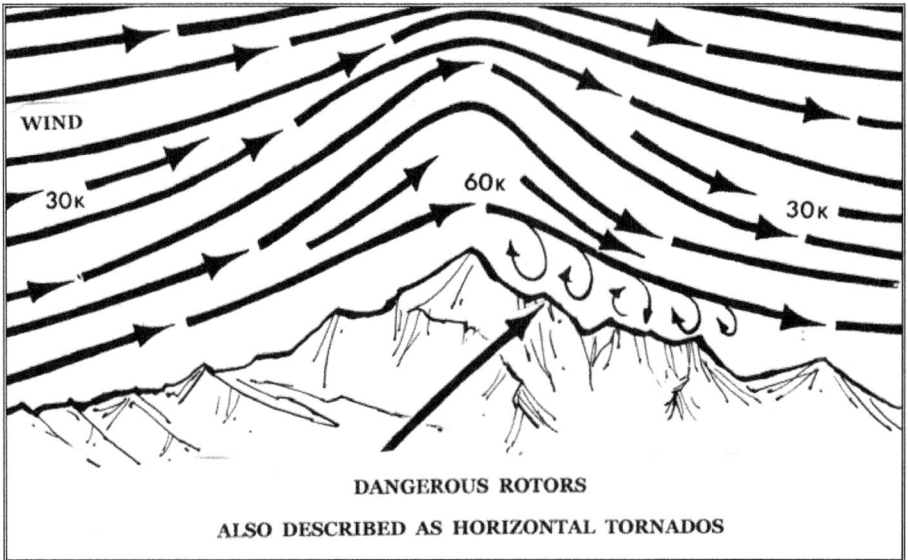

WIND

30ᴋ

60ᴋ

30ᴋ

DANGEROUS ROTORS

ALSO DESCRIBED AS HORIZONTAL TORNADOS

The texts couldn't have called it more accurately for California: the strong Pacific flow of stable air coming off the Pacific Ocean varies in altitude from about 600 to 3,000 feet and it breaks up where the mountains rise to meet it. Like other weather phenomena, it took time and study finally to get an accurate picture of where these rotary winds would be, and they received a name — "streaming and trailing rotors." "Rotor Ridge" would be an appropriate name for some very identifiable mountain ranges in California; every bomber pilot knew which bearing and distance from his base guaranteed a trip he wouldn't forget.

Quantifying this beast is little comfort to the pilots who must fly into the dragon's mouth in the performance of their jobs, but at least we now know the name of what can tear us to pieces. Rotors and downdrafts, and all the unsettling, little surprises associated with what winds stir up in the mountains, are not confined to California. Winds are common on most days in all the mountains of the Western United States and Canada. Calm days are rare.

Thunderstorm

Rotor winds are not the only potentially fatal hazard for an aircraft. Another equally deadly phenomenon called a downburst lurks in the vicinity of thunderstorms. Like every other kind of flying, Fire Bombers fly near thunderstorms. Apart from landing close to storms as scheduled airliners do, we storm-chase. We will often be called upon to bomb fires springing up immediately after a lightning strike. A dry storm passing over a dry forest can leave hundreds of new fires without the accompanying rain to put them out. Action on these spot fires often begins as soon as they are discovered. It means bombing in the vicinity of the storm, despite the fact that the hazards of thunderstorms to aircraft are well known and well documented.

On August 2, 1985, a Lockheed L-1011 (Delta Airlines flight 191) was doing a normal ILS approach to Dallas-Fort Worth Airport. In the final stages of the approach when the aircraft was only a few hundred feet high, it was suddenly slammed into the ground. It hit far short of the runway, rammed through a car on a highway and bounced a number of times before hitting an airport storage tank. The aircraft burst into flames and 137 people died. This happened after an aircraft had landed safely doing the same approach to the same runway only a few minutes earlier.

On July 2, 1994, a DC-9 (Flight 1016) from Columbia, SC to Charlotte, NC crashed on approach to Charlotte-Douglas International Airport. An attempt was made at landing even though there were violent thunderstorms in the area. The crew was losing altitude rapidly on final approach, so they attempted a "go-around." They were unable to climb even with the application of full power. The aircraft stalled and plunged into a field within the airport boundary about one half mile from the threshold of Runway 18 Right. It crashed through the airport fence, impacted a grove of trees and skidded down a residential street that was on the airport boundary. Thirty-seven people died in the crash.

On June 24, 1975, Eastern Air Lines Flight 66, a Boeing 727-225 on a flight from New Orleans arrived in the New York City terminal area, bound for John F. Kennedy International Airport. On final approach to Runway 22 Left, as Eastern 66 passed through 400 feet, the rate of descent went from 675 feet per minute to 1,500 feet per minute. The aircraft rapidly lost altitude and within a few seconds the airspeed dropped dramatically. At 150 feet of altitude, the F/O who was flying the aircraft ordered "takeoff thrust." The aircraft recorder captured the sound of an impact and nothing more was heard from the crew. One hundred and thirteen passengers and crew died in the crash.

On August 7, 1975, Continental Flight 426 took off from Denver-Stapleton International Airport on Runway 35 Left and climbed to 100 feet when it began to descend. The Boeing 727 crashed near the departure end of the runway. Fortunately no one died in the crash. The following likely cause was written by The *Flight Safety Foundation* and reported in the *Aviation Safety Network:*

> PROBABLE CAUSE: *The aircraft's encounter, immediately following takeoff, with severe wind shear at an altitude and airspeed which precluded recovery level flight; the wind shear caused the aircraft to descend at a rate which could not be overcome even though the aircraft was flown at or near its maximum lift capability throughout the encounter. The wind shear was generated by the outflow from a thunderstorm which was over the aircraft's departure path.*

The Dragon's Legs

A thunderstorm is a lightning-breathing dragon continually recharging itself with enormous amounts of heat energy. As water vapour condenses into liquid, an immense amount of heat is released which warms the air and causes it to become less dense than the surrounding air. This causes a low-pressure area under the storm setting up the dragon's pulse, the raging currents of upward and downward flowing air. Wind shear is the extreme and virtually instant change of wind direction between the up and downdrafts that can cause structural failure to an aircraft unfortunate enough to fly into it. The thunderstorm is a mindless beast, ponderously plodding across the country supporting its moiling interior on legs of powerful downbursts. Between its lethal steps are periods of safe air — the green, benign medium when it's safe for an aircraft to be down low, close to the storm.

Aircraft landing in the presence of thunderstorms is a common occurrence. Winds may be strong, but as long as they're within the crosswind limits of the aircraft, such landings are routine. It's the unexpected descent of the invisible dragon's leg that can cause disaster. An aircraft may land safely only minutes before another is bludgeoned into oblivion like a gnat under a fly swatter. An extremely powerful downdraft leaves little time for pilots and aircraft to react.

Flights 191, 1016, 66, 426 and many other crashes were due to severe downdrafts associated with thunderstorms. John McCarthy, a meteorologist from Colorado, coined the term "microburst" to identify these intense columns of descending air, also known as downbursts. They are sudden and unpredictable.

The thunderstorm killer of airplanes is an intense downdraft strong enough to smash airliners into the ground in spite of the immense power available to safely climb a modern jet aircraft. Over the years, over 500 people have died in twenty-six crashes thought to be the result of airliners encountering these deadly winds. In 1982, the phenomenon was finally recognized for what it was when a CBS Television crew at Dallas airport was clearly able to see the dust, water vapour and debris raging downward in a microburst. Several minutes of videotape positively identified this powerful killer.

When the downburst hits the ground, the air splashes out in all directions. An airplane entering it from any direction would experience the same sequence of events: a sudden and large increase in airspeed because of a headwind, followed by a strong downdraft, and finally a large drop in airspeed as a result of a tailwind. These events could follow each other in a matter of seconds. The combination of the downdraft and an instant loss of airspeed because of the tailwind is the killer, two deadly forces that a pilot spends his lifetime trying to avoid conspire against him in the worst possible place — close to the ground.

The Boundary Layer

As aviation in general learned about the air, pilots discovered there were dangers everywhere and especially in that part of the sky that we call the "boundary layer" — the atmosphere from the ground up to about five thousand feet. We found out about wind shear, where aircraft at almost any altitude would suddenly encounter severe turbulence because of winds blowing in different directions shearing off against eac h other. Vertical wind shear, the common condition in and around thunderstorms, could be just as hazardous as horizontal wind shear. Sailors are familiar with gusts and squall gusts, the dramatic changes in wind velocity that rise and instantly fall, creating a headache for sailors and dangerous drops in airspeed for pilots.

We were learning that the boundary layer was a dangerous place. We were also learning that the benign, ever-present air, which is indispensable to life itself, has a deadly nature if we innocently venture into its angry tantrums. We are now aware of the hazards and have a good idea of where they'll lie in wait for us. As much as we try to understand the air, it is still invisible. If only there were a magic fairy or a siren for pilots who would sprinkle pixie dust into the air, green for safe, yellow for caution and red for danger. Unfortunately, all of these air currents are one colour — invisible. You assign your own colour after you enter.

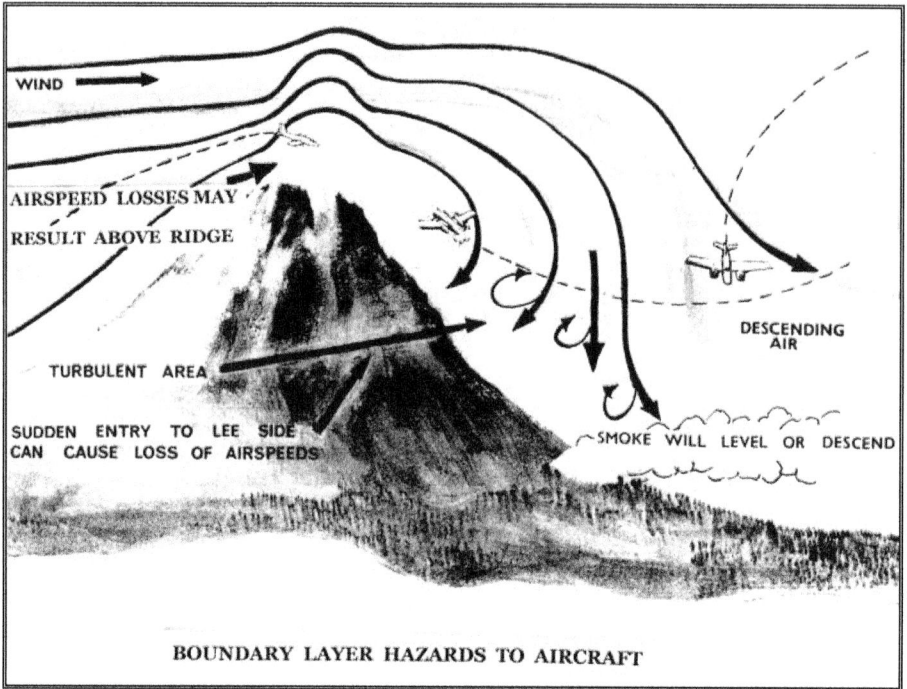

WIND ➡

AIRSPEED LOSSES MAY
RESULT ABOVE RIDGE

TURBULENT AREA

SUDDEN ENTRY TO LEE SIDE
CAN CAUSE LOSS OF AIRSPEEDS

DESCENDING
AIR

SMOKE WILL LEVEL OR DESCEND

BOUNDARY LAYER HAZARDS TO AIRCRAFT

Safe Flying

It hardly needs to be said that the purpose in knowing of these hazards is to avoid them. The Federal Aviation Administration (FAA) and the aviation industry in general take these dangers very seriously. Doppler radar is being installed at airports to help detect severe turbulence and downbursts. Pilots are continually warned about wind shears and shifting winds in the vicinity of thunderstorms. Pilots report turbulence aloft to air controllers and weather stations and to each other. If conditions are severe enough, an airport is closed and flights are diverted. Safe flying demands that the pilot knows where he is likely to encounter danger and do everything he can to avoid it. This is the rule for sane pilots. Fire Bomber pilots fly by different rules.

Chapter Three
Aircraft Overstress and Fatigue

Pilot "squawk": Number three engine missing.
Maintenance fix: Engine found on right wing after brief search.
Quantas Airlines

Failed Wings and Fallen Colleagues

On June 21, 1981, a Hemet Valley Flying Service C-119, Tanker 88 broke apart in mid-air while on a fire action over Frazier Park in California. Both crew members were killed.

On September 16, 1987, a Hawkins and Powers C-119, Tanker 135 came apart in mid-air while flying on a firefighting action near Crags Canyon State Park in Arizona. Three crew members were killed. What is significant about both of these accidents is that the National Transportation Safety Board (NTSB) and the FAA have no records of these crashes. Did they officially not happen? Did people try to hide the reality of Fire Bombing hazards?

On August 13, 1994, an Aero Firefighting Service C-130A, Tanker 82 lost the left wing and came apart while fighting a fire near Pearblossom, California. The wreckage fell in the San Gabriel Mountains onto the north face of Pleasant View Ridge. The three crew members were killed. The NTSB accident report identification LAX94FA323 contained some revealing information as to the probable cause of the crash:

> *A visual examination of the fracture surfaces revealed that most had features consistent with overstress separation. However, on one center wing section, at CWS 186R, two fracture regions displayed thumbnail patterns, indicative of fatigue... The regions aft of the fatigue region, up to stringer 20, displayed features consistent with overstress.*

On July 18, 2002, Tanker 123, a Consolidated-Vultee P4Y-2, operated by Hawkins and Powers lost its left wing while turning to final approach on a fire and crashed six miles southwest of Estes Park Colorado. Both pilots were killed. NTSB accident report identification DEN02GA074 revealed the cause of the wing separation:

> *The Materials Laboratory Factual Report states that microscopic examinations of the fractures found extensive areas of fatigue cracking in both the lower spar cap members, in the spar web and in the lower skin. Close examinations established that both angle members of the lower spar were almost completely separated by fatigue... The fatigue regions in the horizontal flanges of the cap members and in the spar web above the cap transitioned from low stress propagation (perpendicular to the plane of the sheet) to higher stress-mixed fatigue and overstress propagation as indicated by the change in fracture orientation to a forty-five degree plane through the pieces... Aft of the spar area, the fracture propagated on various slant planes through the skin indicative of high stress propagation.*

On June 17, 2002, Tanker 130, a Hawkins and Powers Aviation C-130A, broke apart in flight while on a fire action near Walker, California. The three flight crew members were killed. A witness shot a video of the break up, which was later shown on television news broadcasts. The world was able to witness the horror of an airplane coming apart in mid-air. Each witness could only imagine what the crew may have thought in their last few seconds of life. An examination of the video showed the right wing folding upwards, followed, less than a second later by the left wing.

NTSB accident report identification LAX02GA201 was very comprehensive in its coverage of the aircraft and the accident. The report gave wind speed and temperatures, and also this comment regarding flight conditions:

Mechanical and/or mountain wave induced turbulence and down slope winds most likely existed at the time of the accident. Subsequent metallurgical examination of the right wing disclosed evidence of multiple fatigue cracks in the right wing's lower surface skin panels, with origins beneath the forward doubler at Center Wing Station (CWS) at the stringers 16 and 17 locations.

The report showed the tanker had been exceeding operating limits to cause the failure:

The evidence indicates that the aircraft was operating within placard speeds, but outside the maneuver load factor constraint of 2.0 g with flaps deployed. The results of the performance analysis of the video and photographic evidence are consistent with the aircraft manufacturer's residual strength analysis of the normal load factor required for wing separation. The estimated load factor at the time of the wing separation was 2.4 g based on the combined effects of the pull up maneuver and retardant release. The presence of wind gusts or turbulence would require additional load factor corrections. The airplane was operating at 146 knots, just below its 150 knot limit airspeed.

At the request the safety board, Lockheed performed a residual strength analysis to identify the vertical load factor that would have caused the centre wing lower surface to fail based on the known fatigue damage documented in the metallurgical report. Lockheed concluded from the analysis that

the center wing failed at a load that was approximately 30 percent of the design ultimate strength of the center wing and that the presence of fatigue cracks at multiple locations and in multiple structural elements reduced the residual strength to approximately 50 percent of design load limit and compromised the fail-safe capability of the structure. The report opined that; 'Failure was likely caused by a symmetrical maneuver load exceeding 2.0 g during the final drop of fire retardant.'

The report also addressed a "Firefighting Tanker Airplane Flight Envelope Performance Study:"

An industry study was conducted during the fire seasons 1983 through 1989. The study, Operational Retardant Evaluation (ORE), addressed all phases of aerial firefighting. Excerpts from the study addressed the potential for fixed wing airplanes exceeding their structural operating limitations. Recorders were installed on some airplanes for data collection. Airspeed and g-loading exceedences were recorded. Airspeed exceedences were associated with the normal practice of making down-slope runs that result in an airspeed increase. In one test airplane, a C-119, maximum drop speeds were exceeded over 90 percent of the time, and 2.5 g's were exceeded on 17 percent of the drops. The exceedences on the instrumented airplanes were outside the operating envelope specified by the Type Certificate or Supplemental Type Certificate.

Fire Bomber Fatigue – 5.7 Times More Severe than Normal

The report looked at other Air Tanker Studies:

The Safety Board located studies performed in the early 1970s by NASA on the Lockheed P2V, and the Douglas DC-6, that examined the effects of the low-level fire fighting missions on these converted surplus military airplanes, plus a Canadian study on civilian Fokker F27 also converted to the firefighting mission. The results of the P2V study indicated that there were no adverse effects to the airframe structure due to the tank installation and the mission flown. The data for the DC-6 study drew conclusions that indicated that, unlike the P2V study, the firefighting mission did impact the structural life of the airplane. The severity of maneuver load applications, in both magnitude and frequency of occurrence, is such that significant shortening of the structural life of the aircraft should be expected.

In the 1990s, a Fokker F27 firefighting aircraft was analyzed as part of a Canadian airworthiness study, which found that

the F27 firefighting aircraft operated in a firefighting role is exposed to a harsher loading environment than initially intended for a typical transport role aircraft – the time spent in the firefighting role is 5.7 times more severe than the typical Fokker transport role operation. Because of these findings, the inspection intervals, limitations, mandatory replacement times and remaining airframe life limits for the Fokker F27 firefighting aircraft were modified.

Is it really possible that the effects of undetected fatigue and overstress had rendered an airplane so crippled it was unsafe to fly even without a load and to experience failure at 30 percent of the design ultimate strength of the centre wing? It is incomprehensible that a wing should fail at 2.4 g but this was the reality for an airplane engaged in a business that uses up airplanes 5.7 times faster than it would in a normal transport role. When these airplanes die, the pilots die with them.

In the study, Operational Retardant Evaluation (ORE), it was noted that on "one test airplane, a C-119, maximum drops speeds were exceeded over 90 percent of the time, and 2.5 g's were exceeded on 17 percent of the drops." The report attempted to document the reality; in fact, it may have been conservative in its findings. Pilots exceed their placarded airspeeds and g-loads with frightening frequency since the requirements of the job and the ever-present mountain turbulence make it unavoidable. A Fire Bomber does not fly in the middle of the air; in mountainous terrain its flight is permanently at all of the edges.

Blue River - British Columbia

Stearman

**Pump your own gas, take off and land on a dusty gravel strip.
Photo by author**

Chapter Four
Carelessness, Incapacity and Neglect

**The best way to learn anything is to start at the bottom,
unless you're learning to swim. Anonymous**

My Fire Bombing career began in 1960, shortly after I finished my
Short Service Commission with the Royal Canadian Air Force in
October of 1959. I had just started the building of my ski area and was
looking for a suitable occupation during the summer months. There
were only a couple of choices for a summer-only job: I could go and fly
up North and spend time amongst the black flies and mosquitoes, or I
could fly with Airspray Ltd., an Alberta operator which needed
someone to fly one of their Stearman airplanes on Fire Bombing. Fire
Bombing sounded much more like my cup of tea than pushing barrels
of fuel up a ramp into Beavers or Otters. And it had the sound of
excitement.

I drove the short distance from my home in Red Deer, Alberta to
Wetaskiwin, the home base for Airspray. In the middle of Alberta grain
country, the town owes its existence to the extensive grain farming in
the area and to oil. The large oilfields to the west of the town are
primarily serviced from Wetaskiwin. I meet Don* the owner, a tall,
lean man of about six foot two. He was balding at an early age and
spoke with a high-pitched voice. My first impression was of a highly
nervous man unsuited to be a pilot and even less suited to be in the
flying business. These impressions would turn out later to be correct.

I was then introduced to Brian* the operations manager. He was a
heavy-set New Zealander who knew everything about everything.
According to him, he was also the world's greatest pilot. At the time I
was not aware he had never done any bombing. He gave me a
considerable grilling about my flying ability and whether or not I had

---

*All characters are real but asterisked names have been changed.

the qualifications he was looking for in a Fire Bomber pilot. During a very long and reluctant acceptance speech, he informed me that Fire Bombing was hazardous and tiring and he would be giving me a break later in the summer if we got busy. He didn't actually say the words, but I presumed I was hired.

The Stearman

I was then introduced to a beautiful biwinged airplane, my steed for the summer. I had seen pictures of a Stearman, but this was my first exposure to a real one. I was immediately struck by the airplane's beauty. The wings were perfectly situated toward the forward end of a long, slim fuselage. The vertical stabilizer had an elegant shape that was exactly right for that airplane. It reminded me of the unforgettable lines of the tail on the DC-3. One little windshield appeared along the top of the fuselage, just in front of the rear cockpit. The fuel tank, situated purposefully in an excellent spot in between the upper wings, gravity-fed the fuel, with the quantity shown on a glass sight gauge hanging down right in front of the pilot's face so he had no excuses about not knowing how much fuel he had. A horizontal wood panel behind the fuel tank held the engine instruments: a needle and ball, an altimeter, a magnetic compass and an airspeed indicator.

Having those instruments up there on the top wing made a great deal of sense for the spray pilot; he didn't have to look down to the panel normally holding the instruments. That configuration allowed the pilot to see what he would eventually hit. The now-vacant instrument panel had a thick vinyl-covered pad, presumably a softer place for the inevitable face plant.

Without a radio, the pilot would not be getting altimeter settings prior to landing. It wouldn't matter anyway, as there was no way of reaching the altimeter from the cockpit. One setting in the morning to local field elevation was good for the day. The airplane had a narrow main landing gear and a fully-swivelling tail wheel. It meant that the pilot would have to keep the airplane dead straight on landing: a slight swing one way or the other could quickly result in a series of pirouettes on the way down the runway. This was the involuntary maneuver known as the ground-loop.

Exposed Engines

At the front of the airplane, a circle of finned cylinders pushed their way out of a bulbous nose to which was attached a propeller. More than likely the original engine was a seven-cylinder Continental (220 horsepower) or a Jacobs (225 horsepower). Never considered ugly, the exposed engine is something special on an older airplane. Some of the first radial engines that were installed on airplanes did not have any cowlings. It was thought that having them exposed, just hanging out in the air so to speak, would provide better cooling.

The early engines, and even the one I was looking at, did not have a starter. The propeller was hand swung to start the engine. Beginning with the blade in a horizontal position, the pilot was like a Balinese dancer as he swept the blade all the way down and part way up on the opposite side to get enough movement to fire at least a couple of cylinders. These resolute little engines, more often than not, started on the first swing.

It's easy to picture the awe-struck farm and city boys who never imagined they would ever fly, at the outset of the war now seeing themselves as aspiring fighter aces. They were looking at the graceful Stearman, a two-man, open-cockpit trainer that would make them masters of the air.

The Stearman biplane was originally designed in 1934 and built by the Stearman Aircraft Company in Wichita, Kansas. In 1938 Boeing purchased the Stearman Aircraft Company and a total of 8,428 Pt -17s, as they became popularly known, were built. They became the standard primary trainer aircraft for the US Army and the Navy at the outset of World War Two. The early power plants gave the airplane a cruise speed of about 85 knots. As it turned out, the services could not have picked a better trainer. It was built strong enough to take the destructive antics of the most determined barbarian, as I was later to discover.

The engine I was looking at was a Pratt and Whitney R-985 with 450 horsepower, virtually double the power of the first models. After the war, there was a need for a crop-spraying airplane. Besides being available in large numbers, it was eminently suitable for the job. The airplane was so strong that it easily handled the big Pratt and Whitney engine. And this ruggedness usually kept the pilot alive when he inevitably rolled the airplane into a ball after hitting something. The centre of gravity was kept in the proper position by putting the 125-gallon tank in the front cockpit area.

Now, one would think that doubling the power of an airplane would end up getting the airplane to go twice as fast. It doesn't work that way: with all the flying wires, ground wires, wings struts, tail wheel, engine and other pipes and tubes hanging out, the entire extra horsepower was simply swallowed up by the immense drag. It gave only an extra twenty knots.

I took the airplane for a ride and discovered it had very gentle flying characteristics. The stall was almost a non-stall. The nose dropped gently straight ahead. Pushing the stick forward a bit and adding some power had it flying normally again. The ailerons were slow (in pilot's language it meant that the airplane rolled slowly). It was okay for turns and normal flying, but just barely adequate for aerobatics. Rolls took a long time, but no sweat; I wouldn't be doing aerobatics while Fire Bombing anyway.

Joys of the Open Cockpit

I don't know who designed the windshield on that airplane, but that undersized cosmetic attachment was definitely not for pilot comfort (but it did look kind of racy). If you sat up straight, the slipstream hit you squarely on the forehead. I had the seat up too high on the first trip and as soon as I applied the power for takeoff, the propeller blast forced my mouth wide open in a crazed, full-toothed grin in the middle of bulbous, inflated cheeks. It was impossible to shut my mouth and I collected a splattering of bugs on my teeth.

The virginal beginning of it all. Little did I know of what lay ahead.

One must either hunch over while flying or end up with a neck like a football player. Flying an airplane with an open cockpit has all the joys of sitting on a motorcycle while riding out a hurricane. However, it has that romantic image of breezing along in the wide open air without a care in the world. There is no canopy to obscure the view to the universe. So I had the view and on a warm sunny day it was grudgingly tolerable. On a cool summer day, it was downright freezing. There's a hurricane blowing outside (a 110 knot wind is a hurricane) that rips at each shoulder. To escape that invigorating convulsion of air, the shoulders are pulled in. After a while the Stearman pilot can be recognized by the hunched back, rounded shoulders, head pointed forward and the thick neck, as well as by the hearing aid in his right ear.

Currently, the Stearman has found a new niche as an aerobatic performer at air shows.

I see myself performing aerobatics at an air show in this brilliant red and blue airplane covered with white stars. I'm wearing a brown leather helmet, aviator's goggles, a white scarf, brown leather jacket, World War One cotton britches and high, brown leather boots. I'm the star of the show and when my performance is over, I park at the celebrity stand to receive the adulations from my adoring crowd.

Miss Air Show has been awarded a ride with me in this gorgeous airplane. I help her into the cockpit and generously give her my helmet, goggles and white scarf so that she may comfortably enjoy the ride. I will sacrifice, and fly without those items for this trip. She's a sensitive woman and has requested that we not do any aerobatics. We circle the crowd so she can wave to her family. We land, and I help the delicate young woman out of the airplane to be hugged by her doting parents. It has been a perfect day. I have flaunted my daring and my perspicacious feelings toward this impressionable young woman, so it is now time to depart. The Air Show Band has struck up the Army Air Force Tune... Off we go into the Wild Blue Yonder. I wave as I take off and depart into the wild blue yonder. Unknown to me, I have left a distraught woman behind. Miss Air Show is crying on her mother's shoulder.

"Mother, will I ever see this man again? He's taken off and gone into the wild blue yonder."

I never got used to the roar coming out of the exhaust pipe only a few feet in front of my right ear. It is deafening. It explains why I had to shout into the left ear of the long-time spray pilots from the USA. Another blast of air comes up from under the feet and heads out past the face with its load of dust and ashes. It is all so romantic. The map you're going to navigate by has to be tightly folded to about the size of a postcard and you sit on it since anything you're not sitting on gets sucked outside. You fly off your map about every fifteen minutes, so to get a new read, you have to lift one cheek, grab the map with a

Schwarzenegger grip and fold out the next section. A loose flap buzzes like a hornet's wing and heads outside as confetti.

The airplane has a sound like no other. Once you get over the engine's incessant growling in your right ear, you can hear the airplane's song, the whistle of the wires, which changed with airspeed. It doesn't take long to match the sound to the airspeed and the airspeed indicator becomes redundant. As it turned out, after flying the airplane for a few hours, the airspeed indicator quit working, a little malfunction that was par for this company. It's very easy to approach and land the airplane: reduce the power a little bit or throttle right back, pick any sound you like for the approach and head for the button of the runway. Going fast is no problem. Going fairly slow is no problem either. When you get over the end of the runway, round out and cut the power. The airplane has so much drag it just can't wait to quit flying. You would have to try hard to run off the end of a thousand-foot runway.

My first job with the airplane was to fly to Eastern Canada and do the Budworm Spray in New Brunswick. That whole affair was an adventure in itself taking the month of June. I was then hoping to do some Fire Bombing.

The Call to Fire Bombing

The call came in July to get my ever-so-eager body up to Wetaskiwin and fly out to Kamloops in British Columbia. There was a "fire bust" going on out there and the forest service was looking for all the airplanes they could get. The trip meant flying through the mountain passes and more or less following the highway winding through the valleys on its way across British Columbia to the West Coast. I had never flown this trip before and it was stunningly spectacular. I passed mountains high enough to be hanging with glaciers and saw a thousand breathtaking waterfalls from the meltwater.

The one sight that has stayed with me more than any other on that first trip across was flying down the South Thompson River just east of Kamloops. In many places, the river banks had formed themselves into tall, vertical hoodoos, pillars of sandstone carved out by the erosion of wind and water. Each chiseled obelisk was a testament to nature's sculpturing skills and they went on for miles. What wondrous structures nature creates with the simplest of tools.

What was so striking was the glittering sand below. As a child I had heard the words "Diamond Sand" in an old song titled *Home on the Range*. I always wondered what it meant. Were the words really referring to something real? Was there really sand with diamonds in it? The sand sparkled with a million points of light. I knew they weren't diamonds and I was curious. Later on in the summer, I would meet people who knew the answer. Flakes of mica were ground into the sand during the ice age, and as the glaciers retreated, the sand was deposited along its edges later to become sandstone and beach sand. The flakes reflected the sunlight to give the impression of diamonds. In truth, the sand didn't need to have diamonds. The glitter of that sand is like no other: it has a special magic.

Landing at Kamloops put me in the middle of a circus of activity. There were TBMs, B-25s and B-17s, and all were busy loading, taking off or landing. With all that heavy firepower around, I wondered why the forest service would want small airplanes like the Stearman. The forest service knew that bombers were being used in the United States, so this armada of airplanes had been invited up from the US. Anything that could be found in Canada was also used. Every conceivable resource which might be of value was thrown into what was really a bad situation. There were fires everywhere.

A catastrophic situation always attracts the media, and they were particularly drawn to the new, dangerous activity of Fire Bombing. So along with all the other activity on the ground, the bombers were doing their bit. The reality was that nobody knew anything about Fire Bombing; airplanes were sent everywhere to drop on their own with no supervision or evaluation of results. Fortunately, the media didn't ask embarrassing questions about our tactics or results. The fires raged and the media gave front page coverage to the brave pilot heroes who had the guts to fly into the holocaust. The airplanes didn't do any effective bombing but the media didn't know it.

Blue River

Dispatch at Kamloops told me that our Stearman group was going to Blue River to handle some runaway fires they had to the west. I was sent there the same day, and by the next day the other two Airspray Ltd. Stearmans arrived. Blue River is about 150 miles north of Kamloops and is in the middle of some of the most valuable and biggest timber in British Columbia. Logging is the only industry in this small town of about two thousand people. The town nestles beside a small lake and is closely surrounded on all sides by heavily timbered mountains. The pines and fir easily reach up to 150 feet and higher, a canopy most impressive from the air. I landed on a dirt strip about 2500 feet long, 75 feet wide and surrounded by tall trees. There was not much room for wandering around on takeoff or landing.

The two other pilots that joined me were Bill Perkins* and Sam Fields.* I had flown with Bill in the Air Force. Although we worked at the same Air Force base, we were in different squadrons so I never had the opportunity to watch him fly. He stood about six foot two, had a lanky build and walked with brisk, purposeful strides. His hair was dark brown which the wind rearranged frequently. He sported a slim mustache on a lean face and his smile revealed widely spaced teeth. He wasn't shy about letting his wants known and he seemed confident around his airplane. His stature reminded me of Charles Lindberg.

Sam Fields in contrast was a farm boy from Saskachewan who had spent some time crop spraying with the Stearman. He was about five foot ten inches tall and a balding head belied his young-looking appearance. He talked slowly, befitting his image of the Saskachewan farmer. His demeanor was very friendly but he didn't say much. When he needed something, he got to the point and that was about it. For all of us, it was our first go at Fire Bombing.

We got settled in to our accommodations which were rooms at the Blue River Hotel. When we went to dinner, I got the surprise of my life. My grade five teacher worked at the hotel as a waitress. We recognized each other immediately. I was stunned with surprise; it had been such a long time since we had seen each other. How could she have recognized me? I was a child in grade five. I must have changed considerably in all those years yet she called my name immediately. It was easy for me to recognize her, as she hadn't changed a bit. And there was a reason I couldn't forget my grade five teacher: she was one of the most considerate, kind and patient of people. It took some courage and strength to handle the unruly child that I was. She gave me the acceptance, consideration and love which was lacking from my parents in my childhood years. I was so delighted to see her. I didn't ask what brought her there, but presumed a marriage. It seemed to me what she was doing was such a setback from the wonderful job that she had done as a teacher.

The next day we were called into the forest service dispatch office for the briefing about our duties. It seemed they hadn't really requested to have us because, like everybody else, they had no experience with Fire Bombers. Someone at head office had invited our three little chariots to the party and sent us to Kamloops district for them to decide what to do with these misfits.

Kamloops didn't want us cluttering up their airport. They already had a mess on their hands, so they decided Blue River needed some experience with Fire Bombers. As requested, the next morning our smiling faces appeared at their office ready and eager for our assignment. If we had appeared with a kite under each arm and said we were ready for action, they might have believed us.

Their ignorance of what we should do was matched by our ignorance of how to do it. They dispensed with us with one flip sentence:

"We've got a big fire going west of here at Myrtle Lake. It's about thirty thousand acres. Go and see what you can do with it."

That was it. Those were our instructions: go hit a thirty thousand acre fire west of here. That was the fire description and at the time it didn't mean a thing to me. I had not seen a fire of thirty thousand acres. I had not dropped a load of 125 gallons of water. My drop door was the emergency drop door for the spray load. If the spray pilot got into trouble, he pulled the emergency handle to dump the load. The door measured seven inches by fifteen inches. I didn't know what a load of that size would do to a fire, any fire. I had no idea how long it took to come out or what kind of spread or thickness it had when it reached the ground. I didn't know how high I should be when I let the load go. I didn't know if I should let it go in level flight or pull some g-forces to push it out. These were all questions to be answered later. At the time, I thought that perhaps I had an effective weapon.

Everyone was shooting in the dark when it came to the Fire Bomber. At the briefing, I wondered if they mistook my blank stare for knowing something about fire control. I presumed that they presumed we knew how to get results with the airplane. However it was the blind leading the blind. "Go and see what you can do with it," said they, and they didn't ask embarrassing questions like, "Do you know where to drop the load?" Maybe they presumed Bomber Pilots came pre-programmed, complete with batteries.

I didn't ask any embarrassing questions either. I didn't know a thing about fighting a fire, so I kept my mouth shut.

The dispatcher had one more comment: "Oh— one more thing: start early and hit it all day."

We were to take that licence seriously. We got paid by the hour, so daylight was a good time to start, and dark was a good time to quit. The briefing lasted about fifteen minutes. We got into a truck and headed for the airport.

A fire pump had been set up at a pond at one end of the airstrip where we would get watered-up for each trip. It could hardly be described as a pond. It was more like a small lake and the water was crystal clear. We were told the water had been poisoned to kill off undesirable fish. It would take a year for the poison to wash out, and then the lake would be seeded with Rainbow Trout.

Thirty Thousand Acres and Exploding

I started the airplane, taxied into the watering-up position and a man with a hose in his hand walked up on the right wing with his cork boots and inserted the hose into the loading hole on top of the tank. (Cork boots are logger's boots that are laced with spikes in the soles and heels to keep a man from slipping on the round logs.) After he climbed up, it was too late to tell him that the wing was covered in fabric and was not meant for spiked traffic. Fortunately the thin plywood walking strip next to the fuselage, covered with a rough, black floor coating, miraculously held up under the less-than-tender footsteps of the loggers.

He shouted to the pump operator, blue smoke came up from the shore and I could see the hose stiffening as the leading edge of the water was enthusiastically charging toward the airplane. A blast of air was followed by the torrent of water. I'm not sure why the loader kept his head down looking into the tank because he waited until it overflowed before he gave the stop signal. I was loaded in about two minutes and I was ready for my first "Attack-the-Fire" mission.

Being the first to go, I didn't see the cloud of dust that I left behind. I would see it later as we shuffled positions in and out of the loading area. At each takeoff, a thick cloud of dust enveloped the entire area and took about ten minutes to settle enough for another takeoff. Dusty conditions are very abrasive to engines that don't have air cleaners. Sand in the cylinders grinds the life out of the engine. I did my best to avoid the worst of it and just hoped that the engine would keep running when I needed it. Conditions were calm, so we took off heading south and landed, heading north.

Blue River has fairly high mountains on both sides of the airport so we had a bit of a climb after takeoff if we wanted to go east or west. The procedure to get to the Myrtle Lake Fire was to climb straight ahead to an altitude of about two thousand feet and turn right. I got up to altitude and turned the corner around the south end of the nearby mountain.

My first sight of a fire — thirty thousand acres and exploding
Photo by author

I was awestruck by the sight. One edge of the fire stretched out several miles in front of me. Fire and billowing clouds of white and black smoke were everywhere. I could see the part of the fire that I was approaching and it was reasonably calm. That was the base of the fire and the wind was blowing the opposite way. It was the only area with any kind of visibility. The edges (flanks) were just as hot and this monstrous fire was expanding in three directions. Across the miles of burnt-out area I could see that the front of the fire, where the spread was the fastest, was moving away from Blue River so the town was not being threatened.

My thoughts tumbled all over each other. *What an expanse of fire! If this fire keeps expanding at this rate, it will burn all of British Columbia before the summer is over. This looks hopeless.*

We were to discover that the fire consumed at least five thousand acres a day and developed enough heat to create its own mushroom cloud. I was stunned. I could only look. I had no idea what to do next.

I was the mouse about to rip into a rogue lion. Someone must have known that the Stearman was an effective bomber — why else would we have been invited? So now I'd prove them right.

How much of this fire could I "take-out" with my drop? Would it leave a cold swath of ashes that my load extinguished? Would I be able to see the effect? And where do I begin? No sense going for the head of the fire: I couldn't see a thing. The edges weren't much better. Best go for the base; at least I could see something.

There were flaming hot spots along the base between the main fire and a road that someone had built there. It was an odd place to build a road, but on second thought I realized that men and equipment had to be brought in, so a road made sense. I could help by starting my attack there, to keep the heat away from the bulldozers that I could see below. Their crews would appreciate that, I thought.

The First Drop

I knew the load would start to come out of the tank through the little dump door as soon as I pulled the handle. From there on I didn't have a clue as to how long it took to leave the airplane and hit the trees, or how soon before the target to pull the handle. *I think I'll stay up a little. That way, I can take out a bigger swath of fire.* I circled for at least fifteen minutes trying to settle down from the shock of seeing this behemoth of a fire and finally selected an area where I could be of most help.

I found a good target where the fire and the road were close together. Putting out that hot spot would keep the guys safe down below, I thought. I headed for the target and when I got over it, I pulled the handle. I felt an immense pride in taking my first shot in the battle of the Myrtle Lake Fire. I circled around to see the results of my drop. *That's odd, nothing seems different. Did I get the right spot? There were quite a few. Maybe the load went one way or another, either on to the road or inside the fire on to the ashes. Maybe it took awhile for the load to take effect. No problem, I'll come back and hit it with the next shot.*

In about half an hour I was back. I found the area and saw that the hot spot was no longer there — the area was quiet. *Wow, did I do a number on that one. I knocked it right off.* My Fire Bombing knowledge had just taken a quantum leap forward. I could see that I was carrying an effective weapon. After all, 125 gallons of water is 1,250 pounds, quite a punch. I picked another target next to the road, got over the hot spot and pulled the handle. I knew I'd have to wait for the results, and sure enough, when I checked the area on the next trip, all was quiet — no fire.

Very quickly I had discovered what worked. The 125 gallons that I was dropping really did a good job on the fire. I was duly impressed. I figured I was about 100 feet above the trees; I flew at cruise speed and pulled the drop handle when I was directly over the fire. It was a safe enough place to drop from and I was getting excellent results. This Fire Bombing stuff was fun.

So it went, day after day for about two weeks and all the while I had never seen a drop from another airplane. I could only imagine the behaviour of my own load, and from what I had seen, the results were quite spectacular. I was taking swath after swath out of the fire.

The Backfire

Unknown to me at the time, the "roads" that I was seeing below were in reality the "fire lines." A fire line or guard is a line scraped down to mineral soil. Any flammable fuel is totally removed so it exposes soil that will not burn. It's either done by equipment like a bulldozer or by men with hoes and shovels. It's where the fire ends.

Lines are usually placed (scraped) as close to the fire edge as possible so as to have the smallest amount of burnable material between the line and the fire.

Before the line is left on its own, the material between the line and the main body of the fire must be burned out. With no more material to burn, the line is safe and the fire cannot spread in that area. If there is a fair amount of burnable material between the line and the main fire, and the prevailing wind permits, the crews may not want to wait too long for the main fire to slowly burn its way to the line. They will light the fuel right next to the line and burn out to the main fire. This is called a "backfire." So the flames I was seeing below that were next to the line were backfires that had been lit to burn out the flammable material between the bulldozer line and the main fire.

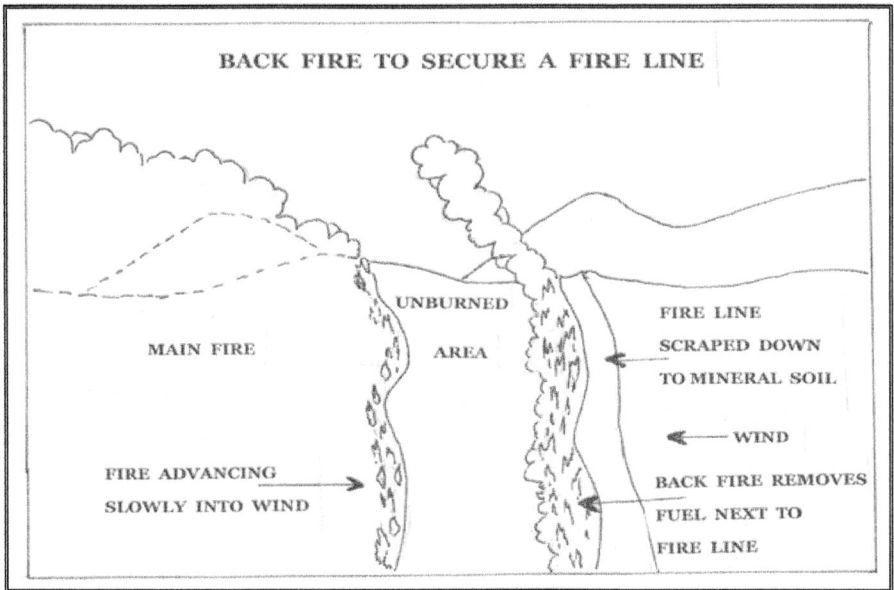

BACK FIRE TO SECURE A FIRE LINE

MAIN FIRE

UNBURNED AREA

FIRE LINE SCRAPED DOWN TO MINERAL SOIL.

WIND

FIRE ADVANCING SLOWLY INTO WIND

BACK FIRE REMOVES FUEL NEXT TO FIRE LINE

My knowledge about my load effectiveness and where to put it on a fire were about equal: non-existent.

Luck of the Ignorant

Later that summer, I spotted an island of trees well inside the burned-out area of the fire torching off with a great column of flame. No one is quite sure why it happens, but islands of trees somehow survive a roaring fire that takes out everything around them. Here and there would be left these clumps of trees: some small (a few trees), others sizable (perhaps hundreds of trees). I already knew I had tremendous fire-killing power in my airplane. This island was worthy of my attention. It looked like hundreds of trees were burning and the flames were at least a hundred feet above the canopy. This looked easy. I thought I could take this out with one shot. What a perfect place to demonstrate the power of the bomber.

Nothing registered in my mind about why I should put out (if I could) a fire that's well inside the burnt-out area. To me, it was an easy target and putting out any flame had to be of benefit to the overall strategy. It's logic that's a bit like throwing a lit match on a blazing bonfire because you want the extra heat. I headed straight for it and pulled the handle just as I entered the smoke above the flames.

The convective blast upward was like an exploding volcano. The airplane was thrown up with such an impact that my head was smashed down on to my hand on the control stick. Fortuitously, the airplane was flung straight up in the level attitude and I could only guess at the g-forces. I was covered in ashes that must have come up through all the openings in the bottom of the airplane as well as the open cockpit. From my experience with pulling g in the Air Force, I figured that I must have been tossed by at least fifteen g or more. At least I flew out in the level attitude and my airplane had just demonstrated how strong it was. There was no effect on that raging column. Did I not hit the target?

It was only because of the ruggedness of the airplane that my first foray into abject stupidity didn't take the wings off. I was learning things the hard way and my Guardian Angel looked after me. I got away with it. I was lucky. But that raging column of fire taught me something that I would never forget. The convection columns are extremely powerful. They're not a safe place to enter – a guy could get hurt doing that. *Wow – was that ever dumb. I won't be doing that again. I'll stick to where I have been so effective– putting out fires next to those important access roads.*

Sharing the Ignorance

Nothing had changed about our instructions to bomb the Myrtle Lake Fire and I wondered why I hadn't seen anyone else doing a drop. With such a monstrous fire, not seeing anyone was not too surprising since they could have been anywhere along the many miles of fire line. Then one day as I was coming back for a reload, I saw Sam the farmer drop his load. The load took several seconds to come out and from his height, which appeared to be about a hundred feet above the trees, most of it just dissipated into nothing. It was a real eye-opener. Very little of the load actually hit the trees and it still had about 150 feet more to go before it hit the ground where the fire was. Also I wasn't sure about what he was trying to hit, as there were hot spots everywhere.

This was a real shock as the same thing was happening to my loads. I stayed "up a bit" to take out a bigger swath of fire. My "up a bit" was to about 150 feet above the tree tops. None of my load was even hitting the trees, let alone descending to the ground. What we didn't know was that the exit door of the tank was too small. Its effect was to spread the load out and break it up into a lot of finer drops and spray, a perfect dispersion for maximum evaporation. The air was hot and dry so evaporation very quickly ate up our 125 gallons. Little or nothing was reaching the ground.

So that night, for the first time since we started bombing, Sam, Bill and I discussed dropping techniques. We didn't know anything about load dispersion or drop pattern. It didn't even enter our minds. We presumed we had an effective drop; we just had to figure out how to put it down. We hadn't talked about it earlier to avoid embarrassment.

No one knew anything, so staying quiet kept the ignorance contained. Everyone was working out their own drop technique.

Sam said, "Just drop at cruising speed from level flight and dump when you get over the fire. Stay "up a bit" so you get a better spread on the fire."

It was obvious that Sam didn't know any more about load behaviour than I did.

Bill countered, "Ya hafta hit it with speed and g's and ya gotta be right down next to the trees. Ya gotta push it down, the more g the better. It's the only way it works."

Perhaps he had a point. Speed and g-forces might be necessary to get the load down. I didn't think that speed would help as the load would string out farther, but I wondered if g-force might punch the load down. I didn't know if he was right or not, but I knew that a drop from level flight didn't do much.

I decided to try Bill's technique. I tried it once and only once. I dove at the target from a few hundred feet and pulled out at the target while dropping the load. I didn't like it at all. There were too many things to judge and get right all at the same time. I also had to take my hand off the throttle because the dump lever was pulled with the left hand. I thought that I had more in common with Sam, but in truth neither one of us had any idea of what we were doing.

We had been flying for weeks and never had any update briefings. When I asked for an update, I was simply told new fires were springing up all over the place. Nor did I get any feedback from the bulldozer operators I was helping so much. No one ever asked us about how we were doing. No one on the fire lines ever mentioned the bombers. All of that lack of attention suited me just fine. I was flying all day, day after day, and making money while I thought I was doing a great job.

We saw the people who had briefed us when we first started only when they wanted a message-drop mission. The radios used by Forest Service Dispatch had blind spots, so their transmitting stations could not contact crews that were hidden behind mountains and out of straight line of sight. When the dispatchers wanted to drop a message to a fire crew, they placed it inside a one foot length of canvas fire hose, clamped both ends and told us the location for the drop. It was fun doing these drops and some of them were in locations of breathtaking beauty.

I recall one site where a small fire (a lightning strike that wasn't doing much) on a steep slope was being sprayed with a powerful stream of water. Where did they get the water? The slope was very steep and there was no pond nearby. Circling a bit higher, I found the answer. The crew had placed a funnel in a stream coming off a glacier above them. The funnel directed water into their fire hose and by the time the water reached the hose nozzle a few hundred feet below, they had a great head of pressure.

The sight was unforgettable. A pale blue glacier ended at the black and orange of volcanic rock. From under the ice, a frothy, white mountain stream rushed to the edge of the tree line to cascade through the lush, emerald green forest. I circled up and down a few times to let my prairie senses absorb a scene of grandeur I never could have imagined.

I had the same problem dropping the messages that I had with dropping the water. How soon ahead of the target do I toss? Just to play safe, I waited until I was directly over the drop zone. With this kind of aim, most of my deliveries on steep mountainsides would have landed thousands of feet below their location. I never did hear if they ever got any of the messages.

Dive Bombing

On a return trip from Myrtle one day, I saw what Bill was doing. I saw his Stearman apparently hanging in space, hovering several hundred feet high above a spot of smoke directly below. I wasn't putting him and the spot together in my mind. It shouldn't be what I thought it shouldn't be. I was transfixed. From what looked like a hover, he suddenly pointed the nose steeply downward. Yes, he was aiming at that smoke. I couldn't believe it. The dive was almost vertical. I don't know how fast he was going just before he began the pull-out but it looked far too fast for a Stearman.

As he pulled out just above the trees, the load came out. It was inconceivable to me that we would have to do this type of maneuver to have the load reach the fire. It was extremely dangerous, but he did say that the dive was his favoured technique. I finally saw it, and the exit of the load looked the same as Sam's. Bill had to have pulled a lot of g to stop that dive and it didn't seem to make any difference to the load pattern. After the drop he pulled up at just as steep an angle as he had come down. He didn't have to do such a steep climb. It was grandstanding and it didn't make any sense. Also, it looked as if he had just missed the trees on the pullout. A few feet lower and he would have hit. What I saw was for real. After he landed, I saw him pulling bits of branches off the horizontal tail wires.

I had been a flying instructor for four years in the RCAF. I knew about flight, and I was experienced at sizing up the talents of my pupils. I could tell very soon into a student's training if they had what it took to be a competent pilot. Did they have the ability to think and work safely with an airplane? What kind of decisions did they make that would make them safe, professional pilots?

Bill's behaviour matched his reckless statements about bombing. I didn't think anyone would put themselves into this kind of danger. If he continued what he was doing, sooner or later he would hit the trees. Earlier, I had had suspicions about his good judgment. One day he took off right behind Sam in a cloud of dust. For some reason Sam aborted his takeoff and Bill just cleared over the top of his airplane. His dive on that smoke completed the portrait I had mentally painted for Bill. He was doing wild and crazy things; he was an accident waiting to happen. I made a statement to Sam and the people on the ground that Bill would run into a disaster if he kept up what he was doing. Sadly, five days later, he hit the trees and was killed.

I had only been in this business for a few weeks and here was the first fatality. It wasn't hard to see that it was totally unnecessary. We didn't know it yet, but the Stearman was not an effective bomber in the big-timber country of British Columbia, and no outlandish maneuvers would make any difference. Bill's and Sam's load exit looked the same, so the safest thing to do was just to fly level and drop at cruise speed. My punctilious logic also concluded that we weren't doing a thing to the targets of our choice.

In the matter of accuracy, I can only speak for myself. My chosen drop timing was to pull the drop handle just as I passed over the target. I figured the load would leave the aircraft, instantly stop and fall straight down. In reality, this was close to what actually happened with the thin spray of the Stearman. I wasn't very far off in my assessment of load behaviour, but it still was not the proper technique. It appeared that Bill and Sam were doing the same thing. We knew nothing of load lead times.

I didn't know the fires right next to the "roads" I was dropping on were backfires lit to burn out the fuel. The roads were actually fire lines. All the help I thought I was giving was totally misplaced; no one wanted those spots to be put out. There was a reason I didn't get any feedback from the boys on the bulldozers. I hadn't done a thing to their fires because my loads weren't reaching the ground. And it's just as likely they never even saw me pass overhead because the dozers had a heavy steel canopy covering the driver's seat, so they couldn't see anything by looking up. I went by fairly silently and they never would have heard me above the roar of their own engines. In this battle, I finally realized I was a non-event.

Three weeks had passed and there was no change to the plan of dropping on the Myrtle Lake Fire, so it continued day after day from dawn till dark. I was flying twelve to fourteen hours a day. It was tiring, but since we had only the summer as an earning period, we were hard at it.

Chapter Five
My Singular Accident

Don't take life too seriously; you'll never get out of it alive.
Elbert Hubbard

The Nose Stand

Aircraft with tail wheels and radial engines have a visibility problem on the ground as the pilot can't see over the nose while taxiing. The solution is to zigzag from side to side to take peeks at what's out front (hopefully nothing). Everyone has seen the procedure in the movies with trainers like the Stearman, the T-6 and fighters like the Thunderbolt. It's also the case with long-nosed airplanes like the Mustang and Spitfire. Consequently, it was necessary for me to weave my way into the loading slot to pick up my load. Although we had never briefed the loading crew to keep the spot clear, they quickly got the idea: nothing was to be put in the loading area.

One day after a routine landing, and the normal snaking on the way to load, all was well. At the last look before entering the loading pit, the area was clear, so in I went. About twenty feet or so from where I was supposed to park, I saw the back of a pickup truck directly ahead. It instantly loomed out on both sides of the nose at once.

I had a choice to make instantly: chew up the truck with the propeller, or stand on the brakes and stop. I stopped so suddenly that the forward momentum sent the tail up in the air and I stood the airplane on its nose. The propeller ground into the dirt, bringing the engine to an instant and involuntary stop. It turned out that a new driver, not familiar with the routine of keeping the spot clear, drove quickly into the area after my last clearing turn when I was going straight ahead. I didn't see him drive in.

It's amazing how high in the air the rear cockpit is when the nose is on the ground. Embarrassment adds ten feet to the height. All the comedians around reminded me that the three-point attitude of the

Stearman meant the two main wheels and the tail wheel, not the nose and the two main wheels. I had to hand it to them. If I could temper my embarrassment, it was funny. There was no easy way to get down from that perch and all the jokers thought I should do it on my own. After all, I got myself up there.

I didn't hit the truck, no one was chewed up, so I made the right choice. The only problem was my propeller: one blade was bent backwards toward the engine at about a thirty to forty degree angle. When it became obvious no one was hurt, the jokers relented and first helped me to get down from my perch and then lower the tail of the airplane to the ground.

To get the airplane back on its normal three points, I had two men lifting on the propeller and more pulling down on a rope attached to the tail wheel. When it did come down, the tail wheel hit with a stupendously loud, dusty crash. It hit so hard it looked to be as much of a disaster as standing the airplane on its nose. We didn't think of a way to let it down gently. It was one comedy after another. I'd probably bent the fuselage. A careful inspection revealed everything looking okay. The Stearman is one tough bird.

Now what? I was out of business. *What to do next? I could get on the phone to the boss and ask him to fly in a new propeller.* First, I didn't know if he had one, and I didn't know how long it would take to arrive. Ideas were flying around everywhere when one of the forest service maintenance people, Robert,* who had watched this whole affair, had an idea:

"Why don't you go down to a machine shop that's in town and Jake* the owner can straighten that blade out for you."

Now that's pretty farfetched, thought I. *Was this merely a suggestion or did this man Jake owe the forest service a favour? Would Jake even consider doing it? And how are we going to do that? We'd have to take the propeller off and we didn't have the proper tools for that. And what does the local machine shop owner know about straightening out airplane propellers?*

"What do you mean by straightening out the propeller, Robert? We don't have the tools to take it off."

"We can wheel the airplane into town, and he can do the job without taking it off."

"Really?"

"I'll get on the phone, Linc, and give him a call."

But first I had to let my boss, Don, know what was going on. I got on the phone and told him the story. He had two airplanes operating out of Kelowna, British Columbia and he was going to drive a truck the thousand miles overnight to be there the next day. He had another propeller, and he would bring it along. He would have to make another arrangement to get it to Blue River. We'd start there.

Straightening the Propeller

I was willing to listen to anything as people in the back woods show amazing ingenuity with limited resources. I don't know what Robert said to Jake when he called him, but it didn't seem that he had to talk Jake into this experiment. It appeared Jake was more than willing and claimed he could straighten the propeller without taking it off. I had never heard of anyone doing something like that and there was no picture in my mind as to how it could be done. But I was game. Why not give it a try?

The entire loading and help crew at the base didn't have to be asked if they would help push the Stearman into town. They had hands all over the airplane as it was pushed backwards down the wide, dusty main drag until our travelling circus arrived at the machine shop in about the centre of town. Robert introduced us.

"Jake this is Linc, the pilot."

"So you fly this thing, huh?"

"Sure do, Jake."

"Whatsa matter, can't fly it the way it is?"

"One blade would provide all the thrust on one side and the airplane would fly sideways."

"What's wrong with that? I thought you fly-boys could do anything."

"The loads would go sideways too and I wouldn't hit the fire."

"Maybe I can do something pretty to make you go straight."

Jake was about five foot ten and had light brown hair, graying slightly on the sides. I expected to see a man in coveralls with a grease-covered face. Not at all as I had imagined, Jake was dressed in a clean shirt and pants that seemed entirely inappropriate for a heavy-duty mechanic.

His deep blue eyes set in a lean, clean-shaven face immediately displayed an unflappable confidence about taking on this or any other task. I wondered if he looked this clean in the midst of changing tracks on a bulldozer. Jake spoke in a soft voice laced with the rough-cut language he used in long-time dealing with coarse-grained loggers and truck drivers. A dry wit and a gentle but no-nonsense demeanor instantly earned him a deserved respect. For some reason, I got the impression that Jake knew much more about airplanes than he was letting on. Jake was anxious to be helpful and I got the feeling he thought that this would be fun.

"I see you brought a few goons along to help."

"Whatever you need, Jake."

He had already dug out an assortment of giant C-clamps and wooden blocks. A C-clamp looks like the letter C. It has a screw on the top side of the C which turns down through a set of threads to clamp anything inside. The size of the C-clamps reminded me that I was in giant logging country. The massive tall trees yielded cumbrous logs that took trucks the size of freight trains to haul them out. And I hadn't seen anything but huge caterpillars in the trees below me. Jake needed humungous tools for the appropriate big-equipment jobs. One of those King Kong C-clamps could have crushed a truck. Why did he haul those things out? Airplanes are delicate items, not logging trucks. He sized up the propeller and the work began.

"I need some of you slopes over here to hold these blocks," he said. ("Slopes" was short for "sloped heads," meaning someone with considerably less intelligence than a chimp.)

Jake asked some of our crew to hold what looked like a ten-inch block on the inside of the blade where the bend began and another near the end of the bend. He spanned a heavy wooden beam across these blocks giving him about a foot and a half clearance at the position of maximum bend. He quietly gave directions about what he wanted while he put two clamps about eight inches apart straddling the middle of the bend. It was now obvious that he could not only pull the propeller straight, but could go well past the straight position and have it bow out.

There was a big rod for turning the screws on the C-clamps, but it wasn't big enough. Jake put a long pipe over it to give the leverage he needed for very heavy turning. He very carefully made sure that each clamp was tightened in turn to apply an even pressure. I was impressed with the fineness of his touch and his delicate care. For a heavy-duty mechanic, Jake was working with the precision of a clockmaker.

I was watching, spellbound. He knew what he was doing and he obviously knew that propellers are made of a very tough alloy. He kept turning until the propeller was straight. Everyone was considerably impressed. This seemed ridiculously easy. *He's now going to take the clamps off and I've got a serviceable airplane,* think I. *I can get back to the airport and go flying.*

The clamps didn't come off and he kept turning the screws so that the propeller was now bowing outwards. *What is he doing? He's going to snap the blade off.* I knew enough to be quiet; he was doing me a favour. He kept applying the pressure and the propeller blade bent further and further outward. It was bent out now almost as much as it was bent in. *This looks crazy, why did he bend it out so far?*

Then he stopped and went into the shop. He emerged with a big brass sledge hammer in his hand. I had no idea why he needed a thing like that. My mind was still trying to catch up to the reason for the huge bend outwards. But the logic of it was slowly sinking in: he bent the blade so far out because the metal was springy. When he let go, it would come back to the straight position.

I was totally unprepared for what happened next. He raised the hammer and landed a tremendous blow right in between the clamps. *What is he doing to my delicate propeller?* And he did it again and again. *This man is crazy. He'll break the blade off.* But equally distressingly, with each hit the entire airplane reverberated with the sound of a drum. The tight fabric over the struts and formers of the fuselage created the boom. After several mighty blows, he put the hammer down and asked us to hold the blocks while he took the clamps off. I couldn't believe it; the blade was still bent backwards although not quite as much as before this brutal abuse. He probably got about ten degrees of curve out of the blade. It was obvious that Jake knew a lot more about metals than the rest of us; hitting the blade allowed the metal to de-stress a little to help it move.

"Okay you jocks, I need you over here again."

It was now apparent that Jake had a plan. The whole procedure started again. We then helped him put bigger blocks up at each end of the bend along with that hefty wood beam. He again bent the blade ridiculously out of whack and again bashed at it with the biggest sledge hammer I had ever seen. Jake was obviously used to using this hammer to coax things into place on bulldozers, skidding machines and logging trucks. He was using the same tactics on my poor little airplane. He repeated the procedure six times to get this blade to track within a quarter of an inch of the other one. I think what amazed me so much was how matter-of-fact he was about the whole procedure. Jake was calm and cool and knew exactly what he was doing while I agonized about this Philistine manhandling of my airplane. If King Arthur had a metal basher the likes of Jake, he'd still be King of England. Finally Jake looked over to me and said:

"I think we got it pretty good. Run it."

"What — here in town?"

"Yup — run it."

We pushed the airplane clear of the shop, pointed it along the street and I gave it the graceful hand swing to start. I didn't want to blow dust around with the propeller slipstream, so I didn't run the engine to any more than 1,500 rpm. I shut it down and went over to the shop. It vibrated a little, but after all that effort I didn't ask Jake for any more tracking bends.

"Ya happy with that, or do we give it some more?"

"Jake, I didn't know you could do it. Thank you, it's going to be okay. I can fly it."

While Jake was straightening the propeller, I had formulated my plan of action. I wasn't going to wait for the propeller to be trucked up to Blue River from Kelowna. That might take a day or two and deprive me of flying time. I could get back to my lucrative bombing a lot sooner if I flew the airplane to Kelowna for the propeller change. Since the whole propeller-bashing process went on until well into the evening, I would have to wait until the next day to fly to Kelowna. I got on the phone to Don, the boss:

"I'll be flying down to Kelowna and you won't have to ship the new propeller up to Blue River."

"What? You said you had a bent propeller and needed a new one."

"It was bent, but we straightened it out. But it still needs a new propeller."

"What do you mean you straightened it out?"

"Jake, the machine shop owner straightened it out and I can fly the airplane to Kelowna."

"Stay where you are. You aren't flying the airplane anywhere. The new prop will be in Kelowna tomorrow and I'll get it trucked up to Blue River."

"It's okay, I ran the engine and I can fly it. I'll be down in Kelowna tomorrow." With that statement, I hung up the phone.

On my run-up the next morning I took the engine to 2,000 rpm. The airplane shook but probably no worse than if a cylinder wasn't firing. I was satisfied to fly the airplane. To this point I hadn't thought too much about what had taken place to straighten the propeller. Jake the gentle, quiet metal-basher knew what he was doing. He straightened it out and I would go flying as if nothing had happened. I was so wired to fly and make money I didn't think about any repercussions to this whole procedure. The airplane shook a little (a fair bit actually), but I talked myself into believing it didn't shake too much and nothing would happen. I wanted to get to Kelowna for the propeller change.

I Must be Crazy

I pointed the airplane down the runway and I was going. As soon as I advanced the power, the airplane took on the buzz it would have for the rest of the trip. I climbed to altitude with the propeller in fine pitch. When I leveled off and pulled coarse pitch to slow the engine down, the airplane vibrated so much I could hardly read the instruments. *Whoa* – I pulled back to fine pitch and the tremendous vibration settled down to a lesser full-airplane reverberation that I have talked myself into believing I could live with. We had tracked the bent blade to within a quarter inch of the good blade but that was in tip travel only. The tremendous vibration at coarse pitch told me we didn't correct the twist in the bent blade. The pitch was out of whack.

I exuded dubious confidence. I would do the trip in fine pitch. It would be a bit slower than normal cruise but so what, I was being paid by the hour. I now had a couple of hours to think about the last day's events. I didn't want to lose too many days' flying time, but now I was going to blow it all. I was up at altitude with a racing engine and there were only the world's most humungous trees below me. Throwing a blade off would tear away the engine from the vibration. The airplane would go out of control and I would crash in some crazy attitude and be shredded into rags before I hit bottom. There was no way to survive that one. The forest canopy would close over me and I would never be found. I was pre-wallowing in self pity early in case I was killed. I couldn't believe that all the bashing with the sledge hammer didn't crack or damage the propeller. Why was I so anxious to fly this airplane when I now knew it was going to fling the blade off?

The rpm was too high, but it was worse to slow it down. *I know the rpm is higher than normal. I can hear the engine winding up to more than 2,000 rpm and it's screaming. The tachometer reads 2,000 rpm, but I know it's not right. It's not working like other things on this airplane. The engine is tearing itself to pieces. What can I do when it does throw the blade off? The engine won't stay on. When the engine flies off, I might be able to come down in a level attitude if I hold the stick full forward. That would make up for the lost weight up front. I could do a soft landing. Why am I here? This is really stupid. I was far too anxious to get down to Kelowna.*

Half an hour had gone by. The engine was still there but in my head it was still screaming way beyond 2,000 rpm. *I'm still here. If it hasn't flung the blade off by now maybe it'll hang on for a while longer. Farther south, I'll find some farm field and do an emergency landing just to play safe.*

I was up for an hour, the propeller hadn't thrown the blade and the engine was whining like a chainsaw even though it was only showing 2,000 rpm. I knew the engine was in wild over-speed but the propeller was still hanging on. That's one tough engine, one tough propeller. I was still flying. *If I get out of this one, I'll be a real good boy and not do anything as stupid as this ever again.*

Kelowna was fifteen minutes away, so I throttled back to save the engine. Save it from what? It must already be garbage.

I was on final approach to the runway and I was going to make it. I taxied in and I was greeted by the boss. He looked at the propeller and shook his head. He was of two minds: I'd saved him some money but what I did was really dumb. He's already lost one airplane, and I could have put in the second. I wasn't sure if he considered me to be much of a loss. Anyway, he was happy to see me and his intact airplane. A crew got on to the business of changing the propeller immediately and I would have the night off in the big city.

There was a flurry of bombing activity going on out of Kelowna, so that night I was able to socialize with a rowdy gang of the troops in a downtown pub. Somehow the word had gotten out that some crazy individual had brought in a Stearman with a bent propeller. Countless beers and a plethora of back-slapping, good natured toasts to my questionable sanity and airmanship morphed my stupidity and recklessness into a bold and daring stroke. As the evening went on, I became more of a nothing-stops-this-guy hero.

Maybe it was a lack of prudence to straighten the propeller, but it all worked out okay. I have to get credit for that. I knew that the propeller was tough; I knew that it would hang on. Now that I think about it, the engine didn't really over-speed, the tach always showed 2,000 rpm and the engine was still as good as new.

I was alive and celebrating with the boys. The guilt was slipping away and I was rationalizing my actions. Everything worked out as planned, just as I thought it would, I kept telling myself I wasn't so feckless after all. In truth I was lucky that I got away with it.

The next day I was on my way back to Blue River. The weather was still hot and dry and the action continued.

The Unwelcome Break

Brian, the big New Zealander operations manager had come to the conclusion I must be tired and needed a break. He arrived in Blue River to fly my airplane for a few days to give me a rest. He got the same one-line briefing I heard for the Myrtle Lake Fire, and he took over my airplane. I didn't like the idea of his taking over for a few days, as I'd be losing out on flying time and pay. That's money. But there was nothing I could do about it, so I went to the airstrip to see him off. He was much bigger than I had remembered and he didn't have an easy time getting into the airplane. He parked himself in the cockpit for quite awhile as he looked for something. I'm not sure what he was looking for; there's no simpler airplane or cockpit. He was finally sure about going ahead and he gave the signal that he wanted a start. I swung the propeller for him and he was ready to load and fly his first trip.

The takeoff looked normal and he was gone. I didn't know what he did over the fire, but he was back for another load. I'd resigned myself to the fact that I'd lose the airplane for a few days before I could get back at it. Maybe I did need the break as I was pretty tired. I'd flown over 250 hours in the last month. He was loaded and off again for his second shot. From the loquacious long-windedness I heard from him when I got hired, he must have really known what he was doing. I thought there might be a real opportunity to learn something from this man. I didn't feel like I could do anything useful back at the hotel so I stayed around the airstrip to watch him enviously do my flying.

Brian was coming back and he was landing in the northerly direction as we had been doing all along. He touched down, gyrated wildly for a swing or two, ground-looped and rolled backwards into the trees. A few of us jumped into a truck and headed down the airstrip. He was already out of the airplane when we get there and he looked unhurt.

The airplane had penetrated into the trees far enough to do substantial damage to the tail planes. The trailing edges of the wings looked pretty ragged as well. There were several broken wing ribs and torn fabric. It looked like a pretty extensive repair job. The airplane would have to be disassembled and trucked back to Wetaskiwin, but it would fly again.

My first summer of Fire Bombing had just ended. How could a man with Brian's fantastic flying ability ground-loop a Stearman? He was still the same gas bag and his Fire Bombing experience consisted of the one trip I saw him make. I didn't know how much more flying he did for the company, but he wasn't there the next season.

The Season's Reality

It was such a frantic pace for the summer I didn't have time to analyze seriously what I was doing. As it turned out, I did nothing of value to fight a forest fire and learned very little. I picked up a little fire jargon — spot fire, head, flanks and base — and that the head was the area of fastest spread. And I found out what those hot spots were next to the fire line. Nobody had any ideas about how to use an airplane effectively for firefighting purposes. It was quickly obvious that nothing my airplane could do was going to have any— beneficial results on the Myrtle Lake Fire. Were there any situations where an airplane could be of help? We didn't do any drop tests and there was no evaluation of results. Nobody sent me on a mission to a specific target because nobody knew what a suitable target was.

Stearman dropping borate on a grass fire in California.
Photo courtesy CDF

In defense of the Stearman, it was a different story in California. There, the Stearman could be effective on a small fire, since the low-lying brush of California lent itself to low-level drops of borate. Borate was added to the water to slow the rate of evaporation. The pattern, as thin as it was, would reach the ground. Early results with the airplane were encouraging, so there was continued interest in the development of larger-aircraft bombing systems.

Maybe the British Columbia Forest Service knew this little airplane was useless long before we knew it, or admitted it. It was flagrantly obvious that the Stearman with the little dump door was totally unsuitable as a Fire Bomber. There was too little load spread out too thinly. Without a big load which could be dropped in reasonable concentration, there was no way to perfect proper drop altitudes, airspeeds and trigger times. My summer of hard flying and earning a decent buck had been a pure gift. I didn't earn it.

Bill had needlessly killed himself in a situation that I didn't regard as dangerous. He made the job even more dangerous by trying drop techniques which called for several simultaneous judgment calls to get the drop right. It was far too dangerous a procedure.

I had seen the awesome power coming out of an immense, out-of-control fire. I had watched daily from a ringside seat. The summer was an unforgettable experience. I now had the fall and winter to think about whether or not this business was something I wanted to do.

Joe Ely, the Man who Started it All

In 1955 and 1956, Joe Ely of the United States Forest Service had commissioned the first Air Tanker "Squadron" at Willows, California, ushering in the beginning of the Air Tanker fleets of today. Bob Fish, who wrote a paper on the activities of Joe and his early "squadrons," had this comment on just how innovative Joe was:

> *What he did struck me when I saw the first "aerial attack map" he hand drew for Mendocino National Forest. He drew "time related" circles around various airstrips (Gravelley Valley, Willows, etc) and overlaid that on a map of the forest. He labeled those bases "farm ships" (which meant the little Stearman and N3N ag planes). Where they did not overlap, he drew in notations called "twin beech" which meant they were special response areas to be handled by the faster twin-engined aircraft that could carry more retardant. He was way*

60

ahead of his time in putting an "architecture for aerial response" together and then coordinating it with the ground strike teams and fire tower operators so they knew which base to call for support to get help in the least amount of time (3 min, 7 min, etc).

In the history of the development of Fire Bombers there is one date which truly marked the beginning of it all – as Joe Ely put it:

On August 13, 1955, a crew was building hand line in the brush on the lower side of the Mendenhall fire on the west side of Bald Mountain on Jack Weddle's Covelo District. They heard a plane coming in close and looked up just in time to see a load of water come down upon them and the edge of the fire. It was the first free-fall drop ever made on a forest fire.

Fate grants few people the singular opportunity to take an initiative unseen by others. At the time of sticking his neck out to try something that looked like it may have potential, Joe may never have realized that he had actualized himself a place in the history of Fire Bombing. Joe deserves recognition as the man with foresight who started it all.

Joe Ely with tanker number one. Photo by author

Reproduced courtesy of Jean Barbaud

Grumman Avenger... TBM

Chapter Six
A Summer of Chaos

Two wrongs are only the beginning. Murphy's Law

Fire Bombing had tickled my sense of adventure and by late winter, I was looking for my next job. About one thing I was certain – I wasn't about to go back flying an open-cockpit Stearman. I wanted to fly a bigger, more modern airplane, and I wanted to fly in the mountains of British Columbia. I had seen the American Grumman TBMs at Kamloops and had heard that a company called Skyway Air Services out on BC's West Coast had bought a few. I possessed what I thought were great credentials: I was Air Force trained and could now claim to be an experienced Fire Bombing pilot. So I applied for a job. Several pilots were needed, and I was hired. I was told to report at Langley, BC in April for training.

Skyway Air Services

By the time I had arrived, the company had purchased a surplus wartime hangar in Abbotsford (the airport later to become home of the famous Abbotsford Air Show) and we did our training there.

Little did I know the first day at Abbotsford would be the beginning of an adventure which would last for the rest of my flying career. On that first day, I met people who would become lifelong friends and others who would soon not survive this business. No one knew what kind of flying was in store for us and no one had done any bombing. On my application I claimed Fire Bombing experience, but I was no more qualified than the other pilots. I knew as much as anybody else: nothing. We were a mixture of spray pilots, bush pilots and ex-military. Fire Bombing was in its infancy and nobody knew anything about how to make the airplanes effective.

The chief pilot, who was also the operations manager, was a short, stocky man by the name of Peter Deck who went by the name of Pete.

He stood about five foot eight and his weather-beaten face made him look well beyond his age, which I would have guessed at around forty. He had a heavy shock of brown hair which also grew liberally out of his nose and ears. I couldn't help but notice because I often wondered how easy it was for him to hear and breathe. Silly thought, but it did enter my mind.

He was the happy combination of lawyer, pilot, judge and solid friend. He loved to debate any topic, even religion. I thought Catholics avoided the topic, but not Pete – he was wide open. He would dissect a topic, advance arguments from both sides of an issue like George Washington and, in measured words, announce his decision. When a discussion finally precipitated something that his mind could accept, he would recite his logic out loud and give the Maxwell Smart – "Ahhh yes – the-old _____ trick." Nevertheless, impressions aside, Pete was a philosopher whose debating prowess could have easily been a challenge to Socrates.

He never made a decision that would use the company's money or would affect his pilots adversely without the recitation of his reasoning and logic. If Pete thought you had the makings of a competent pilot, he was your friend and would go to bat for you with the top brass of the company. He knew that boys would be boys and he looked after us regardless of the antics we often got into. He was my confidant and friend for the several years that I worked for the company.

Seven of us were hired to man the seven TBMs Skyway had just purchased. Although we came from diverse flying backgrounds, all of us had thousands of hours of flying experience and it was anybody's guess as to who had the best credentials for Fire Bombing. Two of our group were spray pilots, so with their low-level flying experience, I thought they might lead the way in helping the rest of us in this oh-so-new occupation. As it turned out, low-level spraying on flat ground had nothing in common with a steep dive down the side of a mountain. As far as any advance advice about bombing with this airplane, there was nothing that Pete could tell us. There were no rules and everyone was on their own. Nevertheless we were all keen, we looked forward to the excitement and we were totally ignorant of what lay ahead.

Tom Wilson, a tall, lean fellow with a perpetual tan, winter and summer, was one of the spray pilots. His lean, boyish face disguised his practical and already seasoned approach to working with an airplane. He had had experience in bush flying in Guyana as well as in crop spraying. When I learned a little about his background, it was obvious that Tom could handle anything flying would throw at him. Nothing shook him up. If a bush plane needed a fix in the middle of nowhere, Tom would get it done.

The TBM was the biggest and heaviest airplane that we were both tackling at the time and he handled it with the hand of a pro. Later in his career, his cool head saved him after a catastrophic ditching of a Tracker into the Fraser River. After being knocked unconscious by the tremendous impact of the hit, he revived in muddy water with zero visibility to unfasten his seat belt, calmly open the roof hatch and climb out. Tom was a pillar of reliability, and a true friend. He never gossiped about anybody, but just told things like they were. If you wanted to know something about Fire Bombing that was happening anywhere in the country, or anywhere else in the world for that matter, Tom was a one-man Google. All information trails led to Tom. He was as concerned about the other pilots as he was about himself. He and I signed the first two membership cards, when, many years later, the pilots recognized the desperate need for a union.

The TBM (Grumman Avenger)

With the use of the airplane manual, we did a short ground school. I was still hot on my flight-planning computer from my Air Force days and could whiz off the aircraft performance once I knew the aircraft weight, its configuration and the horsepower of the engine.

There was nothing pretty about the Grumman Avenger. It was powered by the big Wright radial, eighteen-cylinder R2600 engine which snorted out a respectable 1,950 horsepower. The airplane had a massive, fat fuselage with a belly that just missed the ground sitting in its three-point, tail-dragger position. Some airplanes just don't look like they should be flying, or even could, and the "Turkey," as it came to be known, was one of them. It certainly would never win a beauty contest. It was designed to operate from aircraft carriers with a crew of three: the pilot, a navigator and a rear gunner. The Grumman Engineers were obviously thinking ship design instead of airplane when it went to the drawing boards. Giant rivet heads, big enough for a battleship, were glaringly obvious when looking down from the front cockpit at the centre wing section.

The fat, high-lift wings dropped out a set of long, spindly landing gear that seemed totally inadequate for carrier landings. Just outside of the main landing gear, the massive folding mechanism for the wings would make a swing section for the Golden Gate Bridge. Like all carrier-based planes, it was built for the bone-jarring arrivals that the Navy calls routine landings. The fully swivelling tail wheel made taxiing and parking easy, and could be locked in the "straight ahead" position for takeoff.

During the War, takeoff meant being shot off the deck of an aircraft carrier to head off on a torpedo attack mission, and the TBM certainly saw its share.

TBM with the abstract "Turkey" I painted on the nose.
Photo by author

The TBM was the American answer to the Japanese Kamikaze. That kind of fate for it wasn't envisaged when it was designed as a torpedo-launch platform. It just turned out that way. It was called a torpedo bomber even though, in reality, the airplane didn't bomb anything: it bravely dropped torpedoes into the water.

The method of using an airplane to launch a torpedo involved flying the airplane at a right-angle to the path of the target ship and far enough ahead of it to drop a torpedo destined to sink the nasty villain. Sinking ships with aerial-borne torpedoes was proven to work by the British at Taranto harbour in Italy and by the Japanese at Pearl Harbour. It looked like the torpedo bomber could be a devastating weapon against Japanese ships in the Pacific.

The pilot knew the speed of his target ship and how long the torpedo needed to run to arm itself. He also had to make sure he wasn't too high or too low since the torpedo had to enter the water at just the right angle. So there was a perfect launch "sweet spot" for letting go of the water-borne missile. If the launch were done in the correct spot and the ship dutifully continued on the same course, the torpedo and ship should arrive at the same place in the ocean at the same time resulting in a calamitous bang. It wasn't an easy hit because the ship captains knew the game and were highly uncooperative, able to turn their ships sharply enough to avoid the torpedoes.

The Japanese Kamikaze was expected to fly into the target ship carrying his torpedo or bomb; the pilot was the precision guidance system in the days before "smart" bombs. (Kind of beastly for the pilot, but it worked.) The American torpedo bomber pilot wasn't expected to fly into the ship, but his mission was to fly precisely into a spot known to every gunner on the ship, where he would be enthusiastically greeted by a wall of explosions and shrapnel. One was not quite the equivalent of the other, but the results for the pilots were not far from the same. If they survived the onslaught of the Japanese Fleet Zero fighters, most torpedo bombers met a quick fate on their run to the target. Losses were so bad that the American Navy had the good sense to withdraw them quickly from that role.

Where the airplane really found its niche was as part of a hunter-killer, anti-submarine weapon operating from aircraft carriers, the weapon of George W. Bush Sr. The man who would later become the President of the United States participated in naval battles in the Pacific, flying off the Aircraft Carrier USS San Jacinto. A large number of TBMs were built, so there were plenty of surplus TBMs available after the war.

Set the Throttle Tension

We finished our ground school in Abbotsford and several of us did our check-out on the one airplane the company had ready at the time. Several more were being tanked at Fairey Aviation in Victoria on Vancouver Island. Once we had done our check-out, a few of us were selected to pick up the new conversions as they came ready and fly them back to Abbotsford.

Pete had some advice for those of us who had never flown a single-engine aircraft with that much horsepower. The proper amount of rudder trim had to be selected to counter the horrendous torque that developed as the power was advanced. "Put in the wrong rudder trim" said Pete, "and your leg won't be big enough to hold the aircraft straight." Like all the single-engined airplanes with big engines, takeoff power is advanced slowly in concert with the aircraft picking up speed. The rudder becomes more effective with speed, which allows the pilot to add more power. He suggested that we should have fifty or more knots on before the power was fully up for takeoff, as the rudder wouldn't hold the aircraft straight if full power was applied at slow speed.

During the course, we were told on several occasions to tighten the throttle tension for takeoff. I knew that was pretty standard for piston-powered airplanes which have a throttle quadrant on the left side of the cockpit. Tighten the tension nut – standard procedure – no problem. "What's the big deal?" I thought. The tension nut or screw is designed to put enough friction on the throttle leverage mechanism to make the throttle stay put in any selected position. The "tension nut," perhaps so named for the condition of the pilot just prior to takeoff, is a round knob which is tightened or loosened right at the throttle quadrant and is done with the left hand.

"It must be set tight for takeoff," said Pete, and added a new point, "or the throttle will come right back to idle."

It was now time for me to fly the airplane. I did the walk-around and climbed into the cockpit. Starting a big radial engine has a special magic about it. After sitting for awhile, oil drains into the lower cylinders, so the engine is turned over with the starter for about twelve blades to give the exhaust valves the chance to open a few times to drain the oil. I watched the big blades slowly passing by and counted, One, two...until the requisite twelve have gone by, I then hit the primer switch to send fuel directly into the cylinders. I heard the chug of each cylinder as it fired, watched the cowling twist from the unbalanced firing and, along with the sound, saw an enveloping cloud of blue smoke. The cleaned-out oil was being burned and had the aroma of aviation. As each additional cylinder joined the cacophony, I heard the throaty growl of this prodigious, round, belching engine that would carry me to the ends of the Earth. The immersion in that bouquet of smoke is like the morning shower; life doesn't begin without it. It was the same every time I started that engine. Those few moments bathed in the clouds of pilot's Chanel began another special day.

I did the pre-takeoff check list and I noticed that there was a thoughtful reminder on the check list: "The throttle tension must be set tight." *Here we go again – why all this fuss about throttle tension?* So I tightened the tension nut to what I thought was enough tension to have a tame, obedient throttle. I was not aware that the airplane had a diabolical trick it was going to spring on me (and every other pilot) on his first takeoff. I obediently advanced the throttle slowly and took off in the three-point attitude as recommended.

Right after takeoff at an altitude of not more than about fifty feet, I let go of the throttle to select the gear up with the left hand. The throttle moved back, all the way back – quick as the next Joan Rivers face-lift – to idle. I just let go, and in about two seconds, I had no power. I couldn't stay at "no power" right next to the ground long enough to reach for the gear handle, or tighten the throttle tension. My hand hastily returned to push the throttle back on and I couldn't let go of the stick to let the right hand crank on more throttle tension.

I tried the be-real-fast trick. My left hand came off the throttle again for a quick grab for the tension knob, but I couldn't do it. The power backed off virtually instantly, so I was back to the throttle. I wondered what people on the ground were thinking as they heard the engine roaring up to full power, going back to idle, roaring up to full power, back to idle and back to full power. I tried the-right-hand-off-the-stick maneuver to head for the tension nut, but I couldn't do that either. The elevator trim was not precisely set for level flight. I started to dive, so it was back to the stick.

I couldn't do this two-handed shuffle close to the ground, so there was only one solution: hold on to everything and climb to a few hundred feet where the aircraft at idle power for a short time wouldn't get me into trouble. At altitude, the throttle tension was the first order of priority, and is normally done with the left hand. If I tried it with my right hand and let go of the control stick the nose might have gone up or down depending on how close to neutral the elevator trim was set prior to takeoff.

I didn't want the engine to go to idle RPM again, so I let go of the stick, took the nose-dive the airplane was trimmed for and made a frantic grab for the tension nut. I tightened the tension nut down with the conviction of a plumber on the end of a three-foot pipe wrench, pulled out of my dive, and then got on with the rest of the after-takeoff check.

Now I couldn't move the throttle back to climb power. I had over-tightened the lid on the cookie jar and now couldn't get the cookies out. I couldn't say that I wasn't warned about the throttle. Yes, you do need a lot of tension on it. Yes, it will come back to idle — really fast. Okay Pete, I fell into the same trap as everybody else.

A Gentle Bird

I flew the airplane for a little over an hour and checked out its stall characteristics. It was docile enough and didn't do anything outrageous. To this point in my flying career, the TBM was the heaviest airplane I'd flown. The stall was gentle, but it used up a huge amount of sky in the recovery — not a practice at low altitude. I was learning about the lead times required to accelerate and slow down a heavy airplane.

Flying the TBM with Skyway Air Services, British Columbia.

Applying full power was not an instant go, as it took awhile for the iron to get moving. The controls were stiff and took extra brawn to move, but that was typical of aircraft designed in that era. There were no boosted controls and the design engineers didn't provide aerodynamic booster tabs big enough to give the pilot's muscles a break.

The bomb doors were opened by a set of pull handles on the left side of the cockpit, one handle for each door. It was a poor arrangement as the pilot had to take his hand off the throttle to activate the bomb doors. The airplane carried 600 imperial gallons that could be dropped singly or as a double shot. Experimentation, and considerable experience at fire actions, confirmed that 300 gallons was the minimum effective drop for the forests of British Columbia, so the TBM dropped an effective load.

American experience had already shown the effect of water could be enhanced by adding Bentonite, what is known as a short-term retardant. Bentonite made the drops go down better and inhibited the evaporation of the water in the mix, thereby prolonging the cooling effect of the water. By itself, it was not a retardant.

A safety feature, which first came from the Americans, was the requirement to place load drop and radio control buttons onto primary aircraft controls. That meant drop and radio controls had to be located either on the throttle or control column, or one on each, depending on how easy these installations were on any particular aircraft. With this arrangement, the pilot never had to take his hands off the critical flight controls. We didn't have a similar configuration on our TBMs which became a contributing factor in the death of some pilots.

The company had several bombing TBMs ready for action, but no contract for standby. Without standby pay for the company, there was no standby pay for the pilots, so it was up to us to decide whether or not we wanted to sit around and wait for the chance that we might fly. Happily from a bomber pilot's point of view, we had numerous fires in 1961 and our education truly began.

The Chaos Begins

A series of thunderstorms ignited a particularly dry forest and in July a fire bust was on provincewide. Typically, airplanes were called in after every other resource was all but exhausted. Still, it was a chance for the company to earn enough money to stay in business, and for the pilots to get some bombing experience – and the needed pay. The company was able to put all of its airplanes to work, and a number of different aircraft from the USA were invited to come to Kamloops and assist.

Kamloops airport and the surrounding area bask in what meteorologists term a rain shadow. The mountains to the west divert the moist air from the Pacific around the area so it receives very little rain. It is in fact one of the micro-climates common in British Columbia resulting in Kamloops being a semi-desert and experiencing California heat and dry humidity during the summer.

Kamloops is the area of British Columbia having the most fires, so it's the place to be for Fire Bombing action. I was quite pleased when I got the opportunity to fly out of that base along with the American bombers based there. My first year of bombing with the TBM wasn't much different than my previous year flying the Stearman. We were always called to a big fire and there was no control over our actions. As a result, my Fire Bombing was no more disciplined or effective than it had been the previous season.

None of us were learning much about fires, but I was certainly learning the ropes of how to handle my TBM in the mountains. It's a heavy, underpowered airplane with a load on and only a reasonable performer empty. Because of its weight, every action had to be anticipated well in advance. Unlike the Stearman, I could not slap on the power and do an immediate tight turn to get out of trouble.

Pre-selecting the gear up with the airplane weight still on the wheels results in a snappy gear retraction at the instant of takeoff. This pilot was dazzling everyone with his takeoffs until his gear retracted just before the airplane was ready to fly. The engine was at full power when it ripped the propeller off and caught fire. Photo by author

I also discovered something else: when I dropped the load, the aircraft had a pronounced pitch-up. It was bad enough when I dropped one door, but it got most unpleasant when I let the full load go at a high airspeed. It was my first year in the TBM and I was delighted to talk to anyone who had some bombing experience. At Kamloops, I was exposed to the pilots of the US TBMs, B-25s and B-17s, so it was an opportunity to learn from others. No one had precisely articulated the cause of pitch-up, and there were all kinds of ideas about the best way to get the load into the trees. Everybody was practicing his own theory. Each pilot distilled his own formula for drop speed, drop height, and whether or not to try for g-force output at the time of load release. One of the first discoveries about pitch-up was how much worse it got as the drop speed increased – much worse. We had plenty of theories, but no one knew precisely why.

One day I watched a B-25 as it taxied in after a bombing run. I was told that on board was a newspaper photographer who went on a bombing trip in the B-25 to get some fire footage from an unusual vantage point. He was in an ideal position to get some pictures while lying down shooting with his movie camera through the glass nose. After the engines shut down, and he and the crew spilled out, I headed for the camera-toting individual who happened to have a very anguished look on his face. It was obvious something unpleasant had happened during the flight. He was about six foot two and looked like a movie star: young, well-built with dark, wavy hair framing a perfect face. Other than wearing a waist-length summer jacket, his shirt and tie suggested he was sent on this mission directly from his office. I was curious about his trip and accosted him after he had walked a short distance from the aircraft.

"How'd your trip go? Get some good footage?"

He spoke excitedly in an American accent. "I'll never do that again."

"Why, what happened?"

"When this guy (gesturing toward the airplane) dropped the load I was smashed down into the glass so hard I thought I had broken some ribs."

"Wow, any idea why that happened?"

"I figure he must have pulled sixteen or seventeen g's."

The photographer had a good idea of what he was talking about, as he had been a pilot during the war.

"How did you get into a situation like that?"

"I don't know, but I'm sure as hell not going up with him again."

I already had enough experience to know the pitch-up got worse with speed and I had heard some people were dropping at what seemed to me to be ridiculously high speeds. So I wondered if the photographer knew what the drop speed was.

"Do you know what speed you dropped at?"

"I don't know but it was one hell of a hairy ride."

Our conversation ended there and the photographer went on to talk to other people. A short time later I had a chance to meet the pilot.

This man was every inch the perfect image of a pilot. He was about five foot ten with a stocky build. He had salt-and-pepper wavy hair, suggesting an age of somewhere between forty and fifty. Despite heavy features in roughly-sculpted potter's clay, he still presented a tanned, handsome face complete with a thick moustache. His tan slacks were immaculately pressed with a crease so perfect he must not have sat in his airplane. One side of a crisp pant leg hung suspended on the top of a polished Wellington boot. His brown, leather bomber jacket, along with his casual stride, completed an image of a highly experienced man who knew what he was doing.

"How do you like flying the B-25?"

His soft, slow speech and measured drawl suggested that home was some southern state.

"Very nice airplane, son."

Son? Had he spotted how green I was in this business?

"This is my first year at bombing and I'm flying that TBM over there. I was wondering what you did to get the load in?"

"I like to toss it in from a pull-out doing about 200. That does a real good job of getting it down."

This man sounded so knowledgeable, but I knew plenty about g-forces and what he was doing didn't sound right at all. Dropping the load at 200? Nobody drops at 200. And if he really was getting sixteen to seventeen g on the drop, the wings wouldn't stay on his airplane. What I knew about Fire Bombing at that stage could have been hand-written on a postage stamp, but I certainly knew that diving approaches and dropping at high speeds was not the way to do it. We chatted briefly about the fire bust and then each of us went on to getting ready for another trip.

So far I had been dropping all my loads straight and level. I didn't see any need to try and "toss" the load. But I was a beginner. I was listening and learning.

It Happens Again

I found out later in the summer that the handsome, soft spoken man with whom I had chatted had crashed in Washington State by going into a mountain backwards. It appeared that on one of his drops, the g-forces must have been so severe as to flip the aircraft completely over to fly backwards into the mountain. It was surprising his wings didn't come off. Nevertheless, his behaviour was prophetic: wings were later to come off the B-25 and research into the pitch-up phenomenon would reveal why.

I flew a bag of hours that summer and like the season before on the Stearman, I sensed that I had yet again achieved nothing of value on the fires. However, if the company and our jobs were to continue, I realized we just couldn't go around the country tossing our loads uselessly wherever we felt like it. That was one concern; the other was that I was learning nothing about how to use the airplane effectively. Surely this could be a summer of learning. I was now exposed to a spectrum of pilots flying a variety of airplanes, and I thought if I talked to enough people, I could filter out something of value.

Sadly, nothing of the kind happened. Pilots were dropping at right angles to the fire line, into the middle of the fire, and some just let the load go from a pleasantly high altitude, allowing it to drift wherever the wind took it. Some were doing steep dives at the fire, some bombed up-hill, others dropped in a turn. From what I observed, there was no consistency whatever about drop heights and airspeeds. Many questions went unanswered: drop half a load or drop it all? What about pitch-up? No one had any sensible answers.

Plainly and simply, chaos prevailed. Considering so much downright dangerous flying was going on, it was a miracle no one was killed. We gathered at a local pub every night and, over copious amounts of beer, bragged about our various antics, oblivious to our dangerous behaviour. We flew in fantasy land. Everybody had their own ideas about the best way to use the airplane and nothing of value came out of our nightly bragging-fests.

The summer was hot and dry and we continued to fly as much as we wanted week after week. We literally flew from dawn till dark for several weeks and pilots were getting tired.

Murphy pulled one of his usual stunts later in summer. A B-17 flying out of Kamloops landed with the gear up. The crew had flown ten to fourteen hour days for so many weeks they were truly fatigued. The captain readily admitted that he and his F/O were both dog tired and forgot to lower the gear for landing. I wasn't there to see what I heard was a spectacular trail of sparks that emanated from the retardant tank on the underside of the airplane. There was no fire, the crew was not injured and someone knew who to call to procure whale-like airbags for lifting the airplane. They arrived on the scene the same day. The bags were placed under the wings, inflated with air and gently lifted the B-17 until it was high enough to drop the gear.

After two months of intensive flying, the rains came one day and heavily doused the entire province. The season was over.

B-17 at Kamloops, British Columbia 1961. Oops – forgot the gear.
Photo by author

An Early Obsession

Now as I write about my flying career as a bomber pilot, I have been searching the deepest recesses of my memory to recall when and how it all began. Was I different from anybody else? Do all young boys have an epiphany moment when their profession-to-be suddenly becomes clear? I looked back to see when the desire to fly became an obsession with me.

I was one of those fortunate kids who knew exactly what I was going to be when I grew up, fortunate because there was no uncertainty to my life as there was for so many of my boyhood friends. Life was simple: I had a goal and took each necessary step along the way to achieve it. I was enjoying model airplanes as an interlude until I would be a pilot in the real thing. I studied airplane design so I could create original models of my own. My teenage years were a whirlwind of making and (while practicing aerobatics) crashing my models almost as fast as I made them. But at what age did the infatuation begin? When did I see my first real airplane?

Starting at the age of three, I had seen strange objects in the sky with two boats on the bottom flying over the house without flapping their wings. They made such a loud buzzing sound and didn't look like birds so I wondered what they were. I asked my stepfather about these flying things and he simply flipped off the word "airplanes" and left it at that. By age six, other kids told me what airplanes were, but I had never seen one up close.

I grew up in the town of Kenora, Ontario which is at the north end of Lake of the Woods. Kenora is a pretty town situated among the low, forest-covered hills of the Canadian Shield, itself made up of some of the oldest rock in North America. Volcanism early in the life of the rock forced molten quartz along with its cargo of gold into the many fissures discovered there. Gold mining, the paper mill and summer fishing supported the town then as now. The forever-unchanging population of 15,000 doubles in summer as people from Winnipeg and Minnesota flock to their summer homes and boats to spend time on the lake's countless channels and pristine islands.

I knew about the lake from a very early age because I would see it every time I was hauled off to town with my mother on shopping trips. By then, I was extremely interested in seeing one of the airplanes up close and my mind was making some connections. I reasoned that airplanes with boats underneath had to come from the lake and if I were to go down where the water was, I might get to see one. My mother had no interest in the lake and never took me there. I would have to wait until I could do it on my own.

By the grown-up age of six I was getting brave about finding things out for myself. I was an intensely curious young fellow and this thirst for discovery would take me on long walks from home, much farther than my parents would have allowed. But I always came home for mealtime or before dark so my parents weren't aware of my wanderings. One day on a trip into town I explored down a street that took me to the lake. It knew that this is where I would find what I was looking for.

Gary Powers in his U-2 couldn't have uncovered a more revealing sanctuary. What had been secret to me was now revealed. I had stumbled across the seaplane base where Ontario Central Airlines kept their fleet of floatplanes. I walked on to the dock to find several more that looked just like the one that flew over the house, and they were all floating on wonderful shiny-looking boats. I timidly approached the one closest to me and from my lowly stature as a six-year-old, I gazed awestruck up at a glistening, polished monster, a Fairchild 82.

The airplane engine, on the front of all the shiny metal, was very different from what I expected. I had seen car engines and they were covered with a hood, but this engine stuck out in the open. It was much bigger and looked very complicated. I didn't know what those black prickly-looking cans were that stuck out on all sides. Big kids later told me later that those were the things that made the engine run. They were called cylinders. In front of all the jumbled-up pieces, the sun reflected eye-piercing points of light from a glistening propeller. The airplane was monstrous. How was it possible that something so big could fly?

Once I made the discovery, I would go to the float-base base as often as I could to admire the airplanes. I saw people get in the airplanes, the engines would start and the airplanes would dash across the water before they suddenly jumped up into the air. I didn't know where the people went but I was spellbound. This was magic.

One day, instead of going away, I saw one come back and coast into the dock as the propeller slowly came to a stop. Once the dock boy tied the airplane to the dock, a door opened on the side and men and women and children came out. The airplanes took people away and then brought them back. And they looked happy and unafraid.

I knew then that I could be as happy as they were if I did what they did. I wanted to fly.

My trips into town took me by many store windows and I would glance inside as I went by. Smith's Book Store was at eye level and I would casually look in, but bookstores never had anything of interest for me. But one day I noticed something very unusual. A cardboard box with a glossy picture of an airplane on it appeared in the window. I was enraptured by that box, and for weeks I looked at the picture every time I went by. It wasn't very big, maybe a foot long, half as high and only a couple of inches thick.

From the moment I saw it, I had the feeling that an airplane was inside, but I had a hopeless feeling about it. Something like that was for big guys with money. I went by that box every day for weeks, and it was always in the same spot. No one had bought it. After looking at it for such a long time, my curiosity finally drove me inside to ask what it was. A nice looking, tall lady in a dark blue dress said that it was a Taylorcraft model airplane kit. It was the only one they had and the box had the materials inside to make a model of the picture on the box. I couldn't believe it. It was true; it did have an airplane inside. If I could somehow have it, I actually would be able to make an airplane I could hold in my hand. But I didn't ask the price. It was just a dream. I knew that it would be a fortune that I would never have.

For days on end as I walked past Smith's Book Store, I gawked into the window. The box was still there. I couldn't stop dreaming about it, so finally one day I mustered up the courage to go inside and ask the price. The same lady told me it was ten cents. It was a large amount of money. How could I ever find a way to find such an impossible sum? Since the country was in the midst of the Great Depression, my parents were poor like most people and there would be no dime for such frivolity. If I wanted that model, I would somehow have to find the money myself.

Night and day I thought about how I could earn ten cents and finally the inspiration came. An older farmer with a two-horse-drawn cart made the rounds of Kenora selling vegetables from his rather commodious wagon. It was taller than I was with its four huge wheels, massive wooden spokes and steel tires. To my mind that cart was as long as a truck I had seen. The farmer had grey hair, and the grey hair on his face wasn't like a real beard. His wide shoulders supported blue denim straps that held up his big coveralls. His heavy body didn't have a waist, but was straight and square all the way down. He had a broad, impassive, friendly face and he spoke quietly and kindly in a low voice. He always stopped at our house and my mother bought whatever she wanted of cabbage, potatoes, cauliflower or turnips. The price for a few items was five or ten cents.

One morning at his stop at our house, he came to the door and asked what my mother wanted. A cabbage and a cauliflower would do. She paid the nickel and the farmer went out to get the vegetables. My plan was already formulated and it was time to carry it out. I immediately told the farmer I would go and get what my mother wanted and that I would be his helper for the rest of the day. I didn't ask if I could help. I simply informed him that I was his newfound assistant, his legs for the day. He didn't seem to mind.

After I had made the delivery to my mother, and before he could change his mind, I dashed back to the cart and joined him on his lofty, full-width bench seat. It was a plain, wide, weather-beaten board which was cushion mounted on a set of leaf springs. It sat above and just at the front end of the precious load. I had never been very close to a horse and now two massive horse's haunches were right in front of me. Later in the day I finally found out how all of those brown lumps on the street got there.

At each of his regular stops, he told me to go to the house and ask for what the lady wanted. I returned to the cart for him to place the items in my arms and collected the nickel or dime that was due. This flurry of activity went on for the rest of the day. When he had finished his rounds, he swung back to our house and planted the princely sum of a dime into my hand. I didn't know he would pay me that much money. I was ecstatic. In one day I had earned exactly the right amount to buy the model. But now a dreaded thought entered my mind. Was it still there? I had been away all day with the farmer and maybe someone had come and bought it. I could hardly sleep. It just had to be there the next day.

When the bookstore opened at nine in the morning I was already there waiting in anticipation. To my immense relief, the box was still in the window. That model would be mine. I went inside as soon as the nice lady opened the door and gave her my dime. She knew exactly what I wanted. She carefully wrapped the box in brown paper, took hold of a string that hung from the ceiling and tied the box securely. I hurried home with my prize.

When I excitedly opened the box, I couldn't believe my great fortune. Everything I needed to build the model was in the kit: it held all the balsa wood, the glue, pins, the orange rice-paper, the rubber band to drive the propeller and even the banana oil to slick and tighten the fabric. IKEA must have taken their assembly instruction ideas from the model airplane makers. A series of drawings showing each step of assembly surrounded the templates for the model itself. I found that even as a six year old, the pictures were easy to follow.

Each frame of the model was built directly on top of a real-sized drawing of the part to be made. I soon discovered that I needed a sharp razor blade to cut the delicate balsa. My stepfather provided me with a used Gillette razor which cut skin and fingers every bit as effectively as it did the balsa. As I cut and placed each little strip of balsa and former piece onto the template, I glued the joints and held them in place with pins while waiting for the glue to dry. Most sections were hopelessly overglued and I had to cut some of the plans away to free them from the paper. I couldn't wait for the airplane to be finished; I had to fly each piece separately as it was built. Watching me fly around the house making airplane noises with no more than the vertical rudder of the model in my hand simply verified my parents' conviction that I was doomed to being a no-good for having spent a dime on such foolishness.

My excitement mounted as I attached the tail planes and finally the wings to the fuselage. By then, the little Taylorcraft had flown a million miles even though it had no fabric covering. My mouth often became sore after the countless hours of vibrating my lips in combination with the throat growling that was an airplane engine. After weeks in the making, I finally glued the rice-paper on with the banana oil and my precious model was complete. I had enough of the banana oil left to dab on to the paper to tighten it up and give it a finishing gloss.

It was built with all the skills of a six year old. All the parts of the airplane had fragments of the plans attached to the joints and the horizontal stabilizer had a twist in it. The wings warped after I put the rice paper on, but that didn't spoil the beauty of my precious little airplane. The Taylorcraft became my most prized possession. I didn't dare wind up the propeller enough to let it fly; I didn't want it to crash. It was enough to let it take short dashes across the floor.

Earning the money to buy and then make that little Taylorcraft put me in control of my destiny. I was empowered and knew then that I had the ability to get the things I wanted. I often visited the real airplanes at the dock, and as I gazed in wonder at each one, there was never any doubt in my mind that when I grew up, I would fly those magic airplanes.

Chapter Seven
The Beginning of Effective Fire Bombing

If at first you don't succeed, don't try skydiving. Anonymous

Fire Size and the Initial Attack

Regardless of the prevailing fire hazard, all forest districts employ air patrol as the most efficient means of discovering fires. Even during times of high and extreme fire hazards, intensive air patrol normally finds fires at a fairly small size. In the densely forested areas like Oregon, Washington, Idaho, Montana and British Columbia, the average discovered fire is about one-quarter of an acre. Because of their waxy leaves, California fuels are so volatile and fast-burning that discovery and action must be expeditious enough to prevent the potential runaway fire that can happen in minutes. Consequently, the State of California lays on extra-heavy air patrol in times of high and extreme hazards, thereby finding most fires at about one-tenth of an acre in size. Of course, these are averages. Some are marginally larger and some are campfires still putting up smoke. The reality is that the vast majority of fires are discovered at a small size.

The first action on a fire is called the "initial attack" whether it's by ground forces or by aircraft. At the beginning of the fire season, Fire Bomber, helicopter attack and smoke jumper bases are activated. The idea is to have firefighting crews ready for immediate dispatch and strategically spaced throughout the forest so as to provide the fastest possible action on a fire.

Forest services consider many factors prior to a fire dispatch. What is the fire hazard: low, moderate, high or extreme? What kind of fuel is it in? Are there residences nearby? What is the weather doing: is it windy? Is the fire on flat ground or the side of a mountain? How close is the nearest ground fire station and does it have adequate water resources? Are there ponds or lakes nearby for a helicopter to bucket water?

Initial attack in times of low hazard is an easy call: send out a helicopter with a fire crew on board. They land at the closest clearing suitable for a helicopter and the crew then walks in to the fire. In Canada, if there is no suitable place to land, the crew may rappel from a hovering helicopter down ropes to the immediate fire area. Any such stalwart individual has been appropriately called a "dope on a rope." The United States Forest Service has initial attack crews called smokejumpers, who parachute to the fire area from a transport aircraft if there is no suitable place to land a helicopter. If it looks like there could be more than just a few hours of action, the crew may cut out a helicopter pad for bringing in more men and equipment. I have always admired the bravery of these initial attack crews who either leapt into a fire by parachute or swung down on a rope. My job as a pilot was tame by comparison.

Timing is everything when a forest service decides that the initial attack will be by aircraft. The California Department of Forestry, for example, likes to have a Fire Bomber over any fire in California within fifteen minutes of its discovery. The number and location of the bomber bases makes this possible. In the vast region of British Columbia, bases are more widely spread, but even so, action on most fires can occur within half to one hour.

The first consideration is, of course, to save lives and property. A fire near a residential area will trigger more vigorous and massive action than will a fire out in the wilderness far away from any buildings.

Escalation of Effort

There is little difference in how any forest service handles a new fire in low to moderate hazards. One way or another, the initial attack on the fire is to dispatch a ground crew to extinguish the fire with ground action.

However, in the high and extreme fire hazards, two schools of logic come into conflict: whether the initial attack should be by ground forces or by aircraft. The philosophy of ground attack and upping the fire fighting resources as needed when the fire continues to spread is called "Escalation of Effort." The idea is to fight the fire using the least amount of resources that will get the job done. In the final analysis, it is true that no fire is ever controlled without the presence of a ground crew, so the logic is to put in the ground crew immediately and up the ante as needed. The least financially expensive attack on a fire is to put in a helicopter crew, then wait and see if such an attack with limited resources is adequate. If this type of initial attack succeeds, it will have been done at the cheapest price.

In reality, before Fire Bombers came along, all fires were fought this way regardless of the fire hazard. The airplane now complicates the matter for some fire agencies, the biggest question being: who has control over the initial firefighting efforts? Is the aircraft an initial attack system in itself or is it merely another tool in the arsenal of the ground Fire Boss? I will be discussing the differences between air attack and "Escalation of Effort" and its repercussions in much more detail later.

Long-term Retardant

For the first couple of seasons, we dropped Bentonite, a short-term retardant. While it did work to a limited degree, a far more effective long-term retardant was developed in 1963. A long-term retardant mixed with water attacks all sides of the fire triangle which are heat, fuel and oxygen. A sticky gum, dyed red for good visibility on the ground, holds the load together when dropped and coats the fuel. The sticky coating sealant enveloping the branches effectively removes the fuel by inhibiting the release of flammable gases. The mixture has additional fire-retarding effects when exposed to heat. The ammonium phosphate or the ammonium sulfate in either of the two marketed mixtures releases ammonia and thereby dilutes the oxygen at the fire.

The long-term retardants attack all sides of the fire triangle by removing the heat, the fuel and the oxygen from the fire while water's single fire retarding action is to drop the temperature of the burning fuel to the point of extinguishing the flame.

Further, it was discovered that these retardants were almost as effective dry as when wet, so even when the water evaporates, the effect remains. In addition, both of the mixtures are fertilizers, so they are beneficial to the soil when they are finally washed away by rain. The long-term retardants are the red material seen dropping from airplanes in news reports.

At first, it was thought the best way to use long-terms was the same as when using short-terms: drop the load on the flames. After a great deal of experimenting by forest services using the material, it was found that the better way to use long-term retardant was to place the entire load outside of the fire. That way, all levels of retardant, even the very thin spray on the outer edges of the load, were working to extinguish the fire. It made no sense to waste retardant by dropping it on ashes.

So just how effective is long-term retardant at containing a fire? The critical word here is "containing." A fire is not extinguished until people on the ground have dug up every bit of flame or burning ember and doused it all with water. It's a painstaking process that takes considerable time and patience after all fire activity seems to have ceased. Very quickly infrared equipment was adapted to survey fires from the air to seek out any hot spots. Ground crews use pump cans, shovels and fire hoses to work every edge of the fire. Native firefighters in Canada have a special technique of their own where they are often down on their stomach squirting at dug-up embers using mouthfuls of water. When the ground

process is entirely finished, the fire will get the "extinguished" label and the exhausted fire fighters are able to go home.

Containing a fire means that its spread has been contained inside the line of retardant but ground action is needed to finally extinguish it. Long-term retardant contains a fire very effectively. If there are no breaks in the retardant line and if the coverage of retardant is sufficient, the fire spread will be stopped.

The Basic Initial Air Attack

The chaotic bombing practices of the previous season had not gone unnoticed by British Columbia Forest Service brass at head office, who determined that there would not be a repetition of the pandemonium of 1961. Thus at the beginning of the 1962 season Art Kirk, a forestry instructor from head office in Victoria, and Denny McDonald, the Kamloops District Forester, were assigned the task of evaluating the future of Fire Bombers in British Columbia.

Art was an articulate, methodical instructor on the techniques of fighting forest fires with ground attack. It was hard to tell Art's age. White hair suggested an older man but his youthful face placed him at around fifty. He was friendly, outgoing and his conversation at our nightly pub gatherings alluded to a highly educated background. He certainly knew his business, but was wide open to new ideas. If he could be shown a better way to do something, he would dispassionately analyze it and if it survived his logic, he would accept it. Art was the perfect man for this mission, as he wasn't bound by historical or political dogma. If there was a way to figure out a way to transfer ground firefighting techniques to the air, Art would do it.

Denny had been a tank commander during World War Two and was just as firmly in charge of his forest district as he was in his tank. Denny was about six feet tall, was broad shouldered and a slim mustache adapted itself to perfectly enhance his handsome face. His blue eyes displayed his mischievous nature. He would always have some prank to pull, especially on us younger, naïve pilots. He believed in swift initial attack on forest fires. He had several phones on his desk all of which I think he used at the same time. He saw the potential of the bomber and, movie camera in hand, went flying with the Birddog on every dispatch. Denny didn't settle for anecdotal stories. He wanted proof of the bomber's actions on film. Once he saw how effective the initial air attack was, his favourite expression became "it's all in here" as he pointed to his movie camera.

The people at headquarters could not have appointed two better men to prove or disprove the value of the airplane in bombing forest fires. This was a no-nonsense mission. Either the airplanes could be made to work, or the system would be scrapped. Because of its high fire incidence, the success or failure of using airplanes to attack forest fires would be carried out at the Kamloops Forest District.

It was painfully obvious that bombers were useless on big fires. It was wasted effort. Therefore, a new set of rules were put into place for the evaluation.

Five TBMs were assembled at Kamloops for the tests. Once the hazard was up, the airplanes would be dispatched to all reported fires. If a Mrs. Jones called in and reported a fire, there would be no wasting time to send someone to see if she was right. Her report was cause for an immediate dispatch of the airplanes. There would also be no waiting for a helicopter crew to start an initial attack and then ask for the bombers; bomber and helitack dispatches were simultaneous. (A helitack crew is a firefighting crew delivered by helicopter.)

Also, the bombers would no longer be sent out to bomb on their own. The bombing action was to be directed by a qualified Fire Control Officer. He would call the shots as to where each load would be placed. The "Birddog," as he became known in British Columbia, took off immediately at the fire report and got a good head start toward the fire as the bombers were being loaded.

Fortunately, during the course of the summer a large number of fires were actioned, and at each fire, Denny got the action on film and the Birddog evaluated how much retardant it took to contain the fire completely. The average attack took five TBM-loads of retardant, a total of 3,000 imperial gallons. Also a critical factor in assuring success at the fire was to attack it in exactly the same order as was done with a ground action, which was to stop the fastest rate of spread first, then the next fastest and finally hit the base. The head of the fire is pushed by the wind and has the fastest rate of spread. The flanks are the sides and have the next fastest rate of spread. The base is the lee side of the fire and has the slowest rate of spread. So the idea was to hit the head, flanks and base in that order. Everyone was passionately involved at making the test a success as the future of the company and our jobs depended on it. Not only that, but in Canada we were pioneers. We were the ones that rescued success out of chaos. We made it all work.

But the real heroes were Art Kirk and Denny McDonald. They put the plan in place and the aircrew carried it out. Beyond all

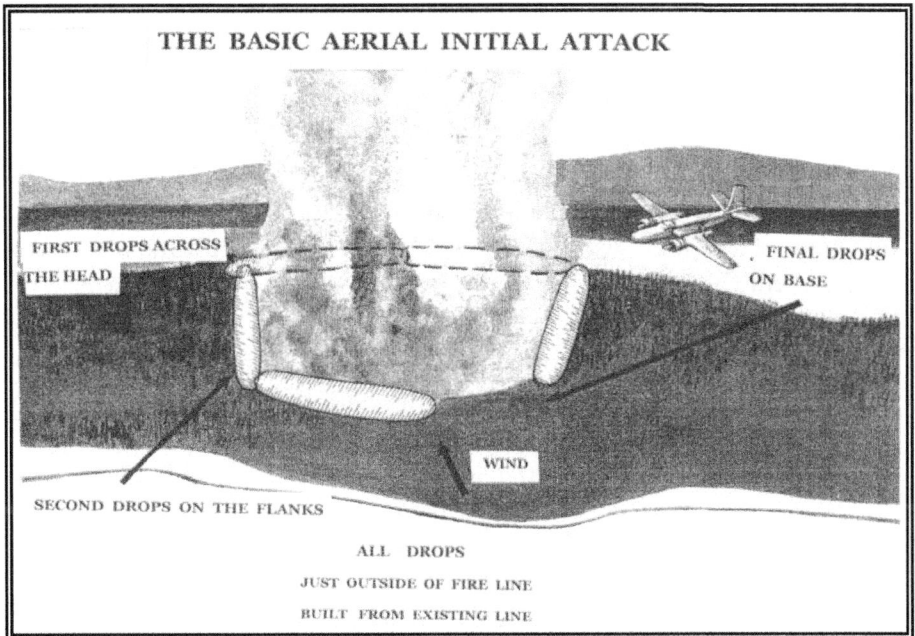

THE BASIC AERIAL INITIAL ATTACK

FIRST DROPS ACROSS THE HEAD

FINAL DROPS ON BASE

WIND

SECOND DROPS ON THE FLANKS

ALL DROPS
JUST OUTSIDE OF FIRE LINE
BUILT FROM EXISTING LINE

expectations, we had a highly successful season. Fire Bombers were here to stay. A new method for initial attack came into being that summer after it was proven that bombers could be effective on a fire.

Denny was completely sold on the swiftness of initial attack dispatch: send the bombers to a reported fire immediately with no waiting. Such decisiveness was to result in an international incident. One day a smoke was spotted near the British Columbia-Washington border, east of Osoyoos and it was a toss-up as to which side of the border it was on.

Denny ordered the bombers to attack, the details about which side of the border it was on to be dealt with later. It turned out that we had attacked and bombed the United States of America. What would happen? Would there be instant and massive retaliation? Would it be war? Would the Americans withdraw the American ambassador from Canada? Maybe the Americans would let us off easily and simply send a strong diplomatic protest. Would they throw mud back at our side of the border? We nervously waited. Nothing happened. We later heard that the United States Forest Service called Denny and thanked him for the quick action.

When the season ended, we arranged to have a party especially for Art and Denny. I made two "Hero" medals, one for each of them, and we had a great presentation ceremony over a tidal wave of beer. The medals were made of aluminum and each had a bar that was three quarters of an inch wide and three inches long. A safety pin was soldered on the back. In felt marker, I wrote the words "For Merit." A skewed, red star hung below the bar at the end of two chains. To imitate the style of Russian medals, I printed "HERO" with the E and R printed backwards on the star in big letters. We could not have presented a better award to two more worthy men. They were delighted. We were all delighted.

The Birddog

There are different names for the Forest Service Officer that directs the air attack. In British Columbia, the aircraft is called the Birddog and two persons are on board the airplane. The contracted pilot flies the airplane, and the Forest Service Fire Control Officer directs the attack. He advises the Birddog pilot of his attack plan and thereafter all radio communications regarding the attack are between the Birddog pilot and the bomber pilot. The Birddog will test the air (a complex technical procedure that requires the Birddog to fly through it) on what will be the bomber's run and advise the pilot if there are any downdrafts to plan for. He is, in fact, testing for dangerous conditions and is the first mouse past the cat. If visibility is marginal and the target is extremely difficult to see, the Birddog may suggest he lead the bomber pilot in to the target.

The OV-10 Bronco, used in California as the Birddog aircraft.
Photo courtesy Clark Cook

Normally, the pilot of the bomber plans his approach and executes the drop at his discretion. The bomber pilot also has the option to request a "lead in" if he thinks he may not find the target on final. Otherwise, all instructions from Birddog about where to drop the load are done while the airplane remains at altitude above the fire.

The California "Air Attack Officer" is called Air Tactical Group Supervisor (ATGS), and is flown to the fire by a contract pilot. Once at the fire location, the aircraft orbits at 1,000 feet while the ATGS directs the bombers in the initial attack or a support action if requested by the fire team on the ground. He remains at altitude and does not do lead-ins or dummy runs on the fire. All communication with the ground team, tankers and helicopters is done by the ATGS.

The United States Forest Service has a position called the Lead Plane. It is flown by the person who also directs the air attack. He gets to do it all. There is also a difference between the Lead Plane method of directing the air attack and how it's done by the British Columbia Forest Service and the California Department of Forestry.

The USFS Lead Plane leads every bomber into his attack run. The bomber is "picked up" at a holding location which is removed from the fire, and thereafter follows the Lead Plane through the entire approach, the final run and escape from the fire area. The Lead Plane will also tell the pilot of the bomber where the load should go as he is on the final run. All of the bombing runs are led in by the Lead Plane.

For the sake of simplicity, I'm calling the person from all agencies who directs the air attack, the "Birddog."

One Strike — The Preeminent Attack

In British Columbia, a number of factors came together which resulted in the creation of an incredibly effective concept of Fire Bombing. First was the invention or formulation of long-term retardant. An unbroken line of retardant can be placed around the fire which can then be left without further action by aircraft. Often, a line of long-term retardant is just as effective at containing the fire as a line dug down to mineral soil. Nevertheless, it will still be under constant observation by air patrol while waiting for the arrival of the follow-up ground attack.

The second factor discovered early in the use of bombers was just how much retardant should be delivered in the first strike. Experience in British Columbia had found that an immediate delivery of about 3,000 imperial gallons of retardant to fires as big as an acre was sufficient resource for a successful containment virtually 100% of the time. Sometimes more retardant was needed, but this assessment would be made during the initial action and more retardant would be on the way even before the initial attack was finished.

Our test group in Kamloops had evolved a highly successful formula which came to be named "One Strike." This attack concept involved hitting the fire with overwhelming forces every time neither guessing about fire size nor waiting to see what the fire would do. The reason was to get the fire at a small size, finish the action quickly and have the airplane or airplanes ready for the next fire occurrence in a matter of minutes.

When using the term airplane or airplanes, I'm referring to the fact that early in the use of bombers, aircraft large enough to carry the three thousand gallons deemed necessary for effective One Strike were not yet available. One Strike also does not necessarily mean the attack has to be carried out with one aircraft. The Department of Forestry in California dispatches more than one bomber from bases near the fire to arrive with a sufficient retardant capacity available from two or more airplanes. When I flew out of Kamloops, British Columbia, five TBMs were sent in each attack. It wasn't long, however, before airplanes like the DC-6, DC-7 and C-130 came along, each with a capacity of three thousand gallons.

The most critical factor for success is the immediate dispatch to every reported fire. It doesn't mean being called by a ground crew when they can no longer handle a fire, nor does it mean positive confirmation of a fire by sending someone out to have a look. One Strike means instant dispatch to every reported fire. This concept recognizes that the time factor is everything. Time only modifies a fire one way: it gets bigger, and in extreme hazards, very quickly.

TBM dropping its two doors in quick succession.
Photo courtesy Sis-Q Flying Service

British Columbia was quick in assigning who had the authority over the use of the bombers. A situation often developed where the helicopter crew and the Fire Boss arrived at the fire before the bomber action was complete. If the Birddog was in the process of initial attack, then he had the final say about the fire he was fighting. He called off the action only when he knew he had effective containment. There were no restrictions on his judgment. Once he finished his initial attack, he assisted the Fire Boss if requested. However, if new fires were occurring, they became top priority and the bombers would be dispatched to the new fires.

Critics of this thinking say that it's like swatting a mosquito with a throwaway Persian carpet. Why hit so hard and with so much initial expense when a far less expensive effort will do the same thing? Why the overkill? By the same token we can ask why a police force should send in an entire Swat Team to eliminate one sniper when one man and one bullet can do it? The idea is to put the odds of success enormously in our favour. Why take chances?

There is no doubt that One Strike has its costs. A bomber or bombers carrying the minimum 3,000 gallons to a fire is far more expensive than a single helicopter carrying seven men to the fire. An expensive air attack takes place and the fire is reduced to stagnation. Nothing more happens. With brilliant hindsight about every small fire, critics can say that One Strike is overkill; with far less effort and expense they could have done the same thing.

There is even more expense to the One Strike concept than initially meets the eye. Fire Bombers are dispatched to every reported fire. As it happens, some are campfires and some are false alarms. Many reported fires are quickly extinguished by a local fire department or local residents. As a result, recalls of the aircraft almost immediately after takeoff are common. A heavily loaded aircraft can't just complete a circuit and land. It has to be at or below its gross landing weight. Quite frequently, the pilot has to fly to a jettison area, get rid of part of the load and then land. Never having seen the fertilizing properties of the retardant, in California I was fascinated to see that the grass in the jettison area was head and shoulders higher than the grass elsewhere.

Proponents of One Strike maintain that if at least fifteen percent of the season's retardant isn't tossed into the jettison area, the airplanes aren't leaving quickly enough: better to be jettisoning retardant than be late to the fire. It's hair-trigger thinking, but the reality is that a single project fire can cost more to fight than the entire season's cost of One Strike.

There is another propitious benefit to using this type of attack. No one on the ground need be exposed to a dangerously explosive situation. There is a truth that has to be faced when fighting fires in extreme hazards: it is far too hazardous for the men on the ground to be fighting a fire with pump cans and shovels in this kind of elevated fire hazard. When the fire crowns (the tree tops ignite and start releasing tremendous heat) and takes off, the men literally have to escape with their lives. In contrast, when the foliage around the fire is coated with long-term retardant it's reduced to quiescence. It merely smolders at the edges of the retardant. It's then safe for the ground crew to enter this area even in times of extreme hazard. They can mop up in safety.

The development of One Strike is the equivalent of the tank being introduced in the First World War: it revolutionized warfare. The tank kept people safe behind its armour, while acting as an effective offensive weapon. Although many people still have not come to this realization, the concept of One Strike has revolutionized the fighting of forest fires. It is not just another tool available for the support of ground action. It is a complete, superbly effective forest firefighting system on its own. All the odds for quick, effective containment of a forest fire could now be on the side of the forest service. If Fire Bombers were only ever properly used in One Strike and never used in support action, it would more than justify their existence and expense.

Significantly, in the early sixties, the Forest Service of British Columbia and the California Department of Forestry independently developed this concept at the same time, thereby becoming the world leaders in effective Fire Bombing. The logic and the use of One Strike is so incredibly simple and effective that it's hard to imagine that any forest service would do anything else.

One Strike, by definition, is the instant dispatch of enough retardant to every reported fire to contain it in a continuous action without the need for the aircraft to make an additional trip. It is a massive and fully complete initial attack on a fire by Fire Bombers (fully complete meaning that the fire has been completely contained by retardant). All normal firefighting procedures then follow. In most cases, continued action by the bombers is unnecessary.

The Bomber Bases in British Columbia

In the summer of 1962, a Fire Bomber base and the crew had to maintain the same kind of readiness as a city or county fire department. The lesson had been learned in previous years. There would be no waiting for a fire bust; airplanes and crews had to be ready as the fire hazard climbed. Contracts had to be awarded for bomber and crew standby, and facilities to mix retardant and to house the crew had to be built.

The sixties were the proving and development years. The Fire Bombers were indeed effective and they were no longer just an experiment. The British Columbia Forest Service and Fire Bombing pilots alike shared the euphoria of having discovered just how effective aircraft can be when used on initial attack. We were having phenomenal success with One Strike. New buildings as well as high-capacity mixing and storage for retardant were built at all of the tanker bases. British Columbia is a big place (three times the size of California) so bomber bases had to be strategically located. The idea was to have bombers over a fire in not more than one hour's flying time. Thick, heavy forests don't instantly flare in the same way as does the waxy brush of California. There is often a short "grace period" after the discovery of a fire when it gradually builds up heat before it leaps to the canopy. This "grace period" was on the side of the bombers. The logs of our arrival times at fires proved that the bases were properly located.

In the design of the base facilities, the forest service had the right idea: offices for the forest service, the radio and dispatch room, the pilots' waiting room and the all-important debriefing room, were all in the same building; we were an integral team. We worked together and we socialized together.

At the beginning of a bomber action, we were briefed by the Birddog, who was already over the fire, about the attack plan. As we circled over the fire and watched the action unfold, each pilot could often predict exactly what he would be called upon to do.

A vital procedure that educated us about fires, and Fire Bombing effectiveness, was the post-fire debriefing. After every fire, we continued to learn about the forest service firefighting techniques, what was expected of us and how to be more effective at our jobs. Pilot input was invited about how to get at the target and place the loads effectively. We weren't simply dropping loads. We became aware of the entire picture. Just as every football player must know the rules of the game and the strategy of each play to be part of an effective team, we had to know firefighting strategy as well as know how to fly our airplane.

A fully equipped kitchen was a highly important feature of the standby building. It gave everyone a chance to prove their ability to create culinary delights. There were the mandatory two refrigerators: one for food and the other for beer. At that time, the forest service gave us the same respect that the British Royal Air Force accorded their pilots — the beer was available at the bomber base for after hours. No one had the slightest concern that we would drink during flying hours. We were honourable gentlemen fully devoted to safe flying. The crew having a beer together came only after the flying day was over.

The end-of-the-day standby was variable. In high and extreme hazards, we could remain on the base until dark. At lesser hazards, standby would end at progressively earlier times, sometimes as early as 6 P.M. At the end of standby, we had a ritual for knocking off the first beer bottle caps. If standby was over at eight o'clock for instance, the countdown began at ten seconds to eight — ten, nine, eight, seven, six, five, four, three, two, one — and the caps would fly off the beer bottles. A dispatch coming even five minutes later would be refused. We already had a drink and none of us would ever consider flying after even one sip.

Having a cold beer after work engendered a special camaraderie. We worked hard and enjoyed socializing after work, even if it was only for a short time. It was a special gathering and it made us a closer team. Those were the halcyon early days.

Once the Fire Bombing operation became a separate government department with its own budget, bureaucracy gravitated to the department like rabbits to a lettuce patch. Bureaucrats had itches they had to scratch, so a cascade of rules began to descend over the Fire Bombing operation. It had long been known that there was a second refrigerator at the base kitchens which was blatantly being used as a beer cooler. The puritanical minds at headquarters must have had nightmares knowing that the boys at the bomber bases were having too much fun. A gaucherie of this magnitude in a forest service building was intolerable: the beer fridge had to go. We couldn't understand what it was about our behaviour that caused such seismic decrees. Were we bad boys? Was it a threat to our work performance? It was a shock, but we weren't to be easily thwarted from one of the few perks we enjoyed.

We made a deal with the engineers. We creatively relocated our beer to the beer fridge in their maintenance shop. For a time, there was clandestine socializing in the engineers' building and we thought our secret was secure. But somehow the having-clandestine-beers police from headquarters sniffed this one out as well. More emergency proclamations descended from on high: "Thou shalt not find devious means to have fun. Can that refrigerator as well."

Like the British Royal Navy that lost its traditional rum ration in July of 1970, ending a tradition begun in 1731, we went down without a fight. We lamented our loss quietly. Unlike the Royal Navy, we wore no black armbands. There was no trumpet sounding of the Last Post, or a gun carriage procession complete with a coffin, drums and piper. Our congenial tradition quietly passed.

Fire Towers with Mountaintop Gardens

The first effective method for finding fires before they were the size of nuclear mushroom clouds was the fire tower. These were high towers with a cupola observation hut on top, set on the top of mountains, which gave the best panoramic view of the countryside. If the mountain top was high enough to present a good view, there might not be a tower. The observation hutch simply sat on rock or windswept grass. Whatever the arrangement, these cabins were above the tree line and exposed to the full force of the prevailing westerly winds. When blowing from just the right direction, the wind blowing through the lattice steel structure of a tower caused a distressing moan both day and night. The lookout's job description was simple: "You will have countless days of boredom looking out over the countryside which will be punctuated on occasion with an opportunity to sit inside a passing thunderstorm." The adventurous man or woman could stay on top of the tower during a thunderstorm if they chose to see and feel the awesome spectacle from inside the heart of the raging beast.

An impending lightning strike begins with an ever intensifying hum as static pours off the mountain preceding the lightning hit. Each blinding lightning strike, only a few feet away from the observer, is simultaneously accompanied by the body-stunning explosion of the thunder's sonic boom. For the brave, it's a disquieting but safe experience as the cupola has adequate lightning protection. For the less courageous, an overnight hut below the tower provided a dubious shelter. Aside from occasionally witnessing the power of nature first hand, most days were peaceful and it was on these bleak, rocky peaks that an amazing horticultural experiment took place.

Towers were located to provide overlapping views. While a single tower could give a bearing to a fire, it could not accurately give the distance. A bearing to the same fire from a second tower solved the problem, and the intersection of the two bearing gave the exact location. The tower system did have some shortcomings. Some towers had blind spots behind mountains and the system was often limited in its coverage during times of restricted visibility due to haze or smoke. However, it was the best at the time and worked reasonably well. It was still in use during my early days of Fire Bombing.

In time, the lookout was replaced with the more effective air patrol. In times of increasing fire hazards and especially when the fire hazard roadside sign has its arrow pointed at "Extreme," numerous Cessna and other light aircraft were put in the air to survey vulnerable areas intensively. Areas in extreme hazard could be visited at least hourly if not more frequently. Air patrol finds fires when they are much smaller.

It was a pity to eliminate the towers, as a certain romance and the opportunity for men to display their chivalry to women in need was forever eliminated. Helicopter pilots were the knights of the air in the days of the fire lookouts. Every lookout had a helicopter pad where supplies could be brought in to the person manning or womaning the tower, as the case may be. While the top of a dry, windswept mountain seems an unlikely place to grow a garden, some female lookouts were exceptionally successful at it. Cultivating a garden was a pleasant diversion from reading, and having fresh vegetables added a nice touch to a meal. The problem with such an elevated horticultural experiment was getting sufficient water to the garden during the dry, hot, dog days of summer.

Enterprising female lookouts conceived an elegantly simple, ingenious solution. In the isolation of the tower, the lady lookouts would often perform their duties in the nude. It was the perfect way to get an all-over, perfectly even tan and to secure the attention of passing helicopter pilots. Discretion demanded the lady not announce her desires over the air, so she displayed her womanhood to a passing helicopter pilot, and used hand signals to indicate her wants. Secret, silent messages like the semaphore signals between warships on the same mission passed between lookout and pilot.

Every lady lookout knew that helicopters carried a Bambi Bucket folded up in the cargo compartment and they could be quickly attached to the helicopter in case of emergency. And a dry, thirsty garden was certainly an emergency. Helicopter pilots also being very enterprising, understood the signals and would go off to fetch a bucket of water. As might be expected, rumours began circulating that it was not the garden that needed attention but the lady lookout who lingered away many lonely days and spent many weeks sleeping alone in total isolation. Neither did the helicopter pilot who spent weeks and months sleeping alone in a tent in the mosquito-infested woods escape the rumour-mongers.

Like an elephant that will unerringly walk a hundred miles to find a watering hole he knows is there, a diversion from the helicopter's route to his destination was sometimes necessary to find a suitable place to pick up water. Helicopter pilots knew the location of every beaver pond and lake in the country. How long the helicopter pilot had been in isolation and how badly the garden needed watering determined how slight the diversion might be. It was the excessively long diversions it took to find and deliver a bucket of water that began to arouse suspicions in the minds of dispatchers. Why hadn't the pilot responded to radio calls when his arrival time at destination was overdue? Helicopter pilots would not be deterred from a noble mission; they went to any lengths to help a lady in need. Like bringing flowers and a bottle of wine to a lady that's invited him to dinner, the thoughtful helicopter pilot brought a bucket of water for the lady's garden.

I had to know the truth about what could have spoiled the good reputations of both the lady lookouts and the helicopter pilots. What went on during these clandestine stopovers? One day I had the opportunity to speak to one of the chivalrous pilots. He was obviously sincere in his testament that no hanky panky had gone on during the visits, as many had rumoured. The pilot was merely helping the lady with her garden and the two had only indulged in casual conversation during his time at the tower. The pilot's help was rewarded with two fresh cucumbers and a bunch of six carrots. I put my mind at ease. One must admire the ingenious women who indulged in pioneering horticultural experiments in hostile, seemingly impossible locations.

Alas, the good deeds of the pilots were overruled by the suspicions of straightlaced dispatchers who were certain the watering of a mountaintop garden was simply a cover for more covert activities. It's a pity they cared so little for the outstanding contributions to mountaintop horticulture made by these enterprising women. The practice of watering the ladies' gardens was ordered to stop.

The Flying Boat

Many areas of Canada are lake county as the retreat of the last glacier generously sprinkled vast sections of Canada with countless lakes. The concept of water pick up by aircraft at lakes near a fire was based on the idea that very large volumes of water could be dropped on fires from a ubiquitous water source.

Eastern Canada, particularly Quebec and Ontario, and the central States, such as Wisconsin and Minnesota, were conveniently ideal places for the application of a water pick up system. The Ontario Department of Lands and Forests were pioneers in this field. Water pick up scoops lowered out of the floats of Beaver and Otter aircraft allowed rapid fillups while skimming on the water. The system was quickly adapted to aircraft like the Canso (PBY) flying boat and later applications would be seen on the Canadair 215 and the Mars flying boat.

Because of this proliferation of lakes in northern British Columbia, the province contracted a second company, the "Flying Firemen," to operate their PBYs in suitable areas. I had not witnessed water dropping in action and looked forward to seeing how well it worked.

During an explosive fire bust, both companies, Skyway and Flying Firemen, were busy attacking numerous lightning ignited fires and a particular action beside a lake gave me an opportunity to witness two Fire Bombing actions involving the different concepts of using bombers. I was part of a group of five TBMs using long-term retardants and we had been dispatched to two fires next to the shore line at opposite ends of a fairly large lake. We were assigned to one of the fires, and a PBY flying boat was assigned to drop water on the other.

As we were making our drops, we had the opportunity to watch the PBY do his water drops. It was rather impressive to watch his quick turnarounds as he dumped impressive quantities of water on his fire. When he quit dropping, his fire was completely subdued with very little smoke coming from it. I was impressed; maybe this water idea did work after all.

PBY on water pickup. Photo courtesy Kenting Aviation

Leaving our fire was almost embarrassing: our fire had its line of retardant around it but it didn't look much different after we had finished our action than it did before we started. It was still throwing up plenty of smoke. We both finished about the same time and went on to other actions.

There was no immediate follow up by ground action to either fire as the ground crews were dispersed to many other fires.

What we learned about these two actions is still true to this day. Water delivery to a fire must remain until a ground crew gets its fire guard down to mineral soil around a fire. This is an inherent weakness of the water-dropping concept. Aircraft are committed to a fire for long periods, working in concert with the ground operation. They cannot leave to attend to new fires. When the PBY left the fire, there was still a little bit of smoke coming from the area — it was not completely extinguished and there was no physical line around the fire. There were still a thousand matches burning under logs or thickets. Within about an hour after the PBY left, the water had fully evaporated and the fire took off up the mountain, consuming several thousand acres that afternoon. We left our fire and the line held — the fire remained quiescent until ground action was able to get to it.

Watching that PBY action proved something else: proximity of a marginally useful fire retardant was not the key to successful initial attack, even though his fire was just a short distance from the edge of the lake and he was able to deliver copious amounts of water.

The water retardant might be cheap but the airplane and runaway fires are expensive. Delivering long-term fire retardants are the only effective fire action worthy of the cost, even in a country full of lakes.

The Canadair CL-215

The Canso was built during the war to be a maritime patrol aircraft. It was in fact a sub hunter. But Cansos were getting old and fewer in number, so a replacement was needed. The Province of Quebec wanted a new, purpose-designed water bomber that had a greater tank capacity and better performance than the Canso.

The job of designing and building the airplane went to Canadair Ltd. of Montreal. The distinctive amphibian design was powered by two Pratt and Whitney R-2800 shoulder-mounted engines of 2,100 horsepower each. The first flight of the airplane took place on October 23, 1967.

Canadair CL-215. Photo courtesy Canadair

Two retractable scoops in the hull can pick up 1,400 US gallons of water in about ten seconds. The first deliveries of the airplane went to the Securité Civilé in France in 1969. Quebec ordered a total of fourteen aircraft. It continues to be used extensively in Canada and eleven other countries.

Three variants of the airplane were built, the CL-215, the CL-215T and the CL-415. The CL-215T and the CL-415 are powered by the more powerful PW123AF turbine engines. A total of 125 aircraft were built, with production ending in 1990.

Purpose-built aircraft for Fire Bombing like these Canadair variants still exposes them to all of the inherent hazards of the occupation. In spite of the airplanes offering excellent visibility and performance to the pilot, the airplane has been involved in twenty-six crashes with twenty-one fatalities.

Chapter Eight
The Learning Curve Continues

A Piper Cub is the safest airplane in the World;
it can just barely kill you.
Max Stanley, Northrop test pilot

The Beginning of the Manual

I was learning about fires and what worked with air attack. Positive air control by competent Birddogs was well established and we were getting excellent results when One Strike techniques were applied. But there was a huge gap of knowledge in how the pilot could do his job safely. All kinds of approaches to the fire and drop techniques were still being used.

I couldn't believe how many pilots were diving at the fire, dive-bomber style, to release the load. It was an exceptionally dangerous maneuver. The pilot would have to fix on the target, try to stay at a safe dropping speed and at the last moment pull out of the dive and release the load. In our TBMs, the pull handles to release the load were on the instrument panel, so the pilot had to let go of the throttle and pull the handles at the same time as he pulled out of the dive. This pullout was done at the same reduced, dive power setting. The airplane would mush in toward the trees at virtually idle power, a configuration inviting disaster.

An airplane like the TBM doesn't suddenly just change direction, especially at reduced power; it enthusiastically obeys Newton's first law of motion: "An object at rest tends to stay at rest and an object in motion tends to stay in motion with the same speed and in the same direction unless acted upon by an unbalanced force."

The TBM was heavy and it took much huffing and puffing (in this case engine power) to get it to change direction. Using the dive-bombing technique, pilots flew into the trees and killed themselves both in practice and over the fire. It began happening during my very first season with Bill Perkins in his Stearman.

In discussing drop techniques with other pilots, I discovered that each one thought his approach was best. We were, after all, highly experienced pilots whether our flying time came from being ex-military, bush flying or crop spraying. In this new occupation, each man was pioneering his own bombing technique and naturally stuck with what was working for him. If dive bombing a fire was a man's preferred technique and he was getting away with it, no one was going to tell him that he was indulging in a very dangerous practice. At this stage, no one had the authority to say how the airplane must be flown while bombing. The forest service controlled where the drops went; they were not telling the pilots how to fly their airplanes. That would be up to the company that contracted the bombers. Unfortunately, there was no pilot's manual.

Over the years I had naturally taken to instructing in just about everything I did. I taught skiing for countless years, as well as scuba diving, hang gliding and teaching NATO students to fly while in the RCAF. I must have done it right because I always got good results. I found it very distressing to see people making fatal mistakes while Fire Bombing. I wanted to be of help, but suggesting to pilots that they were doing the wrong thing was akin to telling the mother-in-law that she wasn't any smarter than her in-laws were about raising kids. Sometimes there was hostile reaction, along with being told that I didn't know any more than anybody else. No one had any more Fire Bombing experience than the next guy and each man was mentally writing his own manual based on his own experience. So far, three pilots that I knew well had been killed while using the dive-bombing approach to the target. Dangerous practices were leading to pilot deaths. Someone had to write an authoritative manual that detailed the safe way to fly Fire Bombers.

I firmly believed that the Americans would do it. After all, they pioneered the use of airplanes as Fire Bombers, and they had a variety of aircraft converted to bombers by the mid sixties. They had to be ahead of everyone, and in my mind, had already worked out the best pilot techniques. But just in case no one was doing it, I started to make notes and I had a note pad strapped to my knee while flying for just that purpose. When the Americans came out with the manual, I intended to throw away my notes.

A peculiar thing happened every time I took off for a bombing run. My mind ran rampant with ideas for the book. All the topics that I thought should be in the book would pour out. If the fire was some distance away, I had time to write. An aircraft trimmed at altitude tends to fly itself and only requires the odd correction. I could relax and make notes and not worry about running into the faraway edges. Often, I could do more than just jot down an idea; whole paragraphs flowed and I could get it all on the pad. There was no continuity in the ideas as they would end up from start to finish in the actual book. I just wrote whatever topic came to mind. This went on in the TBM for the several years flying for Skyway in British Columbia and for the years I flew in California. In actuality, I wrote most of the book *Air Attack on Forest Fires* on my right knee. While on standby, I'd refine what I had written and stash it away for the great sorting that would put it all into meaningful order later on.

The Aircraft Pitch-up

I examined one aspect of airplane behaviour in detail and made sure that it was adequately explained in the book, *Air Attack on Forest Fires*. A phenomenon called pitch-up occurs with Fire Bombers shortly after the load is released. A sudden pitching up of the nose of the aircraft occurs about two seconds after the load is triggered. It didn't happen with the early Fire Bombers like the Stearman since its load came out slowly from a small door. It was first felt with the TBM that dropped a large load all at once. The cause was thought to be the sudden loss of weight at load release, but this idea was quickly dispelled when it was realized that bombers dropping heavy loads of streamlined bombs didn't pitch up. They flew along straight and level, feeling quite undisturbed. The sudden dropping of a heavy weight out of an aircraft wasn't the cause.

It was also thought that a centre of gravity (C of g) shift could be the cause: if the front doors were dropped first, the C of g would shift backwards and cause the pitch-up. However, even with a slight shift backwards, the C of g was still within limits and was not instrumental in causing the large pitch-ups that occurred in some aircraft.

Research into pitch-up by the United States Forest Service, the FAA and the National Aeronautical Establishment of Canada nailed down the cause and the safe way to deal with it. They soon discovered that a number of factors influenced how much an aircraft would pitch up at load release. It varied with how much of the airplane's load was dropped at one time, the speed the aircraft was doing at the time of drop, and with the configuration of the aircraft itself.

A large mass of dense fluid dropped from the airplane is, in effect, the same as suddenly placing a large door into the slipstream: the air pressure behind this "door" drops substantially. Air rushes in from all sides to equalize this area of low pressure. The air coming in from the bottom or sides of the load is of no consequence to what happens with the airplane.

The down-flow of air from above the load causes the pitch-up. It pushes down on the aft fuselage as well as the horizontal stabilizer and elevators. These airflows could be as high as thirty feet per second. True to form, the pitch-up was less with the smaller loads and increased with the size of load dropped. Increased airspeeds caused an exponential increase in pitch-up, since loads dropped at high speed caused a greater drop in air pressure behind the load and resulted in air rushing in with greater force.

Once the investigating agencies determined and precisely measured the cause of pitch-up, the next step was to discover the best drop speed range for each aircraft. A safe maneuvering speed of 1.3 times the drop configuration, power off, stalling speed provided good drop results. As an example, if an airplane stalled at 100 knots, minimum drop speed would be 133 knots. This allowed sufficient airspeed margins that neither g-forces from load drop nor normal mountain maneuvering would induce an accelerated stall. This became the minimum drop speed formula for each aircraft. Aircraft maximum drop speeds are reached when the g-force at drop goes to the aircraft's positive g limit of 3 g. A 20 to 30 knot spread is desirable as it allows for the inevitable airspeed increases resulting from downhill drops.

F7F in pitch-up. Photo by author

Research into the drop range for the B-25 showed a 3 g pitch-up at only 145 knots. Loads dropped above that speed showed a straight-up exponential climb of g-force. I never did figure out what could possibly have induced the B-25 pilot whom I had met into dropping at such high speeds to suffer such excessive g-force. No one in any aircraft dropped at 200 knots.

Pitch-up could not be avoided and it did no harm to the aircraft to take a slight positive g-load. I found the best way to deal with the pitch-up was to put in only enough stick forward to cancel some of the positive g and not get into any negative g-force at all.

Once the load was gone, the aircraft was much lighter. If full power was applied at the time of pitch-up, a fairly steep climb could follow the drop because at that point the aircraft had the respectable empty aircraft performance. This chance for grandstanding was not lost on pilots bombing in the view of bystanders. The bump-up could be used to climb over obstructions that were ahead or to climb up the slope of a mountain. A steep climbing turn away from the drop was also impressive. But it had its deadly side.

If empty aircraft performance was needed to climb a slope after a drop, a hung-up load or a delay in the drop could prove suicidal. This is what happened to one of the giant Mars Flying Boats. The pilot was dropping into the slope of a mountainside, and needed empty aircraft performance to climb over the mountain after he had made his drop. This airplane had the early configuration of having the drop doors on the side of the fuselage. The load took considerable time to exit, far too long, and on this drop he was late. He could not out-climb the mountain. The lesson learned was never to rely on the load leaving the aircraft to save the pilot from his own folly. All bombing runs must be made when flying level or downhill. As hard and fast and sensible as this rule of bombing is, there are promotional pictures of the CL-215 bombing uphill.

The configuration of the aircraft determines how susceptible it is to pitch-up. Short-coupled aircraft like the TBM, the CS2F and the F7F have substantial pitch-up, as the horizontal stabilizer on short aircraft is in the path of the down-rushing air, while the tail and horizontal stabilizer on longer aircraft like the B-17, the DC-6 and the P3 Electra are clear of the down-moving air. The onrush of descending air occurs in the relatively empty space between the load and the horizontal stabilizer and elevator. Some aircraft like the DC-6 show no pitch-up at all when dropping single or even double doors. The displacement of air behind the load is small enough that the slight downward pulse of air on the aft fuselage doesn't affect the aircraft.

Hitting the Target

In order to drop a load of retardant accurately on a target, the pilot must see or know where the target is and he must trigger the load at the appropriate moment in advance of arriving there. Targets can be easily visible in fairly open areas with thin forest or brush cover, or they can be almost totally obscured in featureless, heavy forest. In either case, the exact location of the target must be established. I began to discover techniques for mentally marking targets in heavy cover which can easily be learned. When to trigger the load, however, can only be learned by experience.

Basically, the bomber pilot is asked to hit a couple of different targets: a spot fire, or an area slightly bigger than a spot, and a longer fire edge. The spot fire is the type of target that pilots will be most often attending with One Strike.

To get some idea of what it's like to hit a spot with a bucket full of water, imagine you're sitting out in the open in an ultralight aircraft (equipped with dual controls for the likes of me) and you have the bucket full of water on your lap. You have an unobstructed area out to the side where you can toss the water. The ultralight is flying at 100 mph and up ahead of your flight path, a patch of red cloth about the size of a table napkin sits out in a large open field and dares you to hit it. Your job is to toss the water out of the bucket at just the right time that the spread of water straddles the cloth equally on both sides. The patch of cloth should be in the middle of the spread. Matters can be complicated further by having a crosswind carry the water sideways after it's tossed. Thus, to make a direct hit, you have a few lead problems to solve in your mind before you toss the water. If you miss, some busybody who is flying overhead with a radio will tell the world that this aspiring bomber pilot would be more gainfully employed as a greeter at Wal-Mart.

Accurately placing a load is a real problem, both for the beginner and the experienced bomber pilot, so how to place a load accurately was something I wrestled with from the very beginning of my Fire

Bombing career. How does a pilot make an accurate drop when every shot is different? The wind is variable, and if he does a succession of drops, one drop could be in a crosswind and the others into the wind or downwind. And the wind makes a huge difference as to where the load will eventually end up. The height for each drop is different: there is no way for the pilot to know that he is precisely 150 feet above the trees. It could be more or less. The speed for each drop might be different. There is no way to know exactly what speed he is going to end up with at the end of a steep descent. In addition, the perspective from the airplane is different every time. If the pilot is going more slowly, the nose is up; if the pilot is flying more quickly, the nose is down. Thus there is a huge computation the mind must make for a variety of parameters in order to pull the trigger at just the right time in advance of the target.

If I were going to write the book on bombing technique, I would certainly have to explain how pilots could do what they were being paid to do: hit the target. So when I started flying the TBM, it became a science for me. I was making hits. The loads were going where I was asked to put them, so I was trying to resolve in my mind just what it was that I was doing right. I wondered if I were somehow using parts of the aircraft to aim the load subconsciously. To investigate this thought, I laid lines of tape on the wings, the windshield and on the nose cowling ahead of me. I marked all the areas on the airplane that I might have been looking at when I triggered the load. I wanted to see if I was subconsciously using any of these lines as a sight. Putting lines of tape all over the front of an airplane naturally aroused curiosity.

"Whatcha got all these lines on the airplane for, Linc?"

"Trying to figure out how to drop the load."

"Tried pullin the trigger?"

"I've got a little experiment going."

"Put on a Stuka dive bomber screamer. That might help."

"The lines are really to help me find my way home."

"Looks like you got a few too many bugs on your windshield, Linc."

Numerous trials revealed that nothing even came close. I was not using any part of the aircraft to aim with.

The Dropping Constants

My next thought was to look for constants while dropping. At first glance, it didn't seem a likely area to investigate because every drop is so different. Upon looking at the drop regime closely, however, it became apparent that there were indeed constants with every drop. The time from pressing the trigger button to the doors opening was a constant. The physical action of pulling the trigger (or pressing a button) takes about one half a second and about one half second later the door or doors open. This may vary a bit with each aircraft but this time delay is soon learned. From the time the door opens to the load entirely leaving the aircraft is a constant and is about two seconds. In this time the load will fall about seventy-five feet.

For each aircraft, the time, which may vary slightly from trigger pull to the load being seventy-five feet below the aircraft, is a constant and is about three seconds. While the slipstream tears away part of the load, the bulk of it travels directly below the aircraft. So I had another constant: if the load is dropped at low altitude (seventy-five feet or less) it will hit the trees directly below the aircraft.

These constants gave me something to build on. If I were to fly at seventy-five feet above the trees, or as close to it as I could judge, then from the time I pulled the trigger to the start of the load entering the trees directly below the aircraft would be three seconds. So now I needed to know how far I would travel in three seconds. I knew I must build in another constant and that is the airspeed at the drop. If the ideal drop speed for the aircraft I'm flying is 135 knots, then every effort must be made to drop at this speed. If consistent drop speeds could be maintained, in a no-wind condition the pilot could gain a perspective of his ground speed passage related to time.

It surprised me how fast the mind puts this perspective together. With experience, pilots are actually able to capture it for any speed very quickly. I knew I must, therefore, set up the final approach to give me enough time to capture a picture of the ground speed mentally to see how far I would travel in three seconds' time. I would have to do that far enough back from the target to be able to trigger three seconds in advance of getting to it. In a perfect no-wind, low-level drop scenario where the tops of the trees are the target, I could approach it with any ground speed built into the mind and trigger three seconds in advance of where I wanted to load to start laying into the trees. If a bull's eye marked the middle of the target, then I would want the load to start hitting far enough back for the bull's eye to be in the centre of the load spread.

The pilot knows the size of his load pattern even before he takes off. When dropped from a specific altitude, each door lays a specific pattern of retardant when it lands on the ground. Its width, length and retardant thickness has been determined from numerous drop tests. A single door dropped from a TBM at a height of about 100 feet will put a pattern on the ground about sixty to seventy feet long and about thirty feet wide. If I wanted the spot fire to be in the middle of the load pattern, then the actual aiming point for where I wanted to load to start hitting would be half a load length from the location of the spot.

Dropping a single door to perfectly straddle a spot fire in a windy condition is the hardest shot there is. It's like the circus performer throwing knives at the lady against the wall. A number of parameters have to be mentally fixed in the mind before the magician throws the knife or the bomber pilot pulls the trigger. If I were lucky (or unlucky) enough to be chosen to hit a spot not much bigger than a campfire in a featureless, dense forest, Birddog's eyes would be intently watching. Just how good I really am would be bared for the world to see. With the retardant being a bright red, there is no subtlety about where the load lands, so the accuracy of my shot relative to my target would be as obvious as the accuracy of the magician hitting his.

The easiest target is the laying of a line next to the edges of a larger fire. The Birddog will state where the line should begin and how many doors should be dropped. If the load is to "tag on" to a load already in place, life is easy. That previous load easily can be seen on final and my own load is triggered soon enough to start the overlap at or near the end of that line. From there on, I extend the line with the rest of the requested doors. I have an entire load length to hide my finger trouble so a perfect tag-on or almost any degree of overlap will keep me in the Birddog's good books. Besides, the retardant is all the same colour, so no one could really tell where my line started.

The Big Variables

The easiest way for a bomber pilot to make accurate drops is to drop at low altitude when the only consideration becomes one of timing. For practical purposes, the effect of wind on drops done at low altitudes can mostly be ignored, since a drop height of 100 feet or less above the trees will have the load travel forward with the speed of the aircraft and land directly below it. Low-level drops, however, are frowned upon and are never requested as they can tear the branches off of large trees and even knock them down, and are dangerous to people on the ground.

Drops are normally done from 150 to 300 feet above the ground or, in tall forest, above the trees. Once the drop leaves the airplane, drag and the prevailing wind begin affecting the load. The higher the drop, the more it's affected by the wind and the more difficult it is to place accurately. A drop made from 300 feet will totally lose the momentum given to it by the aircraft and simply free fall, drifting with the wind. I called this condition "terminal velocity." How far loads will drift with the wind is learned by experience. Making allowance for this drift is in the same category for the bomber pilot as changing trigger considerations when dropping in a headwind or tailwind.

The easiest drops to make are the ones a Lead Plane has you drop from the stratosphere – every drop is a bull's eye even though the bull is nowhere to be found.

Accurate dropping with a strong tailwind is by far the pilot's biggest headache. In winds of twenty miles per hour or more, the triggering point is so far away from the target that it's almost impossible to get it right. The mind simply cannot believe that the load will drift as far as it does after it leaves the aircraft. An equally bizarre triggering situation takes place when dropping into a very strong headwind. I've gone completely past a target before triggering and ended up with bull's eyes. The load is shredded and quickly stopped by the wind. It almost seems to stop in the air and then flies backwards. It's not unusual to see retardant on the windward side of the trees.

Built-in Errors

To complicate things for us, Murphy has decreed that bomber pilots should have some built-in errors. Pilots are well acquainted with Murphy and go out of their way to prove that Murphy lacks imagination. The first error occurs when a small target is difficult to see. Dense forest creates the biggest problem. The Birddog explains where the target is and from altitude, it is easy enough to see. On low-level final, however, everything changes. Pilots are looking horizontally through a mass of forest and the real target down on the ground has disappeared. What is visible is the smoke emerging from the trees. If there is a substantial crosswind, this could be a long way from the location of the real target. A pilot's natural tendency is to aim at something he sees: the smoke. He's like a fish chasing elusive bait. It's built in error number one. The next tendency is to wait for the target to become clearly visible through the trees below the airplane, and then trigger the shot. At this stage it's far too late and the load overshoots. Shooting long is built-in error number two and is actually the most common problem. If a pilot shoots long at a smoke well displaced from the real target (as happens all too frequently) Birddog may have an irresistible urge to announce publicly over the radio that this delusional pilot is depriving some village of an idiot.

The cures for these two errors are experience and huge self-discipline on the final run. A difficult-to-see target is marked in the mind with some physical feature right at the target. The smoke must be ignored. The same is true for where the trigger is pulled. The target must be firmly fixed in the pilot's mind and physical features which can be followed and seen on final must be memorized. The trigger point on final could be over dense forest, with any indication of fire well removed from the airplane's flight path. Many times, I have hit the bomb button when it looked like I would miss the fire by a Texas mile. The vindication always came when I heard the Birddog's comforting words: "Bull's eye." When target identification and timing has reached this point, the pilot has come of age in Fire Bombing.

Dry Lightning

A mature thunderstorm passing over a forested area in the afternoon and evening can spawn hundreds of lightning strikes. All have the potential to start a forest fire. In the normal, wet thunderstorm where vast amounts of rain fall, the rain will extinguish most, if not all of the strikes. If some of the fires continue smouldering as they might if they're inside a hollow log or standing tree, they may flare into an active fire when the forest dries and burning conditions are better. Forest services are aware of potential "sleepers" that may come alive a few days after the storm, so it's routine to keep track of storm paths and regularly patrol appropriate areas looking for latent fires. Consequently, fires in the aftermath of wet thunderstorms are normally quickly found and most often easily extinguished.

A phenomenon feared by all forest services in North America is a devil called the dry lightning storm. The most likely time to get a dry storm is when a weak amount of moist air aloft forms into a storm or line of storms as it passes over a deep, entrenched area of hot dry air that may have been in place for some time. The forests are dry and fire hazards may already be high. A dry lightning storm is like any other storm but it will usually have a very high base and most often very little rain may fall from it. The rain that does fall will quickly evaporate as it reaches the dry air below. Still, the storm generates lightning and the lightning definitely reaches the ground. The potential for a rash of new fires without the accompanying rain to put them out can lead to an explosive situation.

The worst possible scenario for any forest service is to have a line of dry storms pass over a forest in extreme fire hazard. I've seen this happen many times and it creates a forest service nightmare. A line of dry thunderstorms can generate many thousands of lightning strikes (fifty thousand and more have been recorded) as it passes over the countryside. These passages are common over the western states like Washington, Oregon and California, and British Columbia. Fortunately, not all strikes will cause fires. Still, hundreds of fires can show up in a matter of a few days. This is the most common cause of the big project fires. There are so many fires showing up so quickly that no forest service can deal with all of them. It's the home run the opposing team can do nothing about. Many will be extinguished at a small size, but if the hazard is high or extreme, some will grow to unmanageable size even in a matter of hours.

Support Action

A bomber's usefulness doesn't end with One Strike. If a raging out-of-control fire is situated away from any communities, little or no bomber action may be used on such a fire. Trying to stop the head would be pure wasted effort. Elsewhere on the fire, the Fire Boss/Incident Commander may ask for a line of retardant in support of a line on the ground.

The bomber comes spectacularly into its own when property is threatened. Bombers can lay a line of retardant next to homes and buildings where ground firefighters don't dare work or cannot reach. Over my years in various bombers, I've flown many actions of this kind in British Columbia and California. These support actions in the defense of property are most often videoed for presentation on newscasts, and the public gets to see how the Fire Bombers work.

When I've laid a line of retardant to protect a home or a subdivision, it has always given me a great deal of satisfaction in knowing that I'm saving someone's memories and lifetime of work. In one pass, I could make the difference between a family losing or keeping their home. And, where I could, I would verify the effectiveness of my load. On a few occasions I was able to drive back to the site of my drop. At other times, I could see whether or not I had saved a home with a flyby the next time I was in the area. Occasionally, fire embers would jump the retardant line and our efforts would be wasted. There is nothing more distressing than watching a home burning and knowing that there is nothing that you can do about it.

But there were lighter sides to support actions. On one occasion I was laying a line of retardant with the DC-6 down a line of homes with swimming pools. What an opportunity for a little harmless mischief. I nudged over far enough to leave a line of red pools. I not only saved the homes but the pools as well.

My Best Miss

Bombing a fire on a windy day in "Happy Valley" was the name we gave to an action in British Columbia's Fraser Canyon. By a windy day I mean a wind that's twenty-five miles an hour or more with high, sudden gusts. The Fraser Canyon, like the Grand Canyon, takes many turns and a myriad of side canyons were carved out by the rivers and creeks entering from various angles. All of these ridges and canyons break up a roaring wind into severe turbulence. While the Canyon is a stunning visual jewel, it's an intimidating black hole for bomber pilots. A fire in the Canyon is indeed a fun time in Happy Valley.

At a place called Kanaka Bar, a fire driven by a high wind was rapidly approaching a group of buildings just below a ridge. Historically, the "Bar" names came from those who worked the river for its gold, and are preserved in the names of the many highway tunnels on the route. Boston Bar earned its name from the concentration of Americans in that area ("Boston" or "Boston Man" was the term for Americans), China Bar from a concentration of Chinese miners in that area, Kanaka Bar from a concentration of

Hawaiians ("Kanaka" being the Hawaiian term for "local person," and the word for a Hawaiian) and Sailor Bar from a group of British sailors who had taken up mining.

It was extremely turbulent and placing a load with any accuracy was almost impossible. I was asked by the Birddog to place a load along the top of the ridge to prevent the fire from descending and igniting the buildings. It was a steep downhill drop and on my descent, I made an outlandish allowance for load drift to try and land it on the ridge. My attempt was pure burlesque. The wind carried the well-dispersed load clean over the ridge (a displacement of at least 300 feet) and all of it landed on the buildings. It turned out to be a very advantageous error. In spite of the fire's mad rush to overwhelm the buildings, none caught fire.

At the end of the season, I returned to Vancouver from Kamloops via the Fraser Canyon and I stopped at Kanaka Bar to see how the drop looked a few months later. When the retardant dries, it's a pink colour and all the buildings around me were "painted" pink, even the inside of the outdoor phone booth. An elderly woman shuffled over to where I was, thinking I wanted some gas.

"You wan gas?"

"No I'm just looking to see how everything looks after you had a big fire here."

"Yes — yes — vee haff beeg fire — terriple — terriple. My hosebeen say it born our house — ve wrrready to ron from house. A beeg plane come — make house roscat (red) an house no born — goot plane — goot plane — safe house from born."

I point to my flight path.

"I flew the plane [TBM] on the other side of the ridge and the load landed here."

"Oooohhh — you fly plane? You safe house? You vonderfool — you vonderfool — you safe house, ees goot — goot — house no born."

"I just wanted to see how it all looked and I'm glad your house didn't burn."

"Tank you — tank you — tank you."

"Okay, everything's fine, I'll be going."

"Tank you — tank you."

It was my best miss and it couldn't have been more gratifying.

The Bomber Pilot's Dream

A series of dry lightning storms in the summer of 1967 at the Kamloops Forest District kept us flying daily for a period of six weeks. An armada of spotter airplanes supplied us with numerous fires every day. Action would generally begin as the day began to warm up at around 10 A.M. and continue until dark. When the pay is by the hour, the bomber pilot's dream is non-stop action. And that's what we were experiencing, day after day. We were euphoric about the pay we were earning, but more importantly we were getting spectacular results. One Strike was working just as it should. We seldom went back for another hit on the same fire. We were a perfectly functioning team and we were in our glory.

The fun we were having during the day was matched by the pleasant camaraderie at night. A long, hot day can generate a mighty thirst, which we quenched at our evenings at the Overlander Pub. Pubs were my favourite place to have a beer and it was our good fortune that the exalted leaders in the governing halls of British Columbia decreed that British and Irish pubs should be transplanted to British Columbia. The Overlander was the quintessential Irish pub. Chunky, dark wooden pillars held up the heavy axe-hewn beams of the ceiling. The Victorian weatherbeaten look of crossed beams set in white plaster decorated the interior. The bartender worked behind a broad, ebony counter to pull endlessly at the tall levers which extracted the various beers from the depths of a subterranean cavern. Massive, leather-covered armchairs, luxuriantly cool to the body, provided the perfect cocoon to relax. Thick oak tables, worn from the traffic of countless beer mugs awaited the next arrival — ours. The pub was slightly dark, providing a warm, inviting atmosphere. It was a nightly affair which we enjoyed immensely.

The first cold beer at the end of a hot day of flying was the time to reflect on how it was that nothing eclipsed man's noblest creation as the perfect primer for exchanging the tall stories of our daily heroics. Beer is the elixir of the gods and a mug of cold, frothy draught beer is the ultimate pleasure, especially the first one. A sweaty body and a dry throat left no option but to take it down almost in one long draught. It may barely have touched the sides of the throat, but there was nothing more refreshing. What fantastic relief to a thirsty, overheated body. After a single pint of beer, all was well with the world. There would be time to drink the other beers more slowly, but that first one was a total ecstasy of the senses. We are a species of genius. It's not surprising that the armchairs of great pubs spawn brilliant solutions to the world's most pressing problems.

It's hard to imagine that our eagerness to fly could actually be tempered, but when the action takes place in intense heat for prolonged periods, the body and the mind get tired. The buildup of heat on a hot, sunny day in an enclosed automobile is familiar. It's even more extreme inside a glass-covered cockpit with no shady roof. The greenhouse effect bakes the interior of the airplane and renders the pilot a sweat-drenched passenger. After several weeks of feverish flying every day, we were actually hoping for a break.

But the frantic pace continued and it looked like even more action was in the making. A line of the blackest storms I had ever seen was herding a migration of lightning strikes just in front of its path. It was gifting us with a practically solid wall of new fires. All of the bombers quickly retreated from this approaching ominous blackness to seek safety on the ground. Shortly after the fireworks hit the bomber base, a Niagara of water followed. None of the existing fires or the thousands of aspiring new ones had a chance. Our season was over.

There was a general euphoria both by the forest service and the bomber crews about our exemplary summer's performance. We knew we were good. The season we just finished demanded a celebratory party to toast our great successes, so we decided to have the party at the bomber base.

To toss this party, the bomber pilots had to throw in their own money as the company wouldn't put a penny into what they considered frivolous entertainment even though it was a celebration by the pilots put on for ourselves and the forest service. Company participation or not, we invited all the top forestry people from the Kamloops and other forest districts. When we had an idea of how many were coming, we discovered that we needed a lot of refreshment, so we had to dig deep into our pockets to ante up the sum.

The liquor flowed freely and as the evening wore on, we were putting our arms around the big kahunas and calling them by their first names. Some were from headquarters and were so important that appointments to see these people had to be arranged with God. We had them where we wanted them and they got our undivided attention. Everyone knows that race car drivers are doused with champagne after winning a race. We had just won a successful season and there was no reason why the upper echelons in the forest service shouldn't be toasted and honoured in the same way. At some dimly remembered, appropriate time in the evening, I offered the first congratulatory toast:

"Here's to a great season, Denny," I said as I shook a bottle of champagne to assure some release pressure. There was a wonderful pleasure in shooting an entire bottle of champagne at one of the forest service's top tank commanders. We were celebrating for us and for them, and it wouldn't do for them to not take it with a sense of humour. My shot at Denny, the District Forester, was just the beginning. Thereafter the sprayed champagne flowed freely even at the exalted few. They all took it in good humour and it was the one and only time that I saw some normally reserved people actually show a sense of humour. It was my most memorable end-of-the-season party. There was also a special ironic twist about it that we all enjoyed. Company management didn't attend. They later found themselves embarrassed as the forest service people talked about the fantastic party and wondered why no top hats from the company were in attendance.

Chapter Nine
Missoula Montana and Back to British Columbia

Learn from the mistakes of others.
You won't live long enough to make them all yourself. Anonymous

The few seasons that I already had with bombing gave me a reasonable income, but in looking south to the good old USA, I knew the pay was better. We were being paid twenty-five dollars an hour and we heard that down south the operators were paying forty dollars an hour. If I went south and got in the same amount of flying as I had in 1963, the forty bucks an hour would allow me — my head was spinning — it was giddy with numbers — allow me to — allow me to take a trip around the world — then make a down payment on an office tower in Calgary. It would be the beginning of a real estate fortune. There was only one step to take to start this dizzying rise to wealth. All I had to do was to find a position with an American operator.

I went to see Johnson Flying Service in Missoula, Montana looking for a job. Missoula was a bit older than I had suspected. Many of the buildings could have been built in the late 1800s. Nevertheless, it had a modern airport and the company facilities were quite new. It appeared the universe was already aware of my plan for riches and placed the first foundation stone: Johnson needed a TBM driver. I got the seat for the months of July and August. I had a choice of two payment methods: I could take a flat $600.00 per month, or I could take forty dollars an hour with no standby pay, but with an advance of $600.00 per month against my summer's earnings. Always being the optimist and "knowing" that the Americans flew much more than we did, I was anticipating bewildering amounts of flying time. I astutely took the flying-pay-only option.

Well, we all know that every summer is different in the great forests of the Northwest. Some summers are hot and dry and some are cold and wet. When I arrived in Missoula it was raining. Not a light rain or even a moderate rain, it was raining hard enough that the giant drops left bubbles the size of soup bowls on the main streets. "Okay," said I to myself, "every area gets a shower or two, but in summer, showers often turn into thunderstorms. They're the fire-lighters." I dismissed this tropical deluge as an unusual, passing phenomenon and knew that thunderstorms would soon be on the way to light a million fires. A break the next day gave Johnson a chance to let me prove that I could fly the airplane. I took off successfully, dropped a load in more or less the desired area and landed. I was ready for the big time. I carefully noted the date in my log book as July 1.

After the one day break, another one of those misplaced tropical cloudbursts came along and took the visibility down to about three feet. I was learning something: it can rain pretty hard in Missoula and the streets can flow six inches deep in water. But I also knew that sunshine and fires were coming. There would be a day or two of no rain but then it would hit − a tropical monsoon with absolutely no hint of lightning or thunder. The fogged-up cockpits were growing mould inside.

As the summer and the rain wore on, we heard that there was a fire or two. I can't possibly imagine how they could have started; everything was wetter than a wrestler's armpit. There were very few fires, and those that did manage to fan themselves into a few hot coals were fought over by hundreds of fire trucks and attack crews. Everyone wanted some action. Needless to say, the demeanor of the pilots was getting pretty touchy.

With each passing July day, it was becoming extremely obvious that the summer was a washout. We knew that in August, the cool evenings settled dew on to the already soaked forest. Soon, cards, reading and our ever-so-polite discussions about religion, sex and politics wore off. The rest-fatigued pilots sat around, read or simply sulked. Tossing soaked paper towels at each other became the highlight of the day. July was almost over. It didn't look good and then it happened. We got a dispatch.

I believe that dispatch was the Dixie Creek Fire. It involved taking off at night to go where no sensible people had gone before to hit a fire that was about forty-five minutes' flying time away. The idea was to arrive at the fire at dawn because it was thought that the early morning calm was the best time for an air attack.

Our flight of TBMs took off in what was almost pitch-black darkness and our route through the mountains had been carefully plotted. The red beacons that marked the sides of the mountains on our route showed up on location and on time, so I knew I was on course. This was the first time I had flown in the mountains at night and, to make it more interesting, we weren't above them: we were flying a valley route. We were in between the rocks. A little bit into the flight I discovered that I could see the complete outlines of the mountains, so it was not totally dark. A sliver of starlight lets us see even in the darkest of nights. Some of the apprehension subsided and I felt better.

This darkness reminded me of the many nights that a boatload of my fellow teenagers and I would take off in a sixteen-foot boat with a ten-horsepower Johnson Outboard on the back, and head for a summer camp belonging to one of our parents. We spent our summers on Lake of the Woods, a huge lake that straddles Ontario, Manitoba and Minnesota. The lake has fourteen thousand islands and probably twice as many reefs. I think half the population of Minneapolis-Saint Paul had summer cottages scattered among the many islands. Privacy was easy to find so the lake was an idyllic place to spend the summer. If one didn't know the lake intimately, it was almost a guarantee that one would get lost or run up on a reef. We had made many long and different trips navigating through the islands and reefs to different cottages in daylight so often, we could find them at night, even with a thick overcast. And back then, we found the same thing that I found on that flight out of Missoula. As black as the night is, the outlines of the mountains show up; it's possible to recognize where you are and not run into one.

Our fleet of TBMs arrived at the fire ready for action and encountered our big problem. The calmness that was supposed to assure easy bombing held a layer of overhanging smoke in place, completely obscuring the fire. We couldn't see anything we might identify as a target. At least the sun was sliding in under the clouds, giving better visibility. We circled the fire for awhile, and finally our loads were placed where the Lead Plane thought we might do some good and flew home.

August was also a washout, but in the Northwest, it's not normally a high-fly month. The thunderstorms are usually over and the dew keeps the grass and the small, more flammable foliage wet until noon. It's called "recovery." However, I did get two dispatches.

At the end of the season, I assiduously tallied my stipend for the flying hours several times to make sure that the company gave me full credit.

July 29 1964	Dixie Creek Fire.....2 hours
August 17 1964	Six Mile Fire...........1 hour 22 minutes
August 24 1964	Canyon Creek Fire. 1 hour 33 minutes
TOTAL...4 hours 55 minutes.	

Amount owing to me...$196.66...US Funds...less tax.

My diligent calculations then confirmed the fact that I indeed did not fly enough at forty bucks an hour to work off my advances. It was then time to point out the fact that I should be paid stress pay for enduring the rain and being in a taut spring-loaded stance ready to sprint to my airplane every day. The company cheerfully informed me that "business was business" and presented me with a bill. No amount of re-calculating on my part could cancel out how much I owed them for the privilege of holding down a TBM seat for the summer. Nevertheless, my pleas caught a sympathetic heart and I was informed I wouldn't have to pay it. I think that exercise about the bill was more a demonstration of the President's warped sense of humour (something like mine). So much for the big bucks in the USA. The next season, I was back in British Columbia.

Standby Pay, Finally

In 1965, I was back in British Columbia and familiar territory. The forest service was serious enough about bombing to want immediate availability for the pilots and airplanes. The company negotiated a standby contract with the British Columbia Forest Service, which allowed them to pay us standby. It wasn't great, but at least it was an acknowledgement that it was worth something to be available. The standby contract included the first forty hours of flying.

That summer I drew a base at a nameless forest district ruled by a District Forester who is best to remain nameless. If it can be said that there is an average year for weather, that summer qualified and there were plenty of fires that needed action. It was soon apparent, however, that the forester judiciously allotted how much bombing would be assigned to each fire so that by the end of the season, they would have used the built-in forty hours and not a minute more. Other pilots who had flown in this district the year before warned us of the predictability of our summer's flying.

Some rather interesting air attack behavior occurs when only so much bomber time is allotted to a fire. When we were dispatched to a fire, we would place bets as to how many loads we would get to drop. We might as well have called it a one or two-shot practice except that it occurred on a real fire. How much containment we had achieved on any fire didn't mean a thing. We flew the time that the forester had assigned for that day and then flew back to base to ponder our bad luck for being there. New fires springing up were none of our business and weren't likely to trigger a bomber dispatch.

The forty hours could easily have been flown in a week, but we were to learn quickly that effective bombing held little sway to a forester quite unwilling to accept a threat to the old way of fighting fires. We were to be dribbled a few hours a week, which would terminate at the end of the season when we flew our forty hours.

As the numerous fires basked in a retardant-free environment, we naturally had to find some suitable behaviour that matched the small thinking of our forester. Sling-shots and grapes were the perfect match and a proper diversion. We were in a ludicrous bombing environment, which precipitated our bird-brained, ludicrous behaviour. We ceased to take bombing and ourselves seriously (that is, less seriously than our normal less-than-serious selves). To prepare for the daily event, each of us would purchase a bag of grapes. Red grapes with seeds were the preferred ammunition as they had those penetrating little bullets called seeds. Each day we would draw two new rival teams and prepare for the blitzkrieg. It was goggles on, shirts off and the carnage would begin. Getting shot at close range with a seedy grape left a stinging, brilliant, round, red welt on the body about the size of a tennis ball. In a few weeks time we all looked like versicoloured leopards.

On one particular fire, the Birddog literally begged the forester to have two more drops on his fire to complete the retardant line around the base. His request fell on deaf ears. The forester was allowing only so much time to any fire, and the Birddog was ordered to stop the attack. The fire escaped where there was no guard at the base and took off up the side of one of the most pristine, even stands of evergreen timber I had ever seen. It consumed thousands of acres that same afternoon. But the stroke of his pen could completely alter the truth of the history of that fire. Time is a great healer, the forest renews itself and such deeds are forgotten.

It wasn't hard to figure out how much flying I got in that summer: forty hours to the second.

The next summer, in 1966, I met an ex-Navy pilot by the name of George Plawski whom the company had hired a year earlier. He was going to university, enrolled in the theatre department at the University of British Columbia doing post-grad studies in directing, and needed a summer job. He didn't seem to be a likely candidate to be a bomber pilot, although I'm not sure what the perfect bomber candidate should look like. He was about five foot nine inches tall, had an athletic build and wore thick sideburns along with dark, shoulder-length hair. George had three priorities in life: life's social pleasures, golf and flying, and I'm not sure in which order. I think just whatever one presented itself at the moment. From our first meeting, it was clear George was not quite a "hippy," but certainly not the clean-cut image of a disciplined naval pilot.

While he was being considered for a bomber pilot position, he was asked to take a TBM out and do a run-up. During the run-up he let the TBM tip on its nose and touched the propeller on to the pavement. That little touch took one quarter inch off each propeller blade. He had never flown a "tail dragger" (airplanes with a tail wheel) and didn't know that the stick had to be held back during high-power settings. Management wanted George fired but Pete took full responsibility, blaming himself for the oversight. It was the lack of a full briefing beforehand from Pete that took George off the hook. It was a measure of Pete's integrity that he stuck up for his pilots if they were right. Staying on board for the summer launched George on a lifetime career.

George is a master of the English language and he has great sense of humour, a merciless wit and a total irreverence for everything people take so seriously. Here was a man with a proper perspective on life: together, we would rip apart all of humanity's sacred cows and were to become lifelong friends.

Pilot's Notes for Fire Bombing — 1966 and 1968

As I continued to gather more information and photographs about Fire Bombing, I was extremely distressed to see the continuing fatalities. I knew they were preventable and wanted to do something about it. The carnage compelled me to put some pertinent pilot guidance into a book that could be used immediately. So, in 1966, I assembled some notes on legal-sized paper which I bound into a soft cover. I gave it the title of *Pilot's Notes for Fire Bombing* and distributed it to the pilots of Skyway. It was to be was the first manual on the techniques of Fire Bombing in print anywhere in the world.

In 1968, I printed a little eighty-nine page blue book also with the title *Pilot's Notes For Fire Bombing*. I sent out a notice of its availability to all the bomber operators and to as many forest districts in the USA and Canada as I could find. I was surprised at the response. I later discovered that the book had been fairly widely read. There was a need for a manual.

When I was hired by Sis-Q to fly in California, one of the instructors at the United States Forest Service Fire Bombing school at Redding held the book up for all to see and suggested that in spite of the fact it was written by a tanker pilot, it was recommend reading. He also made another comment in serious tones: "There is one thing wrong with this book. We should have written it." It met with his full approval.

There is nothing like being the author of a book to establish credibility in one's profession. It was to lead to an invitation for me to act as a consultant during the conversion of the first S2-F Tracker into a Fire Bomber.

Making Notes

Each summer, I continued to gather more material for the book that would become *Air Attack on Forest Fires*. I felt a sense of achievement while I recorded my experience and observations into useful material for the uninitiated pilot. There was much to learn. Pilots were still getting killed: Fire Bombing is unforgiving of mistakes or ineptitude. Mountain flying in particular, with its variable winds and strong downdrafts, separates the professionals from the amateurs. Consequently, I spent considerable time in analyzing and laying out pilot procedures for safe flying in the difficult conditions of turbulence and descending air. The Birddog gives instructions on where he wants the load to go. After that, the pilot has to plan his descent, the final run and the escape from the area.

On relatively flat ground, the entire approach and run out could be fairly easy, but there was far more to talk about for runs down or across the steep face of a mountain. Pilots had to be aware of where they might find the unexpected. The air is invisible – all plans for the run are made from reading the smoke or from educated readings of the prevailing wind. Otherwise, even experienced pilots needed considerable input in what it took to be a proficient bomber pilot. The manual also needed to educate the aspiring bomber driver about fires, forest service tactics and how he should handle his airplane in mountainous terrain from the moment of takeoff to landing. The work continued year after year.

A Guardian Angel or Outhouse Luck

The TBM was an airplane I was quite used to flying and I didn't experience any situations with it in British Columbia that I couldn't handle. I did have a flying "close call" with the airplane, but that was to come later in California. Of course, close calls are quite subjective; what one pilot considers a hairy experience may be an uneventful event for another.

One day I was to learn how long one interminable minute after another could be. Shortly after takeoff in my TBM, the cockpit suddenly and completely filled with dense smoke. In that instant fog, every breath was highly irritating to my lungs and I was tearing so badly I could hardly see. I slid one side of the cockpit open to ventilate and get some visibility. I was at full power and immediately suspected an engine fire. But I wasn't sure. Where there's smoke there's fire, they say, so where was this coming from? I thought if I had an engine fire, there would be little time for whatever course of action would be forced upon me. I quickly checked the engine instrument for trouble. Nothing. All indications were normal. Where else to look? Ever greater volumes of smoke continue to pour into the cockpit, making the visibility worse. As I climbed, I was convinced I had a fire somewhere in the engine compartment. With no fire extinguisher, I had already decided on the option of bailing out. I just wanted to be high enough.

I continued to check around the cockpit and through the tears, I looked down to my right. I saw the source of the "smoke." Hydraulic fluid was being ejected from a hydraulic line as an extremely fine mist. It looked very much like smoke and was billowing out in profuse volumes. Hydraulic fluid as a mist is highly flammable or even explosive. A spark could easily ignite it and a catastrophic fire situation could occur at any second. I was in worse peril than if I had had an engine fire and could end up sitting in the middle of a violent, fireball explosion. The enveloping fog had permeated the entire cockpit – it was a bomb waiting to be lit. Any spark could light it and the most likely source of ignition might be the radio box. I wasn't sure if transmitting would create any sparks, but I wasn't taking the chance that it might. I could not risk talking to the tower.

I had to get on the ground, and fast. I wasn't high enough to bail out, and I didn't want to jettison the load in the airport area, so I quickly enter the approach circuit preparing for a loaded landing. I slid the other side of the canopy open and I didn't touch anything that needed electric power. With both sides of the cockpit wide open, the mist was dissipating somewhat, making breathing and seeing easier. But the real danger wouldn't be over until I was on the ground with the engine and electrics off. I made a tight circuit in nervous, anxious silence and landed. Had the mist caught fire, it would have been an instant inferno or an explosion. I would have been severely burned or may not have made it at all.

There was no fire.

My Guardian Angel dutifully kept the airplane electrics contained.

It was not my time.

TBM Engine Failure

Many pilots, particularly airline pilots, suggested that my flying an airplane with only one engine was the undertaking of the brave and ignorant (I didn't like the word undertaking) or foolhardy, as the case may be. Friends wisely informed me that if I kept it up long enough, one day that thrashing piece of iron up front would decide to stop and leave me with an airplane that glided with the grace of four bricks tied together. At that point in time, I was stuck with one engine, but as soon as I graduated to two engines as on the F7F and the B-26, I quickly saw their logic. Engines do indeed quit now and then. When I later began flying the DC-6, I decided four engines was an even better number. And as Murphy's Law would have it, to defy mathematical odds, four times as many engines gave me far more than the proportionate share of engine failures.

For several years I had no problems with the big Wright R-2600 on the TBM, but one day the inevitable happened. I was on my way to a fire south of Penticton, and, because it was a trip out of Kamloops, I had to climb to 8,000 feet to clear the mountains en route.

As I was nearing the fire, I heard a loud bang, saw the engine shaking wildly and noticed that the cockpit was filling with smoke. *Oooooh – what now?* The engine transferred the prodigious shaking to the airplane and the situation was beginning to get uncomfortable. I checked the instruments to see if I'd lost oil pressure. Nope - oil pressure and temperature indications were normal. *So what's with the smoke? Have I got a fire?* I couldn't locate a fire but clouds of smoke continued to enter the cockpit. I called the Birddog to tell him that I was jettisoning my load and heading for Penticton about twenty miles away.

I knew I had options if a fire developed. I was high enough to bail out. I asked another bomber to stay close alongside of me to let me know if any pieces started coming off, or if he could see a fire I couldn't. I opened the canopy and the smoke dissipated enough for me to see. If I was going to crash, I wanted to see what I would hit. My aircraft diagnosis to that point didn't reveal any major problem, but it soon became apparent that this less-than-smooth-running engine was slowly losing power. I advanced the throttle further to compensate, but nothing noticeable happened. The manifold pressure was slowly fading and the engine continued to die.

Fortunately, I started with eight thousand feet, but it was now nonchalantly bleeding away. I had full throttle on now, but there was no response to the engine. Nevertheless, the situation was under control, if I could call an airplane that's looking for its place to crash as being under control. I received one report from the airplane alongside:

he told me that black oil was gushing out from somewhere and was covering the entire bottom of the airplane. While that was bad, it was good. Oil on the outside doesn't normally catch fire. If the engine ran out of oil and seized, there was nothing I could do about it; I would handle that if it happened. I was hoping things wouldn't change too much because I could see Penticton off in the distance. I was now calculating off my rate of descent versus the distance I had left and it looked like I'd make it just fine if – and that was a big if – I didn't lose any more power.

So much for that thought. The engine was expiring even faster. My mighty radial that would carry me to the ends of the Earth might not take me the next five miles. What was once a throaty roar was being reduced to the muffled, heavy breathing of a steam engine. I was descending faster and my distance-to-altitude eye measurement told me that I may not make the airport immediately on the other side of the beach on Skaha Lake.

Skaha Lake is a blue-green jewel forming the south boundary of the city of Penticton. Its width fills the Okanagan valley from one mountain side to another and it extends southward for about fifteen miles. On hot summer days, thousands of oiled bodies seek the perfect tan on the broad golden beach. Calm winds and the summer's legendary heat make the lake a water skier's paradise.

It was Sunday and the lake was dotted with boats, so another alternative now entered my mind. I could ditch in the lake. I wouldn't even get my feet wet, as the TBM ditches well and floats for a considerable time. I would be picked up by a boat in a matter of minutes. In fact, the whole idea was now more appealing and could be fun. There would be miles of video and numerous pictures of the event. I would probably make a headline in the local newspaper. With luck, their photographer would have gotten some great pictures with me standing on the wing. Ditch in the lake, have a boat tow me close to shore, drop the gear when I'm close enough, and the TBM would settle on the bottom with the wheels down just the way the Vulcan bomber did in the James Bond movie *Thunderball*. The airplane could then be towed ashore or lifted out by a helicopter. No one could fault me for it. I would have said that the engine finally gave up and ditching in the lake was the only alternative.

As much as it was groaning and shaking, the engine was still running. I was now only about half a mile away from the button of the runway and low over the water. I dropped the gear and just as the wheels locked green, I hit the very edge of the runway. At the same moment, I censured myself for not having put it in the lake. It would have been far more exciting.

What had happened? When I heard the bang, an intake valve on one of the cylinders broke off and started to chew its way through the top of the piston. Once the top was eaten out, oil from the crankcase began flooding into the intake manifold and entering the other cylinders. As each cylinder got a big enough dose of oil to foul the spark plugs, the cylinder quit firing. As that process progressed to one cylinder after another, the engine continued to lose power. As is typical for any piston engine, it needs to fire on all cylinders for it to run smoothly. An imbalance of firing caused the engine to shake which was transferred to the airplane. Oil would have been blasted out of the exhaust valves as well, which accounted for the oil on the underside of the fuselage. When I shut the engine down, the oil quantity was down to one gallon out of the twenty-nine that it carried. I don't know how many cylinders were left firing when I landed.

If I had been one half mile farther away from the airport when the engine began its failure, I would have been able to live the fantasy I briefly had on final.

Discontent with the Company

I enjoyed flying TBMs in British Columbia. I had flown with Skyway for several years and was hooked on Fire Bombing, definitely an occupation I enjoyed. What I didn't enjoy was the way the company was treating us; we were being shamelessly exploited by the owner of the company. Bus drivers, Safeway drivers and municipal firemen were paid far more than we were. Even the boys who flew Cessna 180s and Beavers on the coast were making far more money than us. Neither were we treated as respected human beings worthy of some dignity: I spent one entire summer in a single room at a motel with eight other men. It was all the more galling when we knew that the forest service was paying the operator to keep each of us in a single room. The operator was putting the money in his pocket.

There was no advancement to better tanker bases by virtue of seniority. Assignment to a base depended on how "close" you were to company management. The manager's favourites even had their permanent first spots in the loading pit. No matter how the airplanes arrived at the pits at the end of the day, there would be a shuffle of airplanes to put the manager's golden-haired boys first in line.

Of course we talked about our pay; it was a never-ending topic of conversation because we were paid so poorly. Each season we compared notes since we all knew each of us was being paid at a different rate. Each year the signup for people began in winter for the summer's flying. Those who unknowingly took the pay at face value like I did signed up early, usually in January. As spring was approaching and the boss needed to fill the roster, the pay offers got better. Some of the fellows who knew the game would wait until the last minute to sign on. They got the best pay. We had talked about an association or union for several years, but nothing ever came of it.

The operator had a particularly good year in 1967. We flew a bag of hours and the boss made a pocket full of money. Our contract ended at the end of August. We delivered the airplanes back to Abbotsford and it didn't look like we'd be flying any more that season. To relax and enjoy the big city for a while, I was staying over in Vancouver with George for a couple of weeks. I was about ready to head for my home in Alberta when George, who flew out of the same base as I did for the summer, got a call from the boss asking for us to come to work. The weather had heated up again and the forest service asked for a return of some airplanes.

The Mouse Takes on the Cat

Our contract was over, so going back to work meant we weren't bound to the poor pay that we were getting. We got a base pay of $19.35 per day along with $35.00 an hour flying pay. We had known for some time the Americans were getting a better base pay along with $50.00 per hour. No one ever had the courage to ask for more pay; we simply took what was offered. We had all been complaining about the pay for years, so when it was my turn to talk to the boss, I would take it upon myself to get the pay raise we all wanted. I thought I had the boss where I wanted him: he needed us, he had a good summer and he may have an altruistic attitude about giving us a raise. We also knew the post-season flying rates on his airplanes were much higher than the contract hours. I'd mentally rehearsed my demand: *I'll tell him I'll only come and fly if I get a flying hour raise to $50.00 an hour. If he wants people, he doesn't have any choice. He'll make a lot more money, so a little raise for us won't hurt him a bit.*

I was being the brave little mouse thinking I was negotiating and had leverage over a hungry, ravenous cat. I knew how the boss treated his employees, but I naïvely thought he might respond because of his enhanced post-season rates and his urgent need of our services. I had him over a barrel. Or so I thought.

He knew he was talking to me but he never used the pilots' names.

"I need you in Kamloops right away. Can you get out there today?"

"I'll come out if I get fifty dollars an hour."

The boss didn't discuss pay. You took what he offered and he was no different in this conversation.

"I need some airplanes in Kamloops and I want you out there right away."

"I'll come out if I get fifty dollars."

"You're holding me up. Are you coming out or not?"

There was no change in his tone, I knew then this was no negotiation, nor did I have any power of leverage because of the situation. He was calling the shots.

"I'll come if I get fifty dollars."

"So I take it you're not coming."

"I'll come if I get fifty dollars," said I with a wilting conviction in my voice, knowing the outcome of our conversation had already been decided. I then heard the two words that can never be misunderstood or construed to have any other meaning.

"You're fired."

I melted in the chair as the realization set in. My flying with this company was over. It was a considerable shock. I loved the flying, I loved the mountains of British Columbia and this was where I wanted to work. The end came with two words. There was no starting the conversation over again with the benefit of some hindsight. I was not the one man union or the powerhouse negotiator who would get us all a raise. That was not to be, and I was not to be either.

It is one thing to be treated as a dispensable tool for the boss if everyone is treated the same and if you know the boss is honest with you. It wouldn't have mitigated the way we were being used, but at the very least there would have been some satisfaction in knowing the boss was up-front with everybody. I am not one who can watch deceit and injustice done to me and the others around me without doing something about it. I had tried and I paid the price. Fate would later conspire to lay the same circumstances before me and again dare me to do something about it.

I had planned on staying in British Columbia for awhile longer and as the next few days passed I thought about the situation and realized what had just happened wasn't the end of the line or even a bad deal. Out of adversity comes opportunity. I would head south and find a job with one of the American operators. I'd have the chance to fly some of the exotic airplanes the Americans were using. I had also been making copious quantities of notes for my book; this would be an opportunity to see different bombing systems in action and to discover the capabilities of other aircraft. It would give me the broader perspective I wanted for the book.

Chapter Ten
California and Sis-Q Flying Service

Keep looking around. There's always something you've missed.
Anonymous

The summer and the job were over for me with Skyway. I took the next two weeks to visit the operators in each state as I headed south, determined to take the first job I was offered. I hoped it would be in an airplane like the A-26. It's a sleek, fast airplane and apparently they were in use all over the USA.

My first stop was in Oregon to see Rosenbalm Aviation. I had a brief chat with Bill Rosenbalm, the owner of the company. I introduced myself, told him I was from British Columbia, who I had worked for and that I was looking for a job for next season.

"What kind of bombing experience have you had?"

"Seven years on a TBM."

"Any A-26 time?"

"Nobody's operating A-26s in Canada. Nope, no A-26."

"Well you've got enough experience on Fire Bombing (I thought, *What fantastic luck. I'm going to get a job on my first try and get to flying a really neat airplane.*) but I'm looking for A-26 drivers."

"I wouldn't have any problems with the A-26. It's just another airplane."

"You don't understand, Linc. The A-26 is not an easy airplane to fly as a bomber. It has a slippery wing and it takes a special person to fly one. You have to know how it handles and you have to keep it flying."

I knew what he meant by the slippery wing and the words about keeping it flying. Slippery wings are laminar flow wings and you can't let the airplane slow down or get behind the power curve. I was later to find out what he was talking about. The airplane has to be flown with special care, but in the real world of Fire Bombing, so does every airplane. I knew about airplanes and I knew I could handle it. But the boss didn't know that and he placed his priorities on the safe side.

146

"Sorry Linc, but with no A-26, we can't use you."

Thoughts I didn't express raced through my mind. *For some reason, operators look for experienced pilots for their equipment and I'm sure it saves training time. I suppose the experienced pilots are better, safer drivers. But who in hell gives anybody the chance to sit in the seat for the first time? Besides, the A-26 is flown by only one pilot. It doesn't need a co-pilot. Everybody has their first go with an airplane before they get the experience. Okay, this guy wants A-26 experience and I can't argue the point. I don't have it, I'm out of luck here, so I need to move on.*

"Why don't you go and see Aero Union at Chico in California? They're the biggest operator around. They run a lot of different airplanes and maybe they're looking for somebody."

"Okay, thanks for taking the time with me Bill. I'll go and talk to them."

Aero Union at Chico was my next stop. As I drove into the Aero Union parking lot, Bill Rosenbalm's words came to mind. They're the biggest operator and it sure looked like it. I saw aircraft parked everywhere of several different types. B-17s were parked all around and I was becoming more intimidated by the minute. I didn't have four-engine time. *Who am I, a little guy from Canada looking for a job with the biggest of the big, and obviously someone who really knows what to do around a forest fire? Am I hopelessly out of my league?* I walked into a tidy, well-organized office where everybody appeared to be doing their job efficiently. I approach the receptionist.

"Can I see the Operations Manager or the Chief Pilot — whoever does the hiring?"

"That would be the Chief Pilot. I'll call him for you. Please have a seat."

I didn't have to wait long: He came through another door in the office and introduced himself.

"I'm Jim Farrell*. What can I do for you?"

"I'm looking for a job for next season."

"Come into my office."

We entered a spacious, neat office.

"Have a seat and tell me about your experience."

"I've flown a TBM for the last seven years in British Columbia. I'd like to get a job for next season and thought now would be a good time to see if you needed somebody."

"Got any four-engine time, or flown anything else besides a TBM?"

I wanted to tell him that I was taking notes for a book and I was good at Fire Bombing. I wasn't just another driver. But the words didn't come out. I was too intimidated. I was a little nobody asking to have a job with the biggest and the best.

"No, just TBM time."

"Well, we're actually not looking for anybody; we've got a full staff of pilots."

Maybe I was just another one of a long line of pilots that must have been knocking at his door. He was obviously a busy man and wasn't giving me any more of his time. He stood up.

"Thanks for coming in. By the way, I think Sis-Q is looking for somebody and they're flying a couple of TBMs."

Sis-Q Flying Service

Sis-Q was still on contract so I had to go to Santa Rosa to find Bud Davis, the owner. To get to Santa Rosa from Chico, I could take the main highways and swing around close to San Francisco or take some shortcuts that appeared to be more in a straight line and which I thought would be quicker. Getting from Chico across the Sacramento Valley to the west side was an easy ride. It was the trip across the mountains to Santa Rosa that took endless time. The road was a narrow, winding bulldozer trail that someone had paved. The switchbacks in the road were so close together it kept my speed down to twenty to thirty miles per hour. I wondered who would ever take this snake of a road if they knew what it was all about. My suspicions were correct. I never met a single car in the hours that it took me to cross those mountains. Maybe it was a fire road because a good part of the trip was through burnt-out forest. After descending from the mountains, I passed through rolling hills covered in vineyards that nudged up to the edges to the city.

Santa Rosa is quintessential California. It's clean and situated among a combination of tall trees, short desert shrubs and grassy desert. Morning fog often drifts over the city but by mid-morning gives way to the dry, desert heat. Winding my way through dry yellow grass and cactus, I arrived at Santa Rosa airport.

I found Sis-Q Flying Service and Bud Davis. A man of about six feet tall, Bud was casually dressed and had dark, wavy hair. He had a no-nonsense demeanor about him, but the atmosphere around Bud was completely different from what I had encountered so far. He was friendly and I was able to relax and to talk freely. He was also genuinely interested in my experience and was impressed that I was taking the trouble of writing a book about the techniques of Fire Bombing. I think he felt that I would be a real asset to Sis-Q.

"I'm looking for a job for next season, Bud, and Jim Farrell at Aero Union said you might need somebody."

"Well we're actually looking for somebody for the TBM but you're going to need an American license. Are you able to get one?"

"I can if I know I've got a job."

"You've got enough experience on the TBM and that's where we'll put you."

Did I really have a job? Was this real? Besides TBMs, they had the F7F and maybe I'd get to fly one of those at some time. My pulse was up.

"So I take it that I have a job?"

"You're going to need an American license and a Green Card. We can supply the documents that you've got a job so you won't have any trouble getting one."

I did have a job! I was beside myself with excitement.

"You've got the job but I want to pass you by Harry Chaffee. He's my Operations Manager and I want to see what he thinks of you. He's up in Ukiah and you can see him on your way home."

I stopped in at the bomber base in Ukiah and met Harry, a stocky man of about five foot ten with a crushing handshake. His dark hair was cropped just short of a tight brush cut. He either had very dark facial hair or hadn't shaved for a couple of days. A cherubic face held piercing, deep-set eyes that scanned me like a laser. I immediately wondered what he thought of my long sideburns and fairly long hair that covered my ears. He looked me over and said:

"You're going to need a haircut if you want to fly here. We also do fires with the United States Forest Service and your haircut won't sit with those guys."

That comment was basically lost on me. Wasn't everybody flying for the USFS? I would learn later that Sis-Q contracted with the California Department of Forestry, not the USFS.
It was an interesting first observation about the haircut; I wondered if he wanted to know anything else.

"So you're from Canada and you want to fly here. You're going to need an American license and an instrument rating as well as a Green Card. If you can have all that by next season, we've got a seat for you right here in Ukiah."

"Sounds great, Harry. I'll go to work on it."

I couldn't wait to tell George about my successful trip, so he decided to call Sis-Q as well to see what his chances were for a job. As fate would have it, he was also hired.

It was time for me to fulfill the job requirement. Since it seemed so important, my first duty was to get a haircut. Having successfully completed the cut, I was confident the rest would be just as easy. I then headed down to Great Falls, Montana to get my instrument rating. It was getting on to ten years since I had flown instruments in the RCAF. Instrument flying is a perishable skill (do it or lose it) and I had long ago lost it. My friends were very perceptive about my flying ability; they had been suggesting that I lost it for some time. It was going to take considerable effort and concentration to sit under a bag and convert instrument readings to a picture of the real world outside. I gave myself two weeks to get the job done.

After the fourth day I could see I was in trouble. I was almost in a panic. There was a vast amount of material to cover to be able to write the exam, and a gorilla would have done better at flying instruments with the little Cessna. I just couldn't see how I could get this all done in two weeks. So I intensified my efforts. I studied till the wee hours of the morning and took more flights each day. But old skills return. Having done it all once before, the material and the flying suddenly all came together. I wrote the exam and did my successful flight test on day nine. At the same time, Sis-Q had supplied all the necessary documents to the American Immigration people regarding my having a job. I was all done.

Making New Friends

The following spring, George and I decided to drive to California at the same time and show up at the company together. The two of us arrived at Sis-Q Aviation, which at that time was located in Montague, California. Montague is a dusty little cattle town situated high up on a grassy plateau in the shadow of Mount Shasta. Agriculture and cattle ranching are the backbone of the economy sustaining the town's 1500 people. The area is covered alternately in rock mounds and sinkholes resulting from Mount Shasta's eruptions and landslides.

We drove to the airport, located to few miles out of town, for the day of introduction to all of the company management and to the other pilots who flew for the company. We first met Bill Benedict, a retired United States Air Force Colonel who had flown nearly every fighter that the Allies and Germans used. He was the company's most senior pilot and was well known in the business.

George and I met Ed Real, also a veteran of the Second World War. He flew fighters such as the P-38 in the United States Air Force. His boyish appearance totally belied his age; he certainly didn't look old enough to be a war veteran. He was friendly, outgoing, had a great sense of humour and thoroughly enjoyed flying. He was ex-military, as we were, so we each had a sack full of heroics that we could swap with each other. Ed's demeanor was more like our age and both George and I instantly made him a friend.

I watched Ed fly his F7F on many fires and it was immediately recognizable that he was an exceptional pilot. I had my doubts about the survival of some people I met in this business, but I never had any doubts about Ed's survival. He was a true professional. He flew his airplane expertly and knew how to hit the target. I had no qualms about telling people this man would survive his Fire Bombing career. When I heard about his tragic crash in a Tracker in 1984, I thought someone had gotten the name wrong. It couldn't have been Ed. But it was, in a Tracker in California. I would later put it all together.

George, Ed and I were staying at the same motel, so we planned on a drink together later on in the day to celebrate our newfound friendship. We spent the day going through all the formalities of the paperwork and learning company protocol.

Dinner for Three

When the afternoon's introductions and tour of the base were over, the three of us headed over to our motel for a drink. We found a forty-ouncer of Vodka with which to toast our newfound friendship, where, of course, one toast called for another and another and another.

The three of us decided that there should be a pause in our revelry (and besides, we were hungry) so the plan was to go and get something to eat. The day was hot and our motel was hot, so we had taken our shoes and socks off, which seemed quite appropriate as a partial means of cooling off. We decided, however, that we needed to wear shirts if we wanted to get service at the restaurant half a block away from the motel.

Off we went to the restaurant in bare feet. The restaurant was quite a classy place, quite out of character for a little town like Montague. The tables were draped in white linen tablecloths and the seats were massive, slippery, leather-covered lounge chairs. We sat ourselves at a table and waited for service. We waited for quite awhile, yet nothing was happening. Meanwhile, George passed out and just disappeared. Ed and I didn't miss him. We were just waiting for service. Then through my foggy vision, I noticed that George was gone.

"I can't find George, Ed. Where'd he go?"

"Don't know. He was here a minute ago."

I just happened to look down to see two bare feet sticking out from under the table.

"Hey Ed, I see feet under the table. I think it's George."

"Are ya sure it's George?"

"Nobody else was here so it's gotta be him."

"Whadya think we oughtta do, Linc?"

"Could we prop him up for dinner?"

"Don't think so. He's out cold."

"Can't feed him where he is, either. Why don't we order dinner, Ed, and take George home later? I'm hungry."

"Maybe we gotta take him back to the motel."

"Hey Ed, I don't see a waitress. I think they're ignoring us."

"Well, I don't think they'll serve us with George under the table."

"Whatcha think we oughtta do, Ed?"

"Let's take George back to the motel."

"Good idea."

There was no way to get George out from under the table other than feet first. So without talking to each other or formulating a plan, we simply got up, circumnavigated our way around the table to where George's feet were and each tucked a foot under an arm. He was limp and heavy, and we realized that we couldn't lift George up, drape his arms over our shoulders and take him out standing. We were already organized for the task of removing George feet-first and we weren't about to complicate matters by trying to lift him up. We each had a foot and the easiest way to move George was to drag him along on his back, a bit undignified for George, but an easy pull for Ed and me. His head bumped over the metal door sill on the way out to the concrete sidewalk.

The motel was about half a block away and we were on the second floor. We dragged George on his back all the way down the sidewalk to the entrance, bumped over another door sill and then navigated our way up the numerous steps to the second floor. George's head banged on every step.

"Whatcha think about George's head, Ed?"

"Kinda bumpy, ain't it?"

"Whatawa we gonna do, Ed?"

"Nuthin...keep pullin."

"Keeps bangin though."

"Not to worry, he can't feel nuthin."

We rationalize that we were not being cruel to George because he couldn't feel anything, but we didn't feel much either. We were simply concentrating in looking after our buddy. We flopped him on to his bed and the evening was over.

After breakfast the next morning, we showed up at the hangar ready to fly our airplanes out to our bases. Bud wanted to see us. Bill Benedict had observed the scene at the restaurant the night before, and in his position as the chief pilot decided that our behavior was unbecoming of gentlemen bomber pilots. His recommendation was that all three of us be fired before we began. Bud was very understanding. Besides, he couldn't get three more pilots on a day's notice. We stayed.

Not my normal approach to my employer, my grand entrance to my flying career in California was a recommendation to be fired the day after I was hired.

Colonel Benedict

Bill was every bit as aggressive flying his F7F and driving his car as he must have been flying fighters. He didn't slow down for anyone. His favourite expression when driving was, "When you fly a fighter or drive your car, you have to take advantage of your momentum."

He pointed out to me that this was the only way to survive and make kills when flying a fighter. He also utilized the physics of momentum to get around road debris (as he described slow-moving cars) to pass anywhere it suited him. He claimed curves in the road or blind hills were no big deal, saying, "I can get around them in a few seconds."

My only reply was, "Maybe so, Bill, but in a head-on collision it only takes a second to get killed."

One sunny summer day Bill and I and two other members of the department of forestry from Ukiah decided that we would drive out to the coast to do some abalone diving. I was all excited about the prospect until I was told we were going in Bill's car. I took some consolation from the fact I sat in the back seat and would be the last to get wiped-out as Bill applied his driving philosophy down the winding road. Bill hunched over the steering wheel as though he were aiming gun sights and never noticed such trivialities as the terrorized looks on all our faces.

We arrived at the coast where we wallowed in relief that we had survived Bill's driving. We spent several hours getting heaved around in the surf and inhaling a belly full of ocean water through our snorkels. Nevertheless, we managed to pry our limit of beautiful abalone off the rocks. I had ingested enough salt water to have a very upset stomach, which wasn't made any better by the prospect of being Bill's passenger on the way back. The trip reminded me of being in a taxi cab in France or Mexico, but those people were mere amateurs compared to Mr. Benedict. It's not surprising the Luftwaffe couldn't survive pilots like Bill. Despite the prospect of instant oblivion at every corner, we did arrive back in Ukiah. I took great care not to hitch another ride with the Colonel.

When World War Two broke out, Bill had originally joined the Royal Air Force. He quickly trained as a fighter pilot and was assigned to fly the Spitfire. After America joined the war, he transferred to the United States Army Air Force and flew Thunderbolts. Bill could tell great stories about his war exploits and I thoroughly enjoyed listening to them.

I liked his story about his one trip in a Messerschmitt ME-109. Several flyable ME-109s had been captured at an Italian air base. All of the pilots in his squadron naturally had to have a "go" on the airplane to see what they were contending with up in the skies. Bill never held back when he wanted to do something; he was going to take this famous fighter for a ride. No one told him one wing flew several knots ahead of the other one. So during the takeoff run when Bill thought it was time for the airplane to fly, he pulled back on the stick only to find the one wing with lift very eagerly obeying the laws of aerodynamics. That wing with lift simply rolled Bill while he was still on the ground until the airplane stood on the other wing that wasn't quite ready to fly. At that point, the airplane cartwheeled down the runway and destroyed itself. Bill walked out unhurt. And so it went for his entire experience during the war. Luck followed him around.

A few years later after I had left Sis-Q, Bill's luck ran out one day when he hit a giant oak snag with his F7F. (Snags are trees that stand out taller than the surrounding canopy.) Oaks are extremely tough trees and they don't give way to airplanes. The consensus among pilots was that this was the proper way for Bill to go. He was the gung-ho, pugnacious pilot to the very end. He died while doing his heart's passion.

Ukiah, California

I was delighted to be flying for Sis-Q. Bud was a peach of a boss who treated everyone well and the pay was much better than what I was getting in British Columbia. Bud often entertained the pilots at his home and on occasion he and his wife May, along with me and another pilot, would take off in his Cessna 310 to fly to some out-of-the-way airport that had a great restaurant. He ran an efficient operation. Any problem I had with my airplane was fixed immediately and I had virtually no down-time due to unservicability.

Ukiah, home of the "Champagne Springs," is a small city of about 15,000 people tucked tightly up against a ridge of mountains to the west. The airport is located on the south end of the city, with the runway having a north-south orientation.

The valley opens to the east and the land once prized for its hops now supports endless rows of fruit trees and vineyards. The native vegetation had long ago evolved its means for survival. The surrounding, low-lying mountains are covered in manzanita, mesquite, eucalyptus, juniper, ponderosa pines and other trees and bushes that have waxy leaves and needles to resist the blistering-hot summers associated with Ukiah's Mediterranean climate. I was surprised at how thickly the hills were covered. Fires in this oily or waxy undergrowth burned with an intense red flame that billowed huge quantities of black smoke. Given a wind, a fire-start here could become a raging holocaust in a matter of minutes. This kind of explosive forest was very new to me. Farther to the west, the coastal, giant redwoods had evolved their own means of survival. The needle of the redwood was the perfect size to condense the fog into water droplets. Standing under a redwood in the fog meant standing in the rain.

Bud decided that I should be partnered with Harry Chaffee, his chief of operations. I've often speculated on why I was teamed up with Harry. He knew the Fire Bombing business as well as anyone and didn't hesitate to let it be known. Why was I, the man who was writing the book, teamed up with the man who knew everything? Perhaps Bud thought that Harry would be just the man to round out my education about bombing for the benefit of the book.

I spent the summers of 1968-69 on base at Ukiah. I flew my TBM while Harry was flying an F7F. After watching the performance of the F7F, it was an understatement to say that I was highly envious of Harry. That envy was compounded by the fact that the F7F was called out of the Mendocino Forest for longer dispatches that were denied to the TBM. Some days I sat while Harry was flying elsewhere.

I wasn't about to challenge or offer any of my opinions about Fire Bombing to Harry. I simply listened to everything he said. Harry did indeed offer the occasional gems of wisdom, particularly about what I could expect in the way of turbulence in some areas. He was most helpful later on when it came my turn to fly the F7F. As a stranger to California, I was in no position to be offering hotshot ideas to the California Department of Forestry (CDF), which I considered, along with the British Columbia Forest Service, to be the best in the world.

I was learning from this new experience of watching the CDF and the United States Forest Service (USFS) at work. What was interesting about each action that we were on together was Harry's unsought advice to the Birddog on how to conduct his attack. Harry spent most of the day sleeping, but seemed to know the fire situation in the entire state on awakening. I quickly learned that everyone politely listened to Harry, pretended to take his sage advice and then went about their own business.

The summers gave me the opportunity to get to know Harry, one of the most unusual people I had ever met. Shortly after we were on base together, Harry informed me that he didn't take any nonsense from anybody. Almost in the same breath, he told me that he knew where to place the money to have anyone rubbed out, done in, whacked or terminated. The term he used was "buy a life." I'm not sure why he told me that. Perhaps I was supposed to be afraid of him. I wondered if he ordered a hit on everyone he disliked.

His German shepherd dog was at the base daily with Harry and he told me why. The dog had been trained to go for the throat of any person that Harry pointed to when he gave a particular crackling sound with his mouth. He thoughtfully demonstrated the sound one day when the dog wasn't around. I wondered where Harry got his training to make that most unusual sound. I also knew that he carried a pistol tucked in his belt behind his back. He seemed extremely paranoid about something; there must have been people out there that he worried about. He certainly didn't find me to be physically threatening and he was relaxed and sometimes quite talkative with me.

But something about Harry's demeanor always bothered me. I had underlying feelings that there was a great deal about Harry that I didn't know about, and while his behaviour appeared straightforward on the surface, I felt a strong uneasiness that Harry had much more on his mind than flying his airplane and being chief pilot. He sometimes spoke in less than complimentary terms about various people and other operators. He didn't trust anyone and everyone was under suspicion.

Everyone kept asking me in concerned tones about how I got along with Harry. In truth, we got along well. Perhaps there was a lot more about Harry I should have worried about. I wasn't tactless enough to tell him how to fly his F7F and he wasn't telling me how to fly my TBM or what to do around fires, so he was satisfied that I was okay.

TBM flown by author at Ukiah, California. Photo by author

I did have to hand it to Harry that he was a good pilot. He knew how to handle his F7F and he was good at Fire Bombing. I wasn't sure whether he had much of a sense of humour so I didn't test it. I didn't want to give him the occasion to crackle his killer at me.

He was really curious about the odd way that this Canuck spoke. I got the usual razzing that I said "oot" for my properly pronounced word out, and "aboot" for my very correct about. Americans are renegade colonials just like Canadians and we both acquire our different regional accents. Just for fun I'd get very formal with him on occasion:

"I would consider it a pleasure, old cock, if we could betake ourselves to a local pub and quaff a bucket or two of suds this evening...eh?"

"You mean go for a beer?"

"Precisely, old chap."

Harry never had a drink with me. I heard rumour that he was a recovered alcoholic.

The California Department of Forestry

I immediately discovered that the base in Ukiah serves the California Department of Forestry. It was not the same as being on a base operated by the United States Forest Service. Over the summer I found that each agency operates very differently, but I'd lucked out. To my utter surprise I found that the CDF operated the same way as the British Columbia Forest Service. I was delighted, and easily fit into the operations.

At Ukiah, the forestry office, operations room and the pilots' standby room were in the same building. Since the CDF was a strong advocate for using the bombers for initial attack, dispatches were made to every reported fire with no waiting. The Birddog briefed the pilots on the attack plan over the fire and did debriefings when the action was over. The pilots were an integral part of the team.

I heard a philosophy I'd heard before in British Columbia. If, by the end of the season, they hadn't jettisoned at least fifteen percent of the season's retardant, they weren't dispatching soon enough. If the bomber was called off the dispatch immediately after takeoff, we were credited with an automatic twenty minutes of flying time even though we could drop part of our load and land in less time. These people knew how to use the airplanes.

After a few weeks of flying in totally cloudless skies every day, my curiosity about California weather needed some answers. I made a trip to the meteorology office at the airport and asked the lady meteorologist the question: "Why is California weather the way California weather is?"

The Great Pacific High

Briefly, she told me that California has a Mediterranean climate, with a distinct change in the weather from winter to summer. Sometime in late November or December the overcast moves in. Then the rains begin and virtually never stop. In April or May when the skies clear, the state experiences a six-month period of high heat, low humidity and no rain.

I was not used to these sterling, predictable, clear summer skies, but there they were. There had to be much more about the climate than the brief explanation she gave me. I suspected more, because I was experiencing unexpected wind and turbulence behaviour while I was flying. I was told about a stable Pacific airflow passing over the state during the summer that caused problems for pilots in some locations. I wondered what they meant, because explanations were far from complete and I was left with many unanswered questions. I wanted to know precisely what they were talking about. What I was about to discover led me to an explanation of life-and-death significance. A study done by the California Air Resources Board (CAAB) in 1984 describes the phenomenon in simple, understandable terms:

> *The North Pacific high-pressure cell (anticyclone) is the dominant influence on the weather and climate of the eastern North Pacific Ocean and neighboring land areas in middle latitudes, particularly during the summer. It is a semi-permanent feature of the large-scale atmospheric circulation*

pattern in the northern hemisphere and consists of an extensive deep mass of air rotating in a clockwise direction and covering much of the North Pacific Ocean throughout the year.

The basic cause of this circulation feature is the large scale thermal difference between adjacent water and land masses in middle latitudes. During summer, the water mass is much cooler than the neighboring land mass. Through conduction and mixing, the air above the water is cooled and its density is increased, thus producing a vast high-pressure cell. In addition, air from the Equator enters the system aloft to provide additional support for high pressures. East of the ocean, the warm land increases the air temperature and consequently the air becomes less dense, resulting in the formation of a large low-pressure cell or thermal low. The positive differential of pressure from ocean and land causes a gigantic interchange of air. The warming air above the land surfaces rises and is replaced at low levels by cooler air moving onshore from the Pacific Ocean. A further interchange takes place aloft where air sinks in the Pacific High to replace the air that moved onshore. The sinking air in turn is replaced aloft by air from the tropics.

Because sinking (subsiding) air over the ocean is warmed by compression, it becomes warmer at lower levels than the maritime layer next to the ocean surface. The subsidence thus produces a strong, persistent vertical temperature inversion which is another dominant feature of the Pacific High.

This warm air above the cool coastal maritime air is a major influence on atmospheric stability. Atmospheric stability is the primary weather factor that influences the vertical dispersion of pollutants. In general, the more stable the air, the more dispersion is inhibited. An extremely stable subsidence inversion dominates the California coastal areas and effectively caps the maritime layer, providing a ceiling above which pollutants cannot rise. This reduces the vertical dispersion of air pollution, particularly during the summer when the inversion is strongest and most persistent.

The mean height of the base of the subsistence inversion ranges between 600 and 2200 feet above sea level and is persistent throughout the year (inversions are present some ninety percent of the time).

The Pacific High is strongest and most extensive in the summer when the temperature difference between the ocean and land is the greatest.

The North Pacific high-pressure cell produces a predominantly north-westerly flow of maritime air over California coastal waters. This large-scale circulation pattern is modified to a more westerly flow by continental influences as the air approaches the coast of California. Onshore wind flows predominate during the spring, summer and fall at all locations.

Land/Sea Breezes

The large scale climatological wind flows along the California coast as discussed above are modified by the effects of local land/sea breeze circulations. In effect, the local daytime sea breeze enhances the large-scale onshore component of the wind, while the nighttime land breeze retards or on occasion reverses the flow. The land/sea breeze circulations show that the onshore winds are generally stronger than offshore winds.

Fog

The climatic arrangement of warm, stable air over the cool maritime environment that dominates the coastal waters of California produces a relatively high incidence of fog. Fog is frequent during the night and early morning hours, especially during the cold half of the year in the Bay area and during the warm half of the year in the Southern California area. In the latter case, fog is observed more than fifty percent of the time.

Chapter Eleven
The California Cannonball

*There is a measure of insanity about people who voluntarily get into a
flying, pressurized metal tube and hope that it stays in the air.*
Anonymous

The Great Pacific High is the major influence on what the
temperatures do in the California valleys each day. This strong, stable
flow across the tops of mountains creates a box to trap convective air
inside the valley. The sun heats the air on the valley floor and the air
rises. It cannot penetrate through the upper flow and is boxed in by the
mountains. So it circulates down to be reheated. The reheated air rises
and is again blocked from escaping, so it descends for further
reheating. This circulation within the valley is continuous, often
resulting in daytime temperatures of 100 to 110 °F (38-43 °C). This
stable flow is also responsible for holding down the smog in the Los
Angeles basin. I've seen the top of it so well-defined and so thick it
looked solid enough to land on.

I was settled into Ukiah and learning what the California weather
had in store for me and my TBM. What was immediately noticeable
was the terrific heat every day. It was so hot, the daytime heat actually
heated the engine oil warm enough for takeoff. Also, with the airplane
sitting out in the sun, the throttle and stick gave an immediate hands-
off warning as they were hot enough to be untouchable with the bare
hands. We all found it necessary to cover each one with a cloth.

The heat also raised the density altitude, and takeoffs would
sometime use substantially more runway than usual. Grass Valley, with
an elevation of 3,000 feet, always proved to be fun. At times I had the
fastest TBM on wheels. The airport at Grass Valley sits up high,
immediately on the east side of the Sacramento Valley. The town rests
at a lower elevation and is one of the most picturesque small towns I
have ever seen. On my first visit, I drove through waving oceans of
golden, dry grass to enter the small, well-watered town that luxuriated

in greenery and flowers. No water shortage here. It was the kind of place I wanted to put in my pocket to transplant beside some azure lake.

There was another fascination about Grass Valley. It overlooked Beale Air Force Base. When I had the occasion to spend some time there, I would often see a long, black shape take off and climb virtually straight up and out of sight. I was duly impressed – I had never seen anything like it. Everyone at the base had seen it many times and it was the rumoured that this odd-looking aircraft was a secret spy plane. The rumours turned out to be true. The SR-71 was being flown out of Beale on spy missions long before it was revealed to the public.

The stable Pacific airflow aloft was warmer than the lower maritime air when it was over the water; it's the well-known inversion. That, of course, changed when the air moved over land and some of the maritime air was intensively heated in the valleys, the type of thing I experienced in Ukiah. The air aloft was definitely much cooler than the temperatures were at some of the tanker bases. I already had some limited experience with the stable, cool upper air. Harry had suggested I could get up there to cool off. On long dispatches, when there was time enough to climb up or I needed the altitude to clear some mountains, I could cool off in this refreshingly invigorating air. The beautiful Pacific Ocean breeze was cool and the flight was smooth.

The Cannonball

California exhibits a wide variety of topography. The land has everything from gently rolling hills covered in vineyards, to wide open valleys, to tightly packed mountain ranges with barely a wide enough gorge at the bottom to place a road. The orientation of the mountains also varies widely. Some ranges run fairly well north-south and others are a jumble of peaks and valleys that wander in all directions. West of the Sacramento Valley, the strong, stable Pacific flow of air undulates in height just over the top of these mountains. If it was well clear of the tops, pilots would find the air below to be relatively calm and predictable. But when the flow descended to the peaks, it could break over the ridges to create the unexpected rotor winds, downdrafts, turbulence and the instant tailwinds which made life particularly hazardous for bomber pilots. An upper flow of twenty or more knots breaking over a ridge could cause devastating turbulence at and below the top.

Because the stable flow varied in height from day to day and from one location to another, it would burst down in unexpected places. It is this unpredictable and extremely dangerous hazard to pilots that I have named the California Cannonball.

A Cannonball is defined as a communication, a missive, a message, or a poison-pen note, and the air in California was definitely telling me something. Some surprises were alerting me to prepare for the unexpected. When I'd get a downhill bombing run calling for a drop over the top of a ridge, I occasionally encountered some scary airspeed losses, which really caught my attention. It's not that I hadn't experienced these before in British Columbia. If there was a strong wind, its effect was everywhere and it was relatively easy to predict where I would get a downdraft. Most days in California had calm air or light winds. But the strong Pacific flow was always above and it could suddenly change a safe flight condition to one that had me holding on to my seat. On a few occasions, I went from still air to instant, bone-jarring turbulence after flying around a corner among the jumbled, sharp-peaked mountains common in some areas.

I had learned of California's dangerous mountain air currents in time to create some inviolate rules for myself. On every fire, I checked for indications of descending air and for the possibility that a rotor wind would be breaking over the ridge above it. Smoke from the fire was the best indicator. If I thought I could get caught by a tailwind or a downdraft, I would make allowance for it by starting a run over a ridge with extra airspeed. Starting a downhill run with higher than normal airspeeds is so counterintuitive that I really had to force myself to do it.

One day while passing over a ridge to start a downhill run, I had an instant airspeed loss of forty knots. I had predicted I might get a loss and allowed for it, but I had never seen anything so instantaneous and of that magnitude. This particular run brought me close to the stall speed and disaster. Fortunately I was in a TBM and the high-lift wing kept me afloat. The characteristics of the Cannonball would allow me to later explain the death of Ed Real.

In 1956, the pilots of Joe Ely's first squadron immediately met the same demon that has killed so many men in this business. On November 15, 1977, Jan Davis and Donald O'Connell interviewed Dale Nolta, the man who flew Tanker Number One and asked him about his first season's experience when flying out of New Cuyama. Dale Nolta recalled it this way:

"That's where I got rolled over upside-down coming in to a peak on a fire called La Roma. I just dumped my load and this updraft rolled me."

Dale also described watching a fellow pilot, George Jess, become the first fatality:

"He just started going down and hit a snag."

Dale had inadvertently described the malignant reality of the California Cannonball.

Emergency Jettison in Downtown Ukiah

The winds at Ukiah airport often hosted special events for the unsuspecting pilot. I had noticed that the winds could be quite strong on occasion and very unpredictable. The airport had a wind sock at each end of the single runway that we used. The open ends frequently pointed at each other, and, just as often, each showed a headwind at their end of the runway. These capricious winds poured over a mountain range just to the west of the airport and dared anyone to guess what they would do next. Openings to the valley at both ends of the mountain allowed the air to flow out into the Ukiah Valley, curl itself around and indulge in a jousting competition over the middle of the airport. To complicate matters further, the air flowing over the top of the mountain added downdrafts as well.

Taking off northbound took the flight path directly over the downtown section of the city, I had made many takeoffs in that direction with no problems. But with Ukiah's wind condition, I could get crosswinds, headwinds and tailwinds all in the same takeoff. But the TBM was like a bulldozer: it simply charged ahead and sooner or later it would lift off the runway.

On a dispatch to a fire, the idea was to get into the air as fast as possible so we could jump on the fire ahead of a nearby fire department. It seemed to me there was a fire station around every corner of every road in California. If we wanted the action, we had to be fast.

Therefore, everything from start-up to takeoff was done at hyper speed. We started the engine before strapping in, while we were taxiing we did all the checks "on-the-go," we headed for the nearest end of the runway, got takeoff clearance even before arriving there and immediately pushed the throttle forward as soon as we were lined up for takeoff – always toward the city of Ukiah. It's the bomber pilot's equivalent of the fireman sliding down his pole.

One day, on a routine dispatch, I did the usual rolling taxi to position followed by the urgent, pressing takeoff. All was going well as I entered my normal climb. I glanced out the left side of the cockpit because a rather chilling sight caught my attention. I saw a cloud of dust which was following me seemingly at my speed. *Silly boy, you don't get 135 knot tailwinds. The gust can't be that fast.* I was soon to discover just how fast it was. I was climbing at my normal speed of 135 knots and was arriving over the edge of the city when my airspeed started to drop off very rapidly.

There was indeed a powerful tailwind carrying that dust. I had entered it and was losing speed rapidly. As it dropped, I put takeoff power back on and started to rotate the nose up to hold altitude. Even as I continued to rotate the nose up, I was losing more speed and altitude as well. Both were still bleeding off quickly even after I had descended to the roof tops and was looking up at the bottoms of the TV antennas. The airspeed was down to ninety knots and I had nowhere else to go but into the buildings. Full power was only leading me to the point of impact.

There was no more time to see if I was going to fly out of this impending disaster. I hit the drop buttons on the control column and the entire load dropped out, right into downtown Ukiah. With one broad sweep of my air brush, I artistically painted a downtown street red. Getting rid of 600 gallons (which was 6,000 pounds of weight) was what I needed to stop the descent and allow me to climb out.

This event, as unexpected and sudden as it was, still took place over a period of fifteen to twenty seconds. While I was going through this dramatic loss of airspeed and altitude, I was still in control of the airplane. It was responding to my control input. I had time to apply full power and time to wait and see if it would stop my descent. There was still the option of dropping the load. Even though a disaster appeared to be looming, my instinct told me dropping the load would get me out of it and at no time did I feel fear or panic. I completed the circuit, reloaded and took off on the same runway to continue with my dispatch.

The CDF never questioned my decision to drop the load. Fire trucks were immediately sent out to wash the cars, trailers, boats, houses and streets I had so effortlessly painted red. It was the only time in my entire Fire Bombing career I had to jettison a load for a takeoff emergency. And being forced down below the level of the TV antennas over downtown Ukiah was definitely an emergency.

This event drove home a point which had been settling on me since I first started flying in California. This was one of the Cannonball's missives: "Take care when you fly among my mountains, my friend. I will always have a surprise for you."

Soon that missive would send my blood cold in an instant.

Arson Fires

There was rarely a day that we didn't fly in California; fires showed up every day whether accidentally or by arson. Eighty percent of

California fires were arson. I couldn't understand why they had to occur at all. Why are people so destructive?

On one occasion I was dispatched to a string of seventeen fires along the highway from Santa Rosa to Ukiah. It was obvious that incendiary devices where being thrown from a vehicle and the vehicle was heading toward Ukiah. The fire farthest south was the biggest at about a half acre and was growing rapidly. The rest of the fires were smaller in size and were about a half mile apart. The last one was just a spot so the incendiary vehicle wasn't too far ahead of the last fire.

According to the people at the CDF, there were two common incendiary devices. One was a book of matches with a lit cigarette inside. The cigarette was held in place with an elastic band wrapped around the booklet. The other was a length of rope (the length varied according to how long the arsonist wanted to delay the ignition) with a bundle of wooden matches tied or held with a rubber band at the end. CDF fire investigators would frequently find these extinguished devices along side of the highways.

Would it ever stop? Incredibly the answer is yes. One day it did stop: California didn't have a single arson fire occurrence. That day was the day of the moon landing, July 20, 1969. Why does it take an event of historical importance and of such immense pride for a nation stop the lunatics, if only for a day? If the insanity can stop for a day, why can't it stop forever? Why are we civilized enough to call a truce in a war to clean up bodies or observe an enemy holiday yet we're not civilized enough to stop wars altogether? But we are "us" and we do irrational and stupid things.

Prior to flying in California, I had been dispatched to similar strings of fires in British Columbia, where it was called "Horseback Lightning." Some areas in British Columbia had their resident kooks: the arsonist would head out on his horse and drop his devices. Whatever methods he used must have had long fuses. The fires would take awhile to start so he would have plenty of time to ride out of the area. Despite the use of extensive air patrol in searching for these people, to my knowledge they were never caught.

Flaming Squirrels

When I first started flying at Ukiah, the Birddogs had mentioned the term "Squirrel Fire." *Okay, Linc, I smell a joke on me coming up.* I suspected they might tell this Canadian country bumpkin that California had squirrels that went around lighting fires. Leroy Zwicky, one of the Birddogs, wasn't backing off the fire-lighting squirrels. "It's true," he assured me, "squirrels do cause fires in California." He just wasn't telling me how they did it.

Leroy got the name of Kamizwiky (as in Kamikaze) for his requests for suicidal bombing runs straight down a canyon with a two foot wide valley at the bottom.

"Shouldn't be any problem with that, Linc. Whatcha think?"

"Kamikaze attacks aren't in the CDF job description, Leroy."

"Okay, if you're going to be sore about it, you can do your drop across the canyon."

"Always willing to please, Leroy."

I wasn't prodding Leroy for an answer about the flaming squirrels because at first I didn't believe it. I was convinced the entire crew was having me on. I kept silent about it, not wanting to appear too gullible. I wasn't biting, so finally the boys relented and gave me the details of the squirrel's suicidal technique.

The early power lines in California were strung on wooden poles and had short insulators at the towers, quite different from the more modern steel tower power lines and their longer insulators. Power line insulators are in place next to a supporting tower to provide a means for the power line to be routed around the tower. I'm not sure how long the insulators are, or what their arrangement is on the power line, but I was told that the squirrel is just a bit longer than the insulator. When the squirrel made a trip down the power line, he wouldn't walk on the slippery porcelain insulator to get to the pole. He either jumped over the insulator and got airborne, or he straddled himself across the insulator and stepped over. When he jumped, he was safe from the power line current; he didn't bridge himself across the insulator. But if he decided to straddle the insulator and step over, he bridged the power and the tremendous current instantly lit him up like a flare. I was told that this had been witnessed and the squirrel was a substantial ball of fire — the "flaming squirrel." When he hit the ground, there was a very likely chance he'd start a new fire. It was an effective but tough way to be an arsonist.

The First Time

One day at an action west of Ukiah, I did my routine methodical check out of the fire area. What was the smoke doing? Was it going straight up or was it curling down the mountain or blowing up? Was it fairly compact or was it diffused and scattered all over the site? What does the Birddog have to say about his runs? Any downdrafts? What is the prevailing upper wind? Could it be curling over the top of a ridge at my fire?

I had to drop over a ridge fairly high up above the fire to get at my target on the flank of the fire down below. All seemed normal and I determined that my run to get to the fire below would not encounter anything unusual. The smoke was drifting straight up, a pattern I had recognized early as being safe. I thought I had read the smoke signal every bit as well as Sitting Bull. In addition, the area around the fire appeared fairly calm. The Birddog did not report any turbulence or downdrafts, but from his position above the fire he wouldn't have been in a position to be certain about it. All indications showed it should be a normal dive from the top, without any special considerations. That meant starting over the ridge at a reduced airspeed so as not to have too high an airspeed when I flew by the fire. The airplane was configured for dropping and my arming switch was "on."

I dropped over the top of the ridge and the sky collapsed from under my airplane. I plummeted into the sudden emptiness one feels when missing a step high up on a ladder, that flush of fear that your footing is gone and you're going to fall and the fall could kill you. I was at zero g and falling fast. The fall was doing something to the airplane that I'd never felt before: zero g and an airplane that wasn't responding to the controls. The airplane had gone completely limp, as limp as a high school date who finds out you're driving a borrowed car and your daddy isn't rich. I moved the controls and there was almost no response. I wasn't stalled and I wasn't really in control. I had the white heat and dry throat of an all-consuming fear. I was going to die. I was rapidly falling hundreds of feet, out-of-control and heading straight down toward the trees. In a few seconds I would be there and my game would be over. I had time to think only one thought: *these downdrafts sometimes stop above the trees.*

Then just as suddenly, the fall stopped. I was just above the trees. The airplane flew again.

"Tanker Two Six, did you have a problem?"

I swallowed dry saliva while I gathered my composure.

"Can't do that run Birddog. I got a pretty severe downdraft."

"Okay, we'll step your drops down instead. Do you think that will work?"

"Roger, I'll give it a try, Birddog."

The Birddog changed the runs: the downhill flank run was now known to be dangerous. My drop was diverted and would now be horizontally across the flank. As I approached the fire paralleling the mountain, I was fully prepared to drop the load and turn away from the mountain if the downdraft caught me again. But it wasn't there. I made the drop. Although it would not be as efficient as the downhill run, since covering the flank would take several drops instead of one, it would eventually get the job done.

"That run was okay, Birddog. I didn't get a downdraft."

"Roger, Two Six. Reload and return."

On the way home I had time to think about the event. For the first time in my flying career, I was in an out-of-control airplane. Nothing that I did saved me. I really didn't have time to do anything. This brush with death was not the same as the event over Ukiah where a sequence of events happened fairly slowly and I had time to react. The suddenness of this plunge put me in terror overload to the point of incapacity. Other than a few control movements, my mind didn't grasp a single useful thought about survival. I didn't add power and I didn't drop the load. Surprise incapacitates a person for a time, a factor well known to martial arts experts and Special Forces like the Navy Seals or the SAS. This dive caught me completely off guard and I was a helpless passenger until it was over. The Fates had placed my cushion of air just above the trees to save me: it was pure luck.

Then I thought about how I could have prepared for the run differently. What did I miss in my evaluation of the situation? A frightening conclusion came to mind. Nothing. I had analyzed this run every bit as conscientiously as every other run, and I had always been right. All of the conditions around this fire told me my judgment was correct. What was even more frightening was that in spite of my planning, I was completely overtaken by the unexpected from our life's medium, the invisible air.

I now think of the times when I had made compensations for suspected downdraft conditions and had come out alive because my hedges were correct. I experienced huge airspeed losses but my allowances were adequate enough to keep me from stalling. This time I had made no allowance for a possible downdraft and it almost cost me my life. My guardian Fairy had sown green pixie dust into the air to tell me the air was safe, but it changed in an instant and she didn't have time to warn me. The California Cannonball had thrown a lethal karate kick at me – and narrowly missed.

The Golden State – Fascinating California

Life held many pleasures and adventures in California and I was enjoying every second of it. Visiting wineries around Santa Rosa was a favourite pastime. The visit to Corbell Wineries was particularly interesting. The tour guide told George and me that prior to the vineyards being planted, the area had been covered with Redwood trees. The Corbell brothers had bought the location in the 1930s for growing grapes but wondered what to do with all of those big trees.

The area was being logged at the time and each giant Redwood was sold for five dollars. Each tree contained enough wood to build four homes. The wine-tasting room was the most important part of the tour. There was no limit to our sampling and we made sure that their superlative claims about their Brut Champagne were well and properly acknowledged.

Ukiah was located in some outstandingly beautiful vineyard and orchard country and there were many pleasant places to visit. California is an incredibly productive agricultural powerhouse and I could understand why. On flying overhead, I saw that virtually every creek and stream had a dam on it. The heavy winter rains were saved in countless reservoirs to be released in summer as irrigation water. Productivity was so prolific that when harvest time came, it was just not possible to pick all of the fruit in the innumerable orchards and much of it lay on the ground. It's not surprising the state is the biggest producer of agricultural products in the USA.

One moonlit September night, as I was descending a winding road on my way to Ukiah from Clear Lake, one of the turns in the road pointed me directly at the full moon and to a farmer's field covered with a low-lying fog. I pulled over to the side of the road to let my imagination take flight.

A childhood fantasy I had had on many such nights returned and for a moment I lived it again. The field was not merely a farmer's field and the fog was not simply a layer of mist next to the ground. The field became the bottom of an empyrean ocean created for creatures that would inhabit that space and time. As a boy I imagined benign dragons emerging from their secret hiding places in the bowels of the earth and coming alive to swim in this silvery sea. Long, undulating tails propelled them to silently explore a time and space created just for them. This diaphanous sea was alive. These lovely creatures floated in their personal universe, their mission to simply be. There they would swim until the morning sun dissolved them and their ethereal elements back into reality. Then they silently waited for the next time the moon was full and their gossamer universe invited them back.

Being based in Ukiah, it was an easy trip for me to drive down to Santa Rosa where George was based. From there, it was a jaunt to one of the local bars or a trip into San Francisco. George's invitation to go into the big city would go something like this:

"I would like to take this occasion my dear Alexander to invite you to participate in a riotous evening at the Playboy Club. The evening has all the earmarks of pleasant company and conviviality. To avoid the unpleasantness of my possible brush with the local gendarmerie and their rather obtuse sense of humour, it would be most felicitous that the evening's transportation be in your car."

I made many trips to Santa Rosa and a few to San Francisco. One of our fun stops was to go to Zach's Place at Sausalito to watch the turtle races. Sausalito is a picturesque little town sitting on the ocean's edge at the north end of the Golden Gate bridge. The owners of Zach's recognized that the excitement of racing turtles released some pheromone or other unknown intoxicating ether that activated both male and female hormones. Turtle race nights were standing room only. I have since sniffed a few turtles but haven't recognized any aroma that could be put in a bottle and left at my front door.

Bang Bang, Who's There?

Santa Rosa creek varies between ten and fifteen feet wide, averages three to four feet deep, has a gently flowing current and wanders aimlessly through the city of Santa Rosa. Its banks are lined with trees and shrubs, some of which had fallen into the creek as deadfall. George's apartment block backed on to the creek, and flowing water that may contain something edible was an irresistible magnet for George. He inspected the shallow depths for crawdads and to his delight he found the place to be crawling with the little crustaceans. George is an inveterate hunter of anything that crawls, flies, runs or swims that can be eaten, and the hapless crayfish fell into that category.

The crawdad is a little freshwater lobster looking every bit the same as its giant cousin but on a smaller scale. They have bulbous eyes in the front of their head and crawl forward as they seek out food. They swim differently, however, if they're threatened by something. Their escape is to give a quick flip of their tail and do a lightning exit backwards. A creek full of crawdads could not go unfished, so, being of much higher intelligence than the crayfish, George fabricated a fiendish net made of stiff wire screen with an opening wide enough to let the crayfish blast his way in. The next diabolical tool he needed for the entrapment of these unsuspecting morsels was a long stick to point in the face of the little critter.

Crawdad hunting in Santa Rosa creek presented its difficulties. There were deadfalls to be circumnavigated and the creek's depth varied from a couple of feet to six or eight feet. Undeterred by these trivialities, George hunted at night since that was the time they came out of their hiding places and became fair game. After a few successful hunts, George invited me to come join the sport and share the feast to follow.

I couldn't wait to participate in such promised hilarity. All I needed were chest-high waders. I was designated to hold the receiving bucket and operate the flashlight. The technique was to find the critter using the flashlight and then gently place the wire net behind him. It needed to be a slow, delicate maneuver so as not to have the suspicious little beast shoot off prematurely. Once the net was in place, George then guided the stick into the crawdad's face and off he would shoot backwards into the net. He then lifted the net quickly enough to cause enough water pressure to contain the prize. A twist of the wrist sent it into our waiting bucket.

George had perfected this technique on his own and it worked, but it worked better if two people maneuvered the hunting tools. Prior to hunting, it was necessary to limber and loosen up with a cocktail because we couldn't slosh around in the creek without proper preparation. One drink worked well, but more than one worked even better. The preparation continued until midnight and we were then ready for the great hunt.

Prior to the events of this night, we had worked Santa Rosa Creek on several occasions and needed to go farther upstream each time to get the catch of fifty or so it took to make a great meal. We had thinned out the lower areas and were well up the creek in more ways than one on the night in question. We never worried about trespassing on anyone's rights or property because it was our understanding that the creek was public property. In all of our previous hunts, we had not encountered anyone. This night we were going to get a very unpleasant surprise.

George in Santa Rosa creek with his entrapment tools and an unlucky crawdad.

We were anything but quiet in the pursuit of our quarry as the sloshing in the creek and the volume of voice developed after several drinks made our progress quite public. We were enjoying the hunt and were our usual carefree selves when we came to a fence that jutted part way into the creek. It materialized down one bank, left an opening at the water and continued up the other side. We stepped around this obstruction and continued. No sooner had we crossed this sacrosanct line, than a dog barked. He emitted about two and one half barks when someone fired two gunshots then shouted,

"Who's there?"

His voice sounded quite close and he must have been using a shotgun because it rained a shower of leaves on us. The blasts were horrendously loud since we were only a short distance from the front end of a shotgun that was fired directly at us. Fortunately, the banks were about four feet high. We dove toward the bank for cover. Lying with our heads about a foot or so from the top I shouted:

"Don't shoot. We're just fishing for crawdads "

"Get off my land!"

My voice had given him our precise location and the range. His next shot was dead on. It blasted a sizeable quantity of dirt off the bank just above our heads. If we had been standing up, we would have been hit. There was no more conversation; we made a wake of white water on our way downstream. He was certainly a touchy fellow about people invading his land. We had been in mortal danger, as those shots were fired directly at us from a fairly close range. If we were close enough for him to have seen us, would he have shot us under those circumstances? From his violent, irrational reaction to our innocent fishing, I can only think that he probably would have. As it was, our leap for cover and the darkness saved us. We wondered if he had a mass grave of missing crawdad hunters in his back yard.

He and the dog certainly made a coordinated team: a couple of barks and he was blasting away. Just like the style of the old west: shoot first and ask questions later.

We had reached the limits of our crawdad hunting in Santa Rosa creek. After we got back to George's apartment, it was time to dissect the whole scary and subsequently hilarious affair over a few more drinks. Neither of us had known we could walk on water. Jesus had nothing on us.

Reproduced courtesy of Jean Barbaud

Grumman - F7F-Tigercat

Chapter Twelve
The Perfect Fire Bomber

The three most useless things to a pilot are altitude above you, runway behind you and a tenth of a second ago. Anonymous

After two seasons of flying the TBM, the company had a seat open on the F7F to be based at Willows. Willows is a little agricultural town about thirty miles south of Chico, the home of Aero Union, the big Fire Bomber operator. It's strategically situated in the rice-growing area of California which was okay if you grew rice but would definitely not be a place I would dash to for my vacation. The mere mention of the name and the fact that I had accepted to go there brought rounds of laughter and finger pointing from all the other pilots who wouldn't be caught dead at Willows. Could it be that bad?

Bud and Harry had casually informed me that the base was in a less-than-desirable location, but the seat was open and "Would I like to have it?" Did I want the F7F seat? That's like asking a baseball fan is he wants a ticket to the World Series. The idea of basing the airplane at Willows was to have it available for dispatch to either side of the Sacramento Valley. I had already formed a dislike for the place purely from what the other pilots had told me but the F7F was too great a magnet to resist. I wasn't particularly keen on being stationed at Willows, but I couldn't wait to get into the seat of that beautiful airplane.

The "base" was a concrete pad with the retardant mixing and loading equipment off to one side. A weatherbeaten wooden hut of about ten feet square containing a phone served as the base standby facility. As an afterthought, a porch with a slanted wooden roof supported on a couple of crooked poles protruded out from the front door. Two canvas recliners had been thoughtfully placed on the porch floor to give the crew shade and comfort while standing by.

The sea of parched, yellow grass which surrounded the base supplied some interesting diversion from the pleasures of over-relaxing in the sagging recliners. I could sit on the ground in the midst of the grass and watch the praying mantises ever so slowly creep up the stalks of grass on their way to ambush insects. The pace of their creeping matched the pace of my daily standby. But once up top, the bug was dead meat. The mantis grabbed him so fast I could hardly see the strike. Looking through the cracks in the porch floor gave me second thoughts about sitting in the lounge chairs. I could see spiders the size of dinner plates under the floor. I just hoped that there was plenty of food where they were and they didn't have to come after me.

Getting on and off the concrete pad was a test of the pilot's skill and daring. Taxiing across the dirt leading to the pad was a frenzied high-speed dash. Slowing or stopping would have meant sinking in the semi-hard soil and getting stuck.

Amenities were at the other end of the airport. Wanting a drink of water or going to the bathroom meant a visit with John and Dotty Sue Ehorn, the couple who operated the service station at the far end of the runway. Fortunately, they were airplane buffs and liked the F7F in particular. They became good friends. The heat, isolation and Spartan facilities in this ocean of impartial rice made Alcatraz look like heaven. What a guy will do to get a seat in a great airplane.

I was curious about the Stearman and AG-Cats (a Grumman purpose-built aircraft for spraying) constantly flying around, so I asked a farmer about the finer points of growing rice. He told me the rice was water-soaked until it sprouted, and was then seeded by air. All other care was also done by air from fertilizing to insecticide spraying. Almost daily, I could watch the Stearman and AG-Cats flying low next to the rice spraying whatever application was appropriate at the time. When the crop was ripe, the field was drained and combines took off the harvest. Unlike the rice-growing process of Asia, there was no hand labour whatsoever involved with growing rice in California.

F7F at Ukiah, California. Photo by author

The F7F — a Super Performer

The design of the F7F began in 1941 and by 1943 it was ready for its debut as a carrier-based fighter. As it turned out, it was too big and fast for the Essex-class aircraft carriers used at the time. Its use was relegated to land-based operations and the United States Marine Corps selected the F7F-3 Tigercat as its primary fighter. The USMC ordered 500 of the aircraft with deliveries beginning in April of 1944. The airplane did not get its operational clearance for combat duties prior to the end of the war but it later saw action in Korea. The later models of the airplane were equipped with the Pratt and Whitney R-2800-34-W engines, which gave it spectacular performance. It weighed in at 25,775 lbs, had a range of 1200 miles and a service ceiling of 40,700 feet.

I heard nothing but praise about the airplane and had watched the company's Chief Pilot, Harry Chaffee, drop with it on many fires. Chaffee's F7F sat alongside my TBM at Ukiah and I was highly envious as I watched the difference in takeoff and climb performance between our two airplanes. When we had a westbound dispatch and took off heading north over the town of Ukiah, Harry would do an immediate left turn and climb over the 3,000 foot mountain just to the west of the airport. I, on the other hand, would plod on for miles before I had enough altitude to clear the top. Harry could certainly handle the airplane. His target identification was spot-on and he always hit the target. I would later find out why he did so well with it. The F7F was every inch a man's airplane and I waited for the day when I would fly one. The day had finally arrived. After two years of hearing about this fabulous airplane it would be my turn.

The F7F, like many fighters, is a single-seat airplane and Bud showed me number 43, my airplane for the summer. Sheets of shiny aluminum fashioned into its clean lines never looked so good. My 43 was trimmed in yellow, unlike the rest of the fleet that had their cowlings and wing tips in red. To really appreciate its clean lines, one had to imagine it without the ugly external retardant tank. In a head-on view, each engine looked bigger than the slim fuselage. The airplane was obviously meant to eat up whoever might turn out to be the bad guys. It carried four 20 mm cannons, two in each bay just outboard of the engines. Japanese Zeros would have been duck soup to the F7F. The airplane was certainly head-and-shoulders faster and better armed than any other airplane at the time. It was a powerful fighter for the most powerful navy in the world.

The gun bays were roomy and made excellent lockers for carrying baggage and whatever else on a base change. The cockpit, in contrast, had barely enough room for the pilot's shoulders and the legs slid down a snug channel to the rudder pedals on either side of a centre console.

Under the blazing heat of the California sun, dehydration could set in quickly so it was absolutely essential to carry a cold drink in the airplane. The problem in the F7F was finding a place to store it. I'm not sure how it was discovered but the only place to carry a cold drink was in a slot behind the pilot's seat. The drink had to be in a Thermos

Bottle, firstly to keep the drink cold and secondly, because it had a handle. Getting the Thermos into that slot was an equally ingenious discovery. With the left hand, the bottle was held horizontally with the top facing rearward as it was passed by the throttle quadrant. It was then rotated to the upright position to make the corner around the seat. The left arm then had enough movement to turn the bottle upright and center it behind the seat. Getting it out involved the same intricate operation. F7F pilots are a creative lot.

To make a Fire Bomber out of this sleek fighter meant hanging a bulbous retardant tank on the underside of the fuselage. It held 800 gallons which dropped out of two doors. A button and a trigger, both on the control column, activated the drop doors, the button for the left door and the trigger for the right. Activating both at the same time gave a full drop. As ugly and bulky as this tank was, the airplane made a fabulous bomber.

Check-out meant reading the manual and getting some advice from the old-timers about the various do's and don'ts. Bud casually informed me that the fuel gauges didn't work. I would have been just as casual about not knowing when I would run out of fuel but the problem was the airplane falls out of the sky. I hadn't even sat in the airplane so I didn't want to start making ridiculously, outlandish demands about wanting fuel gauges. I discovered that the fuel gauges were considered as non-essential.

"It's no sweat," said Bud, "the fuel gauge is on your wrist; the airplane has enough fuel for three hours' flying. At two and one half hours you should be looking for a place to fuel up."

Bud presumed I had a watch, or would get one.

Now what could be simpler than that?

Harry cheerfully chimed in to tell me the instrument lighting system wasn't working, but no sweat on that one either.

"We only bomb in daylight hours, Linc. You don't need instrument lights."

Of course I won't need them. I didn't bomb at night in British Columbia either. It just so happened that many attacks were completed at dusk and some long flights home took place in pitch-black darkness. So I needed two indispensible items to fly the F7F: a watch and a penlight.

The F7F heavy wheel loading likes steel decks — not thin pavement.
Photo by author

Boost Pumps on High

One critical F7F pre-takeoff item in particular was strongly etched into my mind by both the company owner Bud and Harry the chief pilot. Switch the fuel boost pumps on "high" for takeoff. The switches were "double throw:" flip the switch one way for "high" and flip it the other way for "low." If a pilot simply were to glance at the switches, it would be difficult to tell which position had been selected. He had to switch them consciously and meticulously to the desired position. Both Bud and Harry couldn't emphasize that procedure enough. Boost pumps on "high" for takeoff was an absolute must. It was one of those

controls on an airplane that invited a mistake, a mistake which could
end up in disaster.

Flying the F7F with Sis-Q Flying Service

Grumman, the manufacturer of the airplane, installed an air compressor to pressurize the main tank. There was good reason for it to be pressurized: it assured positive fuel feed at the high power setting used for takeoff regardless of the boost pump setting the pilot had selected, "high" or "low." In the civil application, someone had discovered that fuel flow would be adequate with the boost pumps set on "high," so pressurization for the main tank could be dispensed with. It would save the weight and the expense of maintaining the compressor system. Presumably this inviolate procedure was discovered at altitude because selecting the boost pumps on "low" for takeoff would result in a double-engine failure immediately after takeoff. Pilots had already been killed because of a double-engine failure after takeoff. (After leaving the company, I was informed that pilots whom I had come to know would die the same way.) It was inconceivable to me that life and or death in this airplane rested on the simple, correct selection of two switches. The cause of these deaths and the remedy was known. One would think that one death from this mistake would be enough to restore fuel tank pressurization in these airplanes. But it never happened. Be that as it was, it was a setting that I never forgot.

A Forty-Ouncer of Rye

I had read the manual diligently and sat in the cockpit of the airplane for a few hours going through checks and emergencies in my mind. I made sure I was familiar with the location of all the controls. When I felt confident enough about my knowledge and procedures with the airplane, I was ready for my first flight.

Harry had a standing bet with every new pilot going on his first flight in the F7F.

"I'll bet a forty-ounce bottle of rye you won't get full power on the engines before the airplane is in the air," he said very smugly.

How could I not bet on that one? thought I. *I had flown jets in the RCAF and was well up to speed required for jet flying. Just how long does it take to advance the throttles on an airplane – two, maybe three seconds? Four or five seconds if I'm slow?* Taking Harry's money would be duck soup. But I did notice something when I asked for the bet to be a bottle of Scotch instead. He insisted that the bet should be a forty-ouncer of rye – his favourite drink. No matter, I could choke down the rye. Winning this bet would be child's play.

"You're on, Harry, and I'm sorry I'll have to take that bottle."

Before climbing into the airplane, I noticed that Bud, Harry and several other people had gathered outside of the main hangar to watch the proceedings. *I knew what this was about, they wanted to watch Harry lose his bet for the first time*, I thought, confidently. I squeezed myself into the cockpit, cranked the canopy forward and locked it. I started up the engines and the first thing I noticed was how loud they were. The exhaust stacks barely carried the exhaust clear of the cowling. They're short and there's no muffling of the sharp crack out of each cylinder. Each one sounded like a rifle shot. I went through the check list run-up, the pre-takeoff check, and taxied out onto the runway. The airplane handled beautifully on the ground. The rest of this trip would be a breeze. All eyes were watching.

I started to open the throttles for the fifty-three inches of boost that I could feed to the engines. An ear-splitting roar told me I was in a different kind of airplane. I was immediately nailed to the back of the seat by g-forces while the airplane was running away down the runway. The last time I was held to the back of a seat was in a jet in the RCAF. Everything was happening far too fast – my only thought was to just keep this damn thing going straight. I don't remember pulling back on the stick for takeoff, or if I even did it, but it was now in the air. The airspeed indicator needle hastened past 100 knots and I was rapidly accelerating. *Time to get the gear up or I'll pass the gear-up speed.* The bird wasn't waiting for me; it was charging ahead. I felt like an actor in a silent movie trying to jump into a trolley car that was moving just a bit too fast. I then looked at the power setting. It was forty-three inches, barely half the power I had available. Even at this power setting, I was the passenger in this airplane. It was taking me for a ride.

After nine years of flying a slow airplane like the TBM, my reaction speed matched the pace of the airplane. I had no idea that an empty, lightweight F7F was in the jet fighter category. It's a rocket in experienced hands. This bit of knowledge was not lost on Harry, the Chief Pilot. Harry won his bet. I was told later that this bet was one he never lost. Now I knew why.

The Perfect Fire Bomber

The F7F is a true fighter airplane. Its initial rate of climb is 5,000 feet per minute and it climbs at 3,000 feet per minute loaded. What became immediately apparent to me was that this private office I had for a cockpit had a view of the entire universe. I've never had such good visibility out of an airplane since I flew the T-33 jet. The nose angle dropped down so steeply that it was not visible to the pilot; the world was a vast unobscured panorama in front of me. I could have been sitting in space. I managed to get the gear up and settle down at altitude. I could now play with this toy. I knew the airplane was stressed for nine positive and three negative g. I was in the seat of a perfect Fire Bomber. It was an airplane built to take whatever turbulence the mountains would throw at me. I was to have a great appreciation for that toughness later on. It had plenty of power and a fast enough rate of roll to do fun aerobatics, so I tossed it around for about an hour. I was in a high performance fighter plane and I was sitting on top of the world. This was my element; my psyche wasn't designed for slow, plodding airplanes. I could stay in this airplane forever.

It was time for some single-engine practice. I feathered the right engine and some odd things happened. Surprisingly, the right engine came out of feather but didn't respond to the throttle. I feathered again and that worked, so I un-feathered again and the same thing happened. The engine turned over slowly but wouldn't take any throttle. Time to head home. I feathered the right engine and left it. On my very first flight on the airplane, I had garbaged an engine. When the chief mechanic later tried to rotate the engine, it wouldn't move an inch. It had seized solid. My lovely airplane needed an engine change.

When my bird was ready to go again, I did several practice water drops with the airplane and discovered the pitch-up was mild and easily compensated for with a little stick forward input. What a dream bomber. It was a strong airplane with a prodigious reserve of power to get out of any difficulty, empty or loaded. The F7F was hands down the best conversion of an airplane to a Fire Bomber that I had flown. The fabulous climb performance allowed me to climb up to the cool, stable air coming off the Pacific so I could easily get out of the oppressive heat I wallowed in daily with the TBM. I also now realized why Harry was so consistent and accurate with his drops. On the final approach to a fire, everything I needed to see to make an accurate drop was right out front, just past my feet, clearly visible. It wasn't anything like judging what was going on below the bulbous nose of the TBM.

The airplane had been obviously designed to operate from aircraft carriers as it had a wheel loading that only a steel deck could appreciate. The tires were so loaded and strained, a trail of black rubber followed the airplane while taxiing. As a result, the main tires were good for seven landings and no more. After the seventh landing, red warning cords showed on the tires and new tires already installed on their wheels had to be changed, a pleasant little duty that fell to the pilot. It wasn't like flying the TBM where all the maintenance was done for us. If a pilot wanted to fly the F7F, he paid for the privilege by constantly changing wheels.

The airplane was predictable in the stall and its ample power reserve made it a very safe airplane at virtually any speed. The airplane passed through minimum control speed even before V1, the rotation for takeoff. The airplane's performance was such an incredible change from the TBM. The F7F had so much power that it could literally climb the steep side of a mountain if necessary, yet it could drop through a fair speed range without excessive pitch-up. Downhill drops could be made without picking up too much speed because maneuverability was such that a quick turn to final approach could be made just above a fire. I had only praise for the performance and predictability of the airplane. But one day Harry told me a strange story. The airplane had done something to him it had never done before, and, as long as Harry flew the airplane, didn't do again.

A Mysterious Event

Harry had just pulled out of a descent to drop on a fire. After letting both doors go, the nose suddenly bunted down, causing the airplane to head downwards to crash into the trees in spite of the fact that Harry had full power on the engines and the control column fully back. It was shaking violently with the airplane pointed steeply down in a negative flight attitude. The wings were not developing lift and the turbulence was quite severe. For some reason, the power was holding the airplane in that attitude and didn't allow the controls to take effect. He felt a crash was inevitable so he decided to pull the power off. As he said:

"I didn't think it would help me to hit the trees with full power on, so I pulled the power off so I wouldn't crash too hard. When I pulled the power off, the nose came up and the shaking stopped; I put the power back on and the airplane was okay again."

I was also at a loss to offer any explanation about what could have happened. He was the old-timer and the pro on the airplane and I was the newbie. His story, however, never left my mind and I could only come up with one possible explanation.

When an airplane pitches up at the time of the load drop, the corrective action is to check forward on the control column, but only enough to cancel out part of the positive g. A slight positive g loading should be allowed to happen to avoid bunting the nose down and putting the aircraft into negative g. It's a fine touch and it would be easy to overcorrect and bunt the nose down. I speculated that this is what might have happened to Harry, with perhaps the overcorrection accelerated by turbulence. I never heard of it happening to any other pilot, and I never came close to that attitude in the airplane. Harry's recovery was pure chance. I think every pilot would have kept the power on, as it's the first reaction if a pilot wants to climb or get out of a bad situation. If he had crashed, there would have been no explanation for the cause. The accident report would have stated that he had controlled flight into terrain. For some strange reason, he simply flew into the trees. In the flying game, one listens to every story. I tucked it indelibly into my memory. I knew what to do if it ever happened to me.

Seeing the Demon

The worst turbulence that I ever encountered in my entire bombing career happened that summer while flying the F7F. I was dispatched to a fire to assist another F7F at a mountain west of Ukiah and about three ranges in from the coast. The strong Pacific flow was breaking up while tumbling over a sharp tree-covered ridge just above our fire. Flying over the mountain at altitude without smoke to give wind indications, would provide no forewarning whatever of what would be in store for an airplane that dared to enter the lee side. The wind was fairly strong and the rotor winds below the mountain rendered the entire effort on the fire quite useless. I was circling above the fire in cool air and watched Johnny Alford in the F7F ahead of me do his drop. Johnny was a handsome, quiet man about six feet in height and with a muscular build. He and his wife flew a midget racer at various race meets around the country.

When he dropped down on final approach, he was riding a raging, wild bull. I could see the airplane rocking from side to side and the nose pitching up and down. As quickly as he was thrown to a steep angle of bank one way, he just as quickly was tossed the opposite way. I had never seen an airplane get shaken up so violently. I realized that I was watching the demon that tore BOAC Flight 911 to pieces at Mount Fuji go to work on the airplane below me. But the monster had met its match; the F7F is a very strong airplane, far stronger than its victim at Mount Fuji.

When Johnny let the load go, it didn't fall downward out of the airplane as it normally does. Instead, it was ripped upward in a circular motion to sweep around the top surfaces of the airplane. I could see the rotating tube of the rotor and watched the retardant swirl around the airplane until it dissipated completely.

F7F at a routine fire action in California.
Photo courtesy Sis-Q Flying Service

For a brief moment, the load revealed the claws of the rotor monster. The sides and upper surfaces of the airplane were covered with orange retardant. Not a single drop of the load descended below the aircraft. None the wiser about what his load had done, Johnny Alford flew away. He had escaped the demon's wrath. True to his nature, Johnny would take this smashing turbulence in stride, accept it as a normal drop and say nothing about it.

Then it was my turn. To prepare for what I had just witnessed, I tightened the shoulder and lap harness down so tightly that it cut the circulation to my legs. I knew I needed to stay put in the cockpit or else I could end up in positions of not being able to hold on to the control stick. I saw no well-defined target because the smoke swirled up all over the side of the mountain. I was so thankful that I was in the strong F7F; I could expect the airplane to stay together. From Johnny's experience, I didn't for a moment think that my load would go down, but we never questioned our orders. I knew I had to drop on this fire regardless of turbulence and not to be concerned that the load might be useless. The Birddog would ask for more if necessary.

I descended to final to meet the same monster that devours lesser airplanes. In his mindless rage, he shook me like a shark taking its first bite out of a victim. It seemed that the airplane was pitching and rolling in every direction all at the same time. The tossing was so violent that I just hung on; I was not controlling the airplane. Worse yet, the quick changes from positive to negative g-forces were causing noises that I'd never heard come from this airplane – loud, sharp cracks as if pieces of the airplane were breaking off. I wondered why my radios and other fixtures weren't being torn loose in the cockpit. My head was being bashed on the top and all sides of the canopy. Only the helmet was saving me from being knocked unconscious. I knew what a boxer felt like when body and head blows knocked him to the edge of sensibility. I thought, *Why am I here? This is stupid.*

I let the load go and Birddog told me that my load did the same thing as Johnny's. The tumultuous, twisting air wound the load around the fuselage and carried it above and all over the top surfaces of my airplane. I did my job. I dove into what I knew would be Hell and dutifully opened the drop doors. Now, thank God, I could climb and get out of there. We weren't called back to the fire, not because of the raging turbulence, but because our loads weren't descending.

What can I say about that action that could not be said about the whole business of Fire Bombing? Entering that deadly condition was expected of us, and we didn't question it. We were in a rotor wind that could have rolled us inverted or flung us into the mountain. Entering extreme lee side turbulence is a game of Russian roulette. It is just this condition that could have been responsible for sending other bombers inexplicably into mountains. Investigators would report that it was controlled flight into terrain – cause unknown. Johnny and I stayed upright; the demon only grasped the retardant in its rotor grip and it missed us. We took the severe turbulence naively unaware of how close we may have been to disaster. Thankfully, we were in strong airplanes that could take this demented beating. It was all in a day's work for us.

This is the type of turbulence that airline crews might find once in a career. They don't go looking for it like we do. On the once-in-a-lifetime occurrence, it finds them.

Playing with the Toy

Boys will be boys and if you give a boy a toy to play with, there is no doubt he will play with it. On the way home from a fire one day, I spotted a B-17 plodding along, heading home from a fire as well. I moved into the B-17's nine o'clock position and about a thousand feet above his altitude. I called to tell him to look out to his nine o'clock position. I then dove down to go under him, rolled over the top of his airplane and finished the roll just ahead of his cockpit. As I accelerated beyond him, I did a second roll. It was an irresistible bit of showing off. I was to hear later that the pilot of the B-17 didn't see much humour in it. Not to be discouraged by humourless pilots, I did the same thing another time around a PBY. These were naughty, spur-of-the-moment stunts done out in the middle of nowhere.

There was another show-off stunt that I would get to pull off fairly often for the benefit of a variety of spectators. Several airplanes would often gather at a reloading base just as a fire action was coming to an end. There would be all types of bombers from TBMs to F7Fs and B-17s. When the word came to return to our regular base, the airplanes would depart in their various directions. This was an opportunity to show the other pilots just what kind of airplane I was flying.

Right after takeoff, I would hold the airplane level at full power and let it accelerate to 265 knots. It could then be rotated up to about a seventy degree angle and do a fast climb to 10,000 feet. I was always tempted to roll the airplane to my heading home but I knew that the United Stated Forest Service people were watching and aerobatics were prohibited over airports. A roll would have caught the attention of people with no sense of humour, but no one could argue about a steep climb.

I was flying a beautiful airplane, the consummate Fire Bomber. It was stressed to take this business, had superb visibility, carried a big enough load to put an effective pattern on the ground and it had the turning and climb performance which was ideal for a bomber. If an airplane was purpose-designed for Fire Bombing, the F7F would be it. What a fabulous adaptation for a military machine it was. I enjoyed every second I was flying this wonderful airplane.

I had a little fun with the airplane with each landing. The round-out for landing didn't have the nose too high, but after touchdown I would pull the stick all the way back as far as I could and hold it there. The nose of the airplane would rise high enough to cause the wing to stall. The airplane then gently dropped the nose to settle itself into a level attitude. It still had enough speed for the wing to regain its lift. Still holding the stick back, the nose would rise again until it got high enough to stall again. The nose wheel would again drop gently to the runway. Just enough speed remained that the wing would again develop lift and the nose would come up again. It would again stall and this time the nose wheel would gently settle and stay on the ground even though I continued to hold the stick back. It was a little diversion from the usual landing that helped to slow the airplane.

With its great cruise speed (around 230 knots indicated), the F7F wasted no time getting around California. Sometimes I'd be a long way from Willows doing the last drop of the evening. One evening just at dusk, I had finished an action near Mount Shasta and it was obvious the trip home to Willows would be in the dark. To prepare myself for the lack of instrument lights, I carried a pen light in my flight suit shoulder pocket.

As I was enveloped in darkness for the first time in this airplane, I was able to see the pale blue exhausts as they clung to the side of the cowling on their way out into space. It was such a beautiful, soft, delicate colour. It occurred to me that it was the same pale violet blue as the colour of my astral body but without the million sparkling points of light.

I held the penlight in my mouth to light up the instruments I needed for landing.

Bill Benedict in the F7F over central California. Photo by author

Coolidge, Arizona

"Pack your bag: You're off to Coolidge, Arizona."
This was the concise dispatch one day. It was nothing complicated: "You're off to Arizona." I liked the dispatch and was excited. I had never been to Arizona. I didn't know where Coolidge was, but I was also puzzled about why I was even going there, as I didn't imagine that

the torrid deserts of Arizona would have trees. I was told that Coolidge was south of Phoenix, and, after diligent searching, I found it in the middle of a blank spot on my aviation map. I then plotted how to get from where I was to where I wanted to be. The F7F doesn't have a great range, so it was necessary to stop for fuel in Las Vegas. Before getting to Vegas, I had to climb high enough to fly over the High Sierra mountains. I needed to climb to 13,000 feet and at this altitude I got a close-up view of the 14,505 foot Mount Whitney, the highest peak in the continental USA, passing off to one side. This is where I saw the deficiency of not having a pressurized main fuel tank. The fuel pressure gauges would drop to next to zero if I didn't have high boost on. So it was high boost as I watched the magnificent blue and gray peaks pass below me. Minutes later, I saw a place that wasn't on my must-visit list – Death Valley, the lowest place in North America at 282 feet below sea level and also the hottest, with a temperature of 134 °F (57 °C), recorded in 1913.

After leaving Vegas, I flew over fairly flat ground as I headed for Coolidge. Not far from my destination, I was awed by a sight I had never seen before. A towering wall of blowing dust and sand was heading for the base – a giant sandstorm. I watched its progress and suddenly realized that this ominous ambush was doing its best to beat me to the base. If I wanted to get there before it did, I'd have to get into high gear. I put my nose down and added power. I had to win this race as the visibility in that storm looked next to zero.

On final approach for landing, I saw a forest of what appeared to me to be the burned-out stumps of trees that are common after a forest fire in the Pacific Northwest or British Columbia. It looked like a fire had passed through the area and left this wasteland. But some of these trees did look rather odd – giant branches as thick as the main trunk of the tree, stuck out the sides, turned and pointed up.

I discovered that Coolidge is an abandoned naval training facility that was used during World War Two. It was a sprawling installation obviously meant to process large numbers of flight students. Old, rundown hangars and buildings littered the base. The Arizona heat, age and sandstorms were taking their toll. Paint peeled off buildings that were once white to reveal bleached gray wood. Few windows were unbroken and the wide-open hangar doors provided easy access to man, insects and reptiles. The aircraft parking areas were covered in layers of dust carried there by the wind and sandstorms.

About five minutes after I landed, the dust storm hit and the visibility was reduced to about a hundred feet. It blew for the entire afternoon, blanketing the area with a layer of fine sand. Fortunately, on the F7F it was easy to scoop the dust out of the air intakes. I wouldn't be ingesting that engine killer into the engines.

We began flying the following day to fires north of the base and at higher levels in the mountains. I was bombing fires as high as 8,000 feet in the Arizona heat. One day we had high humidity that caused a radical performance difference in the airplane. Moist air is less dense than dry air and I was to discover that hot, moist air made the airplane far more sluggish in its performance than I had so far experienced. On a pull-out after a dive to a fire, the airplane sagged and wallowed like an overloaded pelican in flight. Fortunately I had plenty of room below the fire for my escape. From watching the sluggish antics of all the other planes, It dawned on me that I was the luckiest pilot at the base: I had a high performing airplane and got around in this incredible heat without too much problem.

I felt sorry for the sweltering guys in the B-17s. To assure themselves of a reasonable chance to get in the air, they picked the longest runway at the airport. I watched the painfully slow acceleration and always wondered if they would actually make it. They groaned on to the very end of the runway and to avoid embarrassment, retracted the gear to give the impression that they were flying. They cleared the brush off the end of the runway by a few feet and slogged on for miles before getting enough altitude to turn to their outbound heading. Oh how happy I was that I wasn't in a B-17.

It didn't take long for me to experience what true desert heat was all about. The temperature went up to 115 to 120 °F (46-49 °C) every day. I couldn't believe how quickly I would dehydrate. It was so obvious and had such a dramatic effect on the body that I timed myself to see how long I could go without a drink. After twenty minutes the thirst was overpowering. There was blast-furnace heat in the cockpit and in only minutes my flight suit was a wet rag. At least it tended to cool me off a little. I could see how people could die in a couple of days if they were stranded here without water. We all drank constantly during our time at the airport and my cold thermos of ice-cold water was never more appreciated.

An Arizona thunderstorm has an appearance and behaviour unlike any I had ever seen. Rain falls out of the storms in straight walls. They had that appearance from the air, but one day I saw it firsthand while standing on a street in the town of Coolidge. Our crew was in town after our flying day was over and a storm approached. A torrent of rain was falling on the opposite side of the street about sixty or seventy feet away and we didn't get a single drop. It was bone-dry on our side. The crews familiar with the area told me that these storms create instant flash floods that come rushing down shallow valleys. Signs on the highways warn drivers to beware of these flash floods. These torrents rush off to nowhere, simply seeping away into the Arizona desert.

On no-fly days, new sights awaited me as I wandered out into the desert. I discovered that the "burnt-out trees" were the giant Saguaro Cactus. They looked impregnable behind an impenetrable wall of thorns until I saw that birds made holes among the thorns to build their nests. That bird is the Gila woodpecker. *Clever bird*, I thought, *what a defense system: he's got 360 degrees of land mines around his house.* I was hoping to see the Gila monster or a rattlesnake, but in the heat of the day there was no such luck. They stayed down in their holes in their cool basement rumpus rooms. What I did see one day was a snake that crossed the tarmac at a speed which would be the envy of a cheetah. I was glad he wasn't heading for me, and I asked some fellow pilots if this one was dangerous.

"It's a Blue Racer, Linc. It can catch anything out there, including that little 100 mile per hour lizard that does push-ups. It's a toss-up who's faster, he or a Road Runner. He eats lizards and other snakes and isn't poisonous."

This guy really impressed me. I had never seen a snake travel at that pace. I had no idea that corkscrewing on the ground could work that well. I was glad that pilots weren't on his menu.

One day I heard what sounded like a strange sort of a bark. I suspected it may have been a fox or some other little desert animal, so off I went to see if I could find what it was. It turned out that there were large patches of watermelon fields not far off the base. I walked over to where I saw what looked like a ten-inch pipe gushing out a torrent of clear water, the irrigation water for the watermelons. I cupped my hand and tasted it; it was cool and delicious.

A fellow of about five foot ten wearing jeans, a long-sleeved shirt and a wide brimmed straw hat walked over to me and asked if he could do anything for me. I explained who I was and my curiosity about the sound. I also asked him about this seemingly inexhaustible geyser of crystalline water. He told me that when settlers first came to Arizona, the sub-surface water was only about forty feet below the desert. Now, he said, this well goes down to 800 feet and the water table goes lower every year.

But, I was still wondering about the bark. He pointed and said that the irrigation water was run off into a pond about half a mile away. I'd find the origin of the noise in that pond. The giant bark turned out to be a tiny, green-mottled frog with an elephantine pouch under his mouth whose bark rather than a croak could be heard for miles. I couldn't imagine how a little guy that could sit in the palm of my hand could make so much noise.

Even though I got in a fair bit of flying, Coolidge was more fun for the discovery of the desert creatures that I had never seen before. After two weeks in this baking desert, I was sent home to Willows.

Oakland/Berkeley Hills

The most distressing fire I had ever attended was the Oakland/Berkeley Hills Fire in September of 1970. On one of my orbits around to the east side of the mountains at Oakland, I saw where the fire had originated beside a curve in the winding road up the mountain. It was lit in the most strategic spot to have the fire go straight up the steep mountain and into the housing development at the top. The arsonist knew exactly what he was doing and acted at the precise time to do the most damage. From a report by *The Journal of Arboriculture*, September 1992:

> *According to historical records, there have been four major fires in the Oakland-Berkeley Hills area and each was associated with the same weather pattern: high atmospheric pressure over the Great Basin desert and a low in southern California. This pattern occurred on September 16, 1923, September 22, 1970, and December 10, 1980. The point of fire origin of the 1970 fire was similar and weather conditions were almost identical to those on October 20, 1991.*
>
> *Wind circulates in a clockwise pattern around a high and counter-clockwise around a low. This strong flow pushes the normally present marine layer off the California coast, followed by hot dry winds coming westward from the Sierras. The air overheats even more as it drops to the valleys, until it reaches the greater San Francisco Bay Area. This pattern occurred on October 20, 1991, when high wind speed and low humidity lasted for several hours. According to thirty years of data collected on the University of California at Berkeley campus, an average of four days of this kind of weather can be expected annually.*
>
> *But besides this weather pattern, another fact remains clear. At the same time the quantity of dead fuel (leaves, twigs and branches) is increasing in the late summer and early fall,*

while the moisture content of the remaining live vegetation is drastically decreasing. Thus, less energy is required for ignition and a destructive fire may start without the presence of Santa Ana winds.

This had to be the worst kind of fire for the Birddog; there was no real plan of attack that he could execute from start to finish. The problem was the roaring wind over the mountain ridge. True to form, it not only generated severe turbulence but it was also laying down the blanket of smoke that covered the entire residential area. The proximity of the advancing fire dictated only one kind of air action: where possible, save lives and property and lay the retardant next to the buildings. As each airplane arrived at the fire, the pilot was placed in a holding pattern to await his turn to drop. While I waited, the occasional, brief clearing of the smoke allowed me to see the walls of fire approaching the homes. There was still some space between the fire and the houses, and this was the perfect time for a drop. Those beautiful homes I was seeing below me still had a chance. If only there was some way to lay down the protective line of retardant instantly that I knew would save them. Unfortunately, these opportune moments were quickly lost. In seconds the houses disappeared again as the smoke closed back over them.

The Birddog and bombers could only wait. If a break looked like it could persist for a few minutes, the lowest airplane in the stack was directed to make his attack. The pilot had to be prepared for an immediate run on his target, as there might only be a few seconds of visibility good enough for his in and out. These dives into the fire and smoke are the very actions photographed for the TV newscasts. On one of my return circuits, the wall of fire I had previously seen approaching some houses had closed the gap and homes were beginning to burn. All we could do was watch. It was a disquieting sight to see the fire and smoke envelop a home and then observe it catch fire. On some orbits I would see several buildings burning at once. While we did some good, most of the time we simply looked on as the fire devoured what it wanted. The smoke paralyzed our actions, we could only watch until the Diablo wind relented. I flew on the fire all afternoon and as it turned out later, the action by all the bombers did save many homes. A total of thirty-seven homes were destroyed in that fire and fortunately, no lives were lost.

What satisfaction does an arsonist get from knowing that so many people are losing a lifetime of work and memories as their beautiful, expensive homes are burned to the ground? It was such a helpless feeling to view the carnage when we knew that with good visibility we could have saved them. Time only granted us the briefest of moments to flail at this monster; all too frequently a pilot's run had to be aborted as the clearing quickly closed. Fortunately, I along with several other bombers managed to get in our shots and most of them were successful. We saved numerous homes. I thanked my good luck for being in my F7F; it was just the tough bird needed for this kind of action.

Landing on the retardant tank works — but you don't get to use the airplane again the same day. Photo courtesy Sis-Q Flying Service

Plywood Approach

Bombing in the northern part of the state often meant re-loading at Rohnerville, located a few miles south of Fortuna. Since it seemed to be foggy there almost all the time, pilots had devised a unique approach to get into the airport. It was called it the Plywood Approach. Harry had briefed me about it earlier but now the time had arrived when I needed to use it.

I did the approach check and set up the airplane ready for landing while I was still east of the airport on the descent, in clear air. There was a highly defined line where the Pacific fog ended and the hot dry air that enveloped the rest of California began. Harry's description of the approach said that it would be necessary to go under that fog bank. As I approached I could see that the ceiling was only a couple of hundred feet. I now had to trust Harry's description of the approach but I wasn't going to trust the fog. I had selected partial flap so if I did run into a brick wall of fog, I could simply put on full power and haul the nose up. I'd be out of the fog and into the clear air above in a matter of seconds.

I began the approach by getting down low between the banks of the Eel River. It was not a long approach and the landing would be done almost immediately after climbing out from between the river banks. I had always enjoyed low-level flying down a winding river but this trip was somewhat anxious because of my uncertainty about the fog.

After a short trip down the Eel River I made the requisite turn up the Van Duzen River as soon as it appeared. A green building then materialized out of the fog and that was the time to turn to a heading of 290 degrees. I flew until two 4 x 8 sheets of plywood, one above the other, showed up. The plywood panels were aligned to put the airplane on the runway heading. It was then a quick climb up out of the river valley, line up on the runway and land. I don't know who figured that one out, but it worked really well and it got easier each time I did it. I don't think I ever got to land at Rohnerville with a clear sky. I never did get a good look at the town of Fortuna. The fog simply obliterated the town out of existence.

One day to get in, I thought I would do something different that might be a bit easier. I decided to fly out over the ocean and let down under the fog and come into the airport following the beacon. The ceiling over the airport was about 200 feet, so I naturally thought that would be the ceiling over the whole Pacific Ocean. Letting down over a flat ocean with the nearest obstruction being Japan had to be a safe bet. I go out far enough to be clear of land and start my let-down.

This will be a breeze, think I, *why isn't this the preferred way to let down?* As the altimeter was showing me getting closer and closer to sea level, I was still in the fog. Down to 200 feet and no ocean. I decreased my rate of descent so I'd lose altitude very slowly. At 100 feet over the water I broke out of the fog. It was then time to turn inland to follow the beacon to the airport and land for a re-load.

Then I had the time to consider my stupidity. The ceiling over the airport didn't mean that it would be the same over the ocean, and no one gave me a guarantee that a ship wouldn't be parked between me and Japan just as I broke out. As it turned out, the air was quite clear below the fog, but it could have been worse with very little visibility. I got away with my gamble over the water, but I never did that again.

The War-Bird

It was the F7F's incredible performance that caused me to reflect on what it was that I was really flying. Yes, it was a perfect Fire Bomber, but that wasn't its original mission. The F7F was purpose designed for something else. It was a killing machine, a fighter designed to shoot other airplanes out of the sky and kill their crews. What an ignoble purpose for an airplane of such performance and beauty. I often thought about the folly of man. We design and build sleek, high-performance airplanes, each generation being far superior to the last of their type. They carry the latest of electronics. They are wonder machines that fly to the edge of space and survey an area the size of a country. The enemy is detected hundreds of miles away and a missile is dispatched to kill him. Every new, ever-more-elegant and futuristic fighter that comes along with its ever-more fantastic performance is, nevertheless, a new breed of killing machine. It always struck me as extreme irony that man's most beautiful and incredibly maneuverable flying machines were designed for one purpose, the purpose of killing each other.

These were my thoughts in later years. It was different when I was young. When I joined the RCAF, the flying world changed for me. The three-dimensional world of airplanes was no longer comprised merely of the slow climbs, descents and level cruising I had known while flying small commercial aircraft. The high power-to-weight ratio, and the full aerobatic capability of military trainers and fighters now allowed adventurous pilots to use the entire airspace from the ground to the stratosphere as their exclusive playground. I determined I would make full use of it. It was a dream come true and it would now be my play-space to experience the wonder of flight in full 3-D.

It was a fabulous adventure: no one was shooting at me and the taxpayer was footing the bill. Later, I would be flying a jet airplane to learn to shoot its machine guns and fire its rockets. These were the weapons with which to kill the people my country named as enemies. But the fact that this wonderful jet airplane I was flying was designed as a killing machine wasn't something I thought about then; those thoughts would come later, when I learned more about "us."

At my age I was full of the idealism and patriotism that is useful to a country's leaders, be they tyrants, religious zealots, or the leaders of a democracy. I had the perfect conditioning to be a killer; I would go and destroy the enemy at the orders of my leaders to defend my country. If I were to serve and die for the purpose of defending the freedom of the citizens of my country, they would remember me forever and be eternally grateful that I sacrificed my life for them. How little I knew about my fellow man.

The insanity of it all comes home with such devastating impact when I know that the fighter pilots who were trying to kill each other during the Second World War are now friends. They honour each other's memorial days and drink toasts to their lost buddies together. Men followed and fought for Hitler until the money, resources and lives ran out. They killed us and in defense of our freedom, we killed more of them. Then it finished. It was time to put the guns away and park the fighter aircraft. It was time to become friends.

The history of man has been a history of conflict. Invaded countries will naturally take up arms to defend themselves. The world fought the tyrannies of Germany and Japan and it would have been folly not to have superior arms in the face of Stalin's desire to make the world communist. Nuclear weapons kept the tyrant at bay. But we must be honest with ourselves. Every society at the apex of its power has indulged in conquest. None of history's dynamic societies can claim innocence. When we have power and think we can get away it, we go on rampages of conquest and murder. Nevertheless, even in the nuclear age, nations and alliances are armed to protect themselves from neighbours who regard war as a legitimate means to achieve their aims.

All conflicts are so incredibly barbarous, senseless and wasteful. How stupid does the killing sound when in retrospect we can so easily see the insanity of it all, and how useless is this kind of behaviour. No one comes out the winner. Every society wants to live in peace, yet a rising tyrant can lead the society to suicide. Every rational person wants to be friends with his neighbour, if our leaders would only let us.

But I was a military man flying for my country, and if it came to war, I just knew that I would be among the best-scoring fighter aces, for I would put everything I had into flying and shooting with the best killing machine my country had to offer. I would be counted among my Air Force's greatest heroes.

Fortunately, I didn't have to go there. When my term in the RCAF was finished, I began this fabulous career of Fire Bombing. As well as the F7F, I flew the TBM and the CS2-F, both torpedo launchers, and the A-26, a bomber. These were all surplus military aircraft conveniently having a bomb bay. The bay was the perfect place for a new, benign weapon, the retardant tank. At least we can show some sanity with the beasts we create. What a different place this world would be if man didn't have his enemies upon which to waste enormous killing resources. But they never go away. There is always another. And we always need bigger and better weapons. Walt Kelly revealed his great insight into the human psyche when he used his cartoon character Pogo to utter his own profound observation about humanity: "We have found the enemy, and he is us."

In spite of my thoughts, the F7F gratified my adventurous spirit. I loved flying the airplane—I was in the perfect Fire Bomber. I was fully prepared to stay and fly for Sis-Q when a unique and irresistible offer was presented to me by Kenting Aviation in Toronto.

FIRE BOMBER INTO HELL

Reproduced courtesy of Jean Barbaud

Grumman S-2F – Tracker

213

Chapter Thirteen
The First S2-F Conversion to a Fire Bomber

Pilot "Squawk": Aircraft handles funny.
Maintenance fix: Aircraft warned to straighten up, "fly right"
and be serious.
Quantas Airlines

In 1970, my third year of flying in California, I received an unusual invitation. Kenting Aviation based in Toronto called me and asked if I would demonstrate the capabilities of the A-26 to the Ontario Department of Lands and Forests. I hadn't flown the A-26 so I wondered why they were asking me. I was to find out later when I learned that a grand plan for using land-based bombers was in the works. Dropping retardant was hatching in the mind of Bill Foster, head of the Department. He had heard about the use of retardants and thought land-based bombers would be a great complement to the water-dropping system used in Ontario. The land-based system did make sense in the area of Sudbury were lakes were few and widely separated, and they had a special problem with fires.

Land-Based Bombers for Ontario

The nickel mines of Sudbury had been sending their pollutants into the atmosphere for decades and included in the smoke were generous quantities of sulfur. It blanketed the countryside for miles around. It killed the trees and coated the entire landscape, rocks and all. Forest fires in that area burned with their own special intensity. Barren areas didn't stop the fire. The sulfur burned with its light blue flame even over the treeless rocky outcrops. As the people with the forest service described it, "even the rocks burned." Bill had reasoned that fires in this condition could be better controlled with long-term retardant instead of water. Sudbury would be an excellent location for a fleet of retardant-dropping land-based bombers. That was the plan.

During a break in the flight testing of the Tracker, I had the honour of flying Apollo astronauts Eugene Cernan and Ron Evans up to Sudbury in a department King Air. Apparently, several of the astronaut crews had been taken there to view what was considered a moonscape right there in li'l ole Sudbury.

The system long in use by the Ontario Department of Lands and Forests was the modified floats of the Beaver, Otter and Twin Otter aircraft used to pick up and drop water. Ontario lies almost entirely within the Laurentian Shield, so the landscape is dotted with a million lakes. Every fire was within easy access of water so it made sense to convert the forest service's utility airplanes for water pick-up and bombing. Ontario had pioneered the float pick-up systems and their water-dropping capability with these airplanes was the pride of the forestry service.

Kenting Aviation was asked to demonstrate the A-26 because that airplane would be closest in its capability to the airplane the Ontario Department of Lands and Forests really had in mind which was the Tracker, the CS2-F. No one had yet converted a Tracker into a bomber, but the groundwork was being laid. It appeared that members of the forest service had contacted Field Aviation in Toronto about the feasibility of converting the Tracker. First, they wanted to have a look at what it took to operate the land-based system and see the capabilities of the A-26. So Kenting needed someone who knew about land-based bombers to demonstrate the A-26. As it turned out, Knox Hawkshaw, the Chief Engineer with Field Aviation had read my little blue book *Pilot's Notes for Fire Bombing* and suggested to Kenting that I might be the man.

It was to be a two-week demonstration conducted from Dryden, Ontario. Dryden was a pulp and paper town that reeked with the rotten-egg smell of hydrogen sulfide, a byproduct of producing pulp. The residents were obviously quite used to it, or they put on a good front for visitors. I wondered how long a resident would have to breathe that nauseating smell before they themselves had dragon breath. Nevertheless, it was the smell of employment. Kenting had indicated to me that with a successful demonstration, the department would be ordering several bombers and I would get the job of managing the operations.

The issue of pay came up and I wouldn't think of doing it unless I was being paid much more than I was getting flying for Sis-Q. I was also flying the F7F and didn't want to give up that great adventure. When I secured the pay assurances I wanted, the next step was to get a check-out on the A-26. Sis-Q gave me a two-week leave of absence and I headed for Rosenbalm Aviation in Medford, Oregon to check out on the A-26. I then got my very curious body up to Edmonton where the airplane was leased from Airspray for the demonstration.

It was indeed an unusual exhibition to members of the Ontario Lands and Forests. I was to demonstrate to a group of foresters who knew nothing about retardants as to how they were to be used to put a containment line around a fire. They created a fire for me out in the middle of an open field as the place for the show. When dropping water, the smoke and fire is always the target and the Ontario bombers always dropped directly on the fire.

Now they were watching someone who supposedly knew about advanced techniques of using aircraft as Fire Bombers. This airplane and pilot had come all the way from Western Canada to demonstrate a superior system that would soon be used in Ontario. I began my usual procedure of containment expecting admiration and wild applause. Apparently I hadn't shown them a thing. Why would Bill Foster send someone who obviously didn't know what he was doing and couldn't hit the target to demonstrate some magic, unknown firefighting system? Neither could they understand why anyone would go all the way back to the airport to have a load of water pumped into the airplane when a Beaver with floats could deliver unlimited quantities from a nearby lake. Word came back to base faster than the spread of a California brush fire that I couldn't hit the target and why would anyone put water around the fire instead of on it? Obviously a great deal had been left out on their initial briefing about the purpose of this presentation.

It didn't appear that anyone knew that I was putting a "line" around the fire the same way I did with retardant. Naturally, I was not making any attempt to hit the fire; it was purely a demonstration of how retardant was employed. The locals were not impressed. They had water on the brain and were applying my illustration to the use of water. On the other hand, I couldn't understand their lack of imagination. All they had to do was believe in their boss who had obviously wanted them to see a superior method of controlling their fires. I was dropping a wondrous substance that was impenetrable to fire; of course I would diligently apply it around the fire to let the interior of the fire burn itself out. Surely their visualization would have them accept the land-based bomber as the perfect, all-in-one complete fire control system: containment, burn-out and extinguishing in one swift action. I'm sure these people out in the field were wondering about my hopeless incompetence at hitting a target and about Bill Foster's sanity.

Nevertheless, someone high up had declared the demonstration a success. The Tracker program would proceed.

Tracker Pitch-up

The Tracker is a short, squat airplane with wings that fold in order to fit on aircraft carrier elevators. Grumman had designed the aircraft as a Cold War hunter-killer of submarines. It first flew in 1952 and entered service in 1954. It had avionics and sonar buoys with which to track the sub, as well as an internally-carried torpedo with which to kill its prey. It was powered by two Wright R-1820-82WA engines of 1525 horsepower each. While the American, Australian, Argentine, Dutch and Canadian navies flew the airplane from aircraft carriers, the Air Forces or navies of Japan, Argentina, Brazil, South Korea, Peru, Taiwan, Turkey and Uruguay used the airplane from land-based operations to perform the same role. To extend operational life and effectiveness of the airplane, Argentina and Brazil updated their versions with new turboprop engines and avionics. A large number of Trackers are currently in use.

In the conversion to a Fire Bomber, the internal "bomb bay" became the place for the 725-imperial gallon retardant tank. The retardant drops, one or two at a time or all four, were to be triggered by a button on the control column. While it had excellent visibility forward, side visibility was restricted somewhat due to the engines. The piston engines gave it a very distinctive sound; close the eyes and farm boys would say it sounded little different than a John Deere tractor.

In this whole approach to the Tracker conversion, I had wondered whether or not the Ontario Department of Lands and Forests or Field Aviation had considered that the configuration of the airplane might render it unsuitable as a Fire Bomber. It was very short-coupled, so its pitch-up characteristics might have been too violent. Ontario had either been advised by someone, Field perhaps, that there would be no problems with pitch-up or they were moving ahead with the first conversion in blind ignorance.

There was also a rumour that the airplane was considered unsuitable as a bomber by the United States Forest Service precisely because of this configuration. Pitch-up was an unknown phenomenon to the Department of Lands and Forests because it didn't occur with their float planes. And it was obviously a non-factor in their thinking as work on the Tracker proceeded. Knox Hawkshaw of Field Aviation would design the tank and once the airplane was ready, it would be handed over to DeHavilland Aircraft of Canada and Bob Fowler, the Chief Test Pilot, for flight testing and evaluation.

During the winter, the conversion began. In April I received a frantic call from Frank Smith, the general manager of Kenting, telling me I had to get on the next flight out of Calgary and get my puzzled body down to Toronto. The program had run into a real problem. He wouldn't discuss the trouble over the phone. He just wanted me down there immediately. Apparently he thought I could solve the problem. *Wow, top secret stuff*, I enthused, *I'm in the big league.*

When I arrived at DeHavilland, I met Bob Fowler, the chief test pilot. He stood about six feet tall, had an average build and I had an immediate liking for the man. His aura exuded professionalism combined with an engaging friendliness. One of the first things I noticed was the crow's feet framing inquiring, smiling eyes. I also had the sense those smiling eyes pierced my inner being every time he looked at me to see if I really knew anything about flying. I would soon be put to the test. He had an ebullient personality, a great sense of humour and life didn't throw him any curves. I guess I liked him so much because he took life as one big fish story. He was a serious professional at his work, but nothing was so serious that he couldn't laugh about it. Bob was in a dangerous occupation (insurance rates on his life would be sky high) but he sure didn't act it – as if I knew how a man in a dangerous occupation should act. All the bomber pilots that I knew didn't act as if they were in dangerous occupations either. We were all ordinary guys pretending to be in an ordinary occupation.

He was the perfect test pilot, methodical in his approach to everything in life yet when he was stuck for an answer, he didn't hesitate to call in some help. On this occasion, he asked for my input. I was flattered. How could I possibly help a man who was an aeronautical engineer and who knew so much more about flying than I did? Bob wouldn't tell me what the problem was. No one did. I was to learn later that no one wanted me to have any pre-conceived ideas before the problem was presented to me. Bob was to the point.

"Linc, we're going to load the airplane and take it up to drop the load. Are you okay with that?"

"Sure Bob, let's do it."

We were going up to drop a load. *So what's the big deal?* I was not sure why I was being asked along. He had already flown the aircraft and dropped loads, so why this trip? When we arrived at our test altitude and were ready to drop, Bob, in carefully measured words said, "I want you to drop the load at the speed you would normally drop and then do what you would normally do."

"Okay, Bob."

I slowed the airplane down to 125 knots and set up for a drop. I hit the button and did my normal input of pushing the control column forward just enough to cancel out some of the positive g. I left a little bit of g on to keep it in the positive range. Bob immediately asked:

"Is that what you do every time you drop?"

"Yes."

"How did you find that? Is this the way other airplanes you've flown pitch-up?"

"Yeah, it's not bad at all."

"So you don't leave the airplane to pitch-up on its own? You always check forward on every drop?"

"Yes."

"And you find that this pitch-up is acceptable with the input that you've just given?"

"Yes."

An immense look of relief came over his face. He had been dropping the load and letting the aircraft pitch-up without any pilot input. As a result, he was getting excessive g and a very high nose attitude, most disconcerting to say the least. No Fire Bombing pilot does that. In aircraft that do have a pitch-up like the TBM, the A-26 and F7F, every drop needs pilot input to check the control column forward. With no input, the pitch-up is wild and can exceed positive g limits.

We flew several more trips as he watched me cancelling out some of the g by checking forward on the control column, and I watched him do the same thing until he got the hang of it. He asked for my assurance a number of times that this g loading and pilot procedure was normal and acceptable for a Fire Bomber. I assured him it was. Bob knew of my experience, I had written the book that got me there and was well into *Air Attack on Forest Fires*, so he accepted my judgment about the safety of the Tracker pitch-up. After those sessions Bob was satisfied that the Tracker was safe to use as a Fire Bomber. In pronouncing the CS2-F as an acceptable Fire Bomber for the Ontario Department of Lands and Forests, it was pronounced suitable to the world. Little did we imagine the avalanche of conversions that would follow.

First flights for the Ontario Tracker. From left — Bill Nash,
Bob Fowler, and me

Handling Pitch-up

Bob then told me about the pitch-up problem that top dressing pilots in New Zealand had with the Beaver aircraft. Top dressing is the dumping of fertilizer on nutrient-poor grasslands in New Zealand on a vast scale. Their habit was to release the load all at once, much the same as we did in Fire Bombing. From altitude, it falls far enough to disperse and give the desired coverage on the ground. When the pilots released the load, they checked forward on the control column far enough to put some negative g on the airplane with the object of trying to cancel out all of the positive g which would follow. The drop sequence encompassed negative g from pilot input followed by the positive g from the load release.

Wings had come off two Beavers so Bob was sent down to New Zealand to find the cause. He asked the pilots to show him what they did when they dropped a load, the same as he did with me. They showed him the procedure and he immediately ordered the wings to be removed from a number of airplanes used in top dressing. He needed to see the pilot procedures only once for his analytical mind to tell him what the problem was. He wanted to check the joints where the wing strut was attached to the wing. The wing strut is attached to a bracket in the wing with a tight-fitting bolt. There is no play in the joint. What he found was that some of the brackets were elongated to the point where failure was imminent. Each time the wing flexed both negative and positive, the elongated joint would slap both ways against a steel bolt to cause further elongation in the softer bracket. It was only a matter of time before the hole in the wing bracket stretched far enough that little metal was left holding it, and it would fail at the next drop. All Beavers used in top dressing were immediately grounded and the strut-wing joint was ordered to be inspected on all Beaver aircraft. Several wing joints were found on the verge of failure.

Bob knew the cause of the problem even though there was only a small amount of g both in the positive and the negative. The sequence of positive g followed by negative g is deadly on aircraft wings. Bob indicated that research done by universities and aircraft manufacturers showed that this combination is the same as applying the sum of both forces both ways on the wings and wings aren't built to take substantial negative g. If there are three positive g-forces on the pitch-up and one negative on the pitch-down, then the wing, in effect, takes 4 g both ways, positive and negative. While aircraft can safely sustain minor overloads in positive g, they aren't built to take big negative loads.

This combination of minus and plus g loading on the Beavers caused a strong flexing on the wing both up and down, enough that the wing joints were overstressed and the action began the elongation that led to failure. He not only advised the operators of the problem, he suggested the solution: the pilots must not check forward on the control column so far as to induce negative g, they were to check forward only enough to reduce some of the positive g once the load comes out.

This was the procedure I was using to cancel out some of the positive g when Fire Bombing but I wasn't sure that everyone else was doing it. So Bob now gave an aeronautical engineer's approval to a procedure that I had been using all along. Bob's explanation of the cumulative effect of g-forces if induced both ways was written into *Air Attack on Forest Fires* exactly as he described it. There was a safe way to handle g and I wanted to be sure everyone knew it.

The Tracker conversion was supposed to be ready by June, so that was the time for me to come to Toronto to do drop evaluation and to demonstrate the airplane to various forest districts.

Check-Out

Other than the trips with Bob Fowler resolving the acceptability of the CS2-F pitch-up, I didn't have any time in the airplane, so it was time to go fly the bird. "Time you got endorsed on the Tracker," Bob said as he pointed to the airplane. "Go get used to it."

Kenting had hired Bill Nash, an ex-navy pilot who had bags of time on the Tracker. He was to fly with me during the drop tests and demonstrations of the airplane. The plan was that he would be one of the pilots when the fleet came on line. Bill was a stocky five foot eight inches tall, had a short-cropped haircut typical of a military man and oozed the confidence of a seasoned naval pilot. He had good reason. He was one of the few who had handled the CS2-F on and off Canada's tiny aircraft carrier, the Bonaventure. If a pilot could handle a CS2-F on the shortest of all runways, he could fly it anywhere. Bill was keen to learn Fire Bombing. He always had a determined look on his face which seemed to signal that he was ready to meet all challenges.

I took the airplane up to get familiar with it. As it was going to be used as a Fire Bomber it was important that I knew how it handled in the Fire Bombing mode. I particularly wanted to know what it did close to a stall in a steep turn, the type of thing I'd be doing next to a mountainside. So I stalled it with power off and power on in steep turns to determine how much warning I would get before it stalled and what would it do when it did.

If we want to fly we have to keep moving, just like the birds. The air moving over the wings provides lift and the consequent joys of flying. As long as we have smooth, undisturbed air flowing, the wing develops lift, the airplane keeps flying and everybody's happy. A stall occurs when the smooth-flowing air over the top of the wing breaks away and becomes turbulent. The wing no longer provides lift and the airplane starts its fall out of the sky.

At some time in a pilot's distant past when he first learned to fly, he was taught the symptoms of the straight-ahead, power-off stall — reduce the power, hold the nose up and stall the aircraft. The air on the upper surface of the wing breaks away and the stall occurs. The recovery procedure is to put the nose down and apply power to get the airplane flying normally again. The recovery is quick and can be done with little or no loss of altitude.

Knowing everything about how the airplane stalls is life-and-death when flying Fire Bombers. We spend all our time flying next to mountains where a variety of different conditions can cause a stall. We must learn how each different type of airplane we fly behaves as it gets close to stalling. The idea is to know the speeds and symptoms so we don't even get close to that happening.

Each airplane has its own personality and quirks in different circumstances, just like people. Some airplanes, like the DC-6, give a week's notice. The airplane begins to shake long before the stall occurs and the shaking slowly gets worse until the airplane, realizing that the dummy at the controls isn't going to do anything about it, finally gives up and stalls. But if he relaxes the control column even slightly, the wing flies again. Others aren't so nice. I've flown airplanes that exhibit very nasty stalls: a wing instantly drops and the aircraft rolls upside down.

In Fire Bombing, we set ourselves up for a stall in the worst possible places and in the most stall-prone configurations: doing steep, low-level turns with a loaded airplane inside a mountain bowl while making approaches to a target. And all the while we're exposed to the possibility of a downdraft, tailwind or turbulence suddenly robbing us of our life's airspeed. It's the situation bomber pilots put themselves into almost on a daily basis.

Bill Nash and I climbed to altitude and I did some single-engine procedures to see what it took to be safe on one engine. I went through all the emergency procedures and did an emergency landing gear drop, something I'd end up doing quite often. As I was turning the airplane through medium and steep turns to get the feel of the airplane, I discovered that it was a toy, light on the controls and capable of doing extremely tight turns. It's very responsive to the controls at all speeds even right up to the stall. With wheels and flaps down, it gives an excellent rate of descent without picking up speed, a great bonus for downhill bombing runs.

Then it was stall time. Unfortunately, Grumman's Tracker wing doesn't transmit any aerodynamic warnings that it was about to quit flying, so an artificial stick shaker had been installed in the airplane to let the pilot know when the stall is a few knots away. The airplane flies beautifully as it gets close to a straight-ahead power-off stall. Then it happens: the airplane goes from perfect flight to a stall in an instant. The smooth air breaks completely away from the wing and the nose takes a steep dive. The recovery takes a big chunk of airspace.

I had discovered the most important piece of handling that I needed to know about the Tracker. The airplane was a delight to fly and behaves like a Super Cub (a Piper Cub with an obscenely oversized engine in it) through all the speed ranges that would be used in Fire Bombing.

For the next stall I had power on, rolled to about eighty degrees of bank and pulled g in a steep turn. The Tracker was about to reveal its dark side. The g-force induced an accelerated stall. The stall was violent and the airplane snap rolled upside down. (A snap roll is a roll of the airplane without using the ailerons to do it.) Air show pilots often do snap rolls because the airplane rolls much more quickly than by using the ailerons. It's done by pulling substantial g-force at speeds well above the normal stall and pushing hard on a rudder pedal at the same time. The airplane will instantly roll around the side of the applied rudder. '

First Tracker conversion to a Fire Bomber, 1972. Photo by author

Bill and I spent the rest of the summer doing drop tests while DeHavilland got the bugs out of the bombing system. To save weight, they had made the classic mistake of having the bomb system hydraulics as part of the airplane hydraulics. It was a brand-new design full of leaky hydraulic joints which would drain away all of the aircraft hydraulics. It meant emergency landing gear and flap-lowering on many occasions.

The system soon got its own hydraulics and the bugs were worked out. The Ontario experiment with the Tracker as a Fire Bomber was a success.

Bill and I were to fly the airplane together for about 100 hours during the drop tests and the subsequent demonstrations to other forest services across Canada. The most fun were the demonstrations in the mountains at Kamloops. The Tracker proved itself in all environments. It made a great Fire Bomber. As there were plenty of surplus airplanes available, it made an ideal choice for several other forest services.

Tracker and Kenting A-26

In anticipation of the next season, Kenting had acquired two A-26 aircraft. These were being used by a number of operators in the USA, which led to A-26 acquisition by Kenting Aviation in Toronto and Conair Aviation in Abbotsford, British Columbia. The A-26 was designed as an "Attack Bomber," hence the designation as an A-26. Starting in November of 1944, it served in the European theatre during the Second World War. It was also sent to the Pacific shortly thereafter. In 1948, the Martin B-26 Marauder bomber was deactivated and this designation was given to the Douglas A-26 which then became the B-26. It held this title until 1962 when it was re-designated the A-26. For awhile we weren't quite sure what to call it in British Columbia, but the A-26 handle stuck.

The airplane was powered by two Pratt and Whitney R-2800-79s of 2000 horsepower each. The most significant feature of the airplane was the high speed, laminar-flow wing. It made the airplane fast but required the pilot to know how to fly that type of wing in a business which required the airplane to be flown fairly slowly in a high-drag configuration. The airplane could get behind the power curve quite easily if it was flown too slowly with gear and flaps down. The enormous drag would overcome the power available for normal flight. It could only be recovered by pointing the nose down as well as using full power while the gear and flaps were retracted.

In pilot's jargon, it was a slippery airplane; the pilot had to keep it moving. It was not an airplane that he could pull off the runway for a short takeoff. The proper procedure was to let it stay on until takeoff speed and then let it climb at a shallow angle as it gained momentum. There was a big gap between takeoff speed (V1) and the minimum control speed, fully loaded (Vmc), on one engine. If an engine failure did occur, the load could be dumped, which would back up the Vmc to a lower, empty-configuration speed. That action could save the emergency, but closing that gap between the two speeds while loaded seemed to take forever. It wasn't like the F7F where I attained the fully loaded minimum control speed in event of an engine failure even before takeoff.

As far as visibility was concerned, it wasn't any better than the TBM. The A-26's bulky nose restricted forward visibility and the engines restricted visibility to the sides.

The airplane did make a decent bomber, and its 800 imperial gallons were dropped out of two doors. A feature I really appreciated about the airplane was its "legs," which meant that it had a great range. We could carry full fuel along with a full load of retardant. If the weather closed in while we were doing an action somewhere in western Canada, we could easily divert to Alberta, Wyoming, Montana or Colorado if that proved necessary. It was a nice "ace-in-the-hole" that I used on several occasions.

The idea was to have these aircraft dispatched along with the single Ontario Tracker in order to create a One Strike force. I was sent to Scottsdale, Arizona to fly both airplanes back to Toronto. Both were purchased from Don Madsen,* the previous operator of the airplanes. Don was about five foot ten and had very light brown hair, almost red. He was a quiet, methodical man who spent his time helping Kenting's chief mechanic and me ready the airplanes to fly away. While I was in Scottsdale, Don told me an interesting story.

He had started into a takeoff run in the A-26. As he described it:

> *The airplane got up to about eighty knots and if I hadn't been in the airplane, I wouldn't have believed what happened. The airplane started to shake so hard that the instrument panel along with the control pedestal became a blur about two feet wide. The whole airplane was shaking so hard and with so much noise that I thought it would fly apart. I had a hard time grabbing the throttles somewhere in that huge vibration so I could stop the airplane. I had to get a tow back to my parking spot and that's when I noticed that the scissors were undone.*

The nose wheel scissors keep the nose wheel straight, especially when retracting into its forward compartment. However, if the operator wants to tow the airplane and move it around on the ground, the scissors need to be undone. It's done by simply pulling out a spring-loaded bolt on each side of the scissor connection. The nose wheel can then rotate freely. Another one of aviations "must-absolutely-do-before-takeoff" checks is to make sure that the scissors are connected; the bolts must be in place. As it happened, Don had forgotten about the movement of the airplane and the undone scissors prior to taking the airplane for a flight.

He showed me the airplane. The horizontal stabilizers were twisted from the level position by about twenty degrees and the fuselage showed the huge wrinkles of the twist. The airplane had been turned into a piece of junk. That unimaginable vibration is known by the simple name of "nose wheel shimmy." It's such a banal description for such a violent shaking. It should be called "vibrating terror in a sealed coffin." I would experience it later in the DC-6.

A Ball of Fire

Some emergencies don't announce themselves. They just arrive. One caught up to me while I was delivering the second A-26 from

Scottsdale to Toronto. Just outside of Peoria, Illinois I heard a pop out the left side of the airplane. Nothing loud, just a barely audible pop. I looked out and saw that the engine was a raging ball of fire. I could not have even imagined anything like it. There were brilliant red flames engulfed in dense black smoke starting from just behind the propeller and extending all the way down the nacelle and trailing out about ten feet behind. As there were no previous engine indications that pointed to trouble, I wondered what created this sudden fiery explosion of such epic proportions. The propeller behaved normally and the hub wasn't gushing oil. I couldn't imagine what would have caused a fire that started at the engine nose case and engulfed so much of the nacelle and wing. While it was spectacular, it was a very unnerving sight.

This is the type of emergency that's constantly rehearsed in check rides but I never thought that I would see such an enormous blaze in real life. There was no time to admire the spectacular sight. I did the fire emergency procedure, which first involves moving the mixture to idle cutoff and shutting off the fuel supply to that engine. There was nothing more to do as the A-26 doesn't have an engine fire extinguishing system. The fire went out instantly and I feathered the engine. In real situations, training takes over and the necessary motions happen almost automatically. The entire event was over in a matter of seconds.

I'm one of those nauseating tourists who always has a camera in tow waiting to capture a perfect picture of something, which, in my case, would be a close-up shot of a UFO, complete with an alien leaning on an outside railing. The camera was sitting in the right seat and I surprised myself that I didn't reach for it.

I was tempted to get a picture before I dealt with the emergency, but this fire was burning too fiercely. It needed quick action. If that failed there was no other emergency recourse to be carried out with the engine or airplane. It would have meant taking to the parachute that every bomber pilot carries. Peoria was now only about eighteen miles away and I received a clearance for an emergency landing.

The problem with the engine turned out to be a fractured automatic mixture control (AMC) diaphragm located in the carburetor. It's a surprisingly large disc, several inches in diameter, and I could readily understand that if it completely fractured and collapsed, copious amounts of fuel would flood in and out of the carburetor. The airplane had sat in the desert for so long that the rubber was brittle and it gave way. The tank and engine booster pumps forced far more fuel into the engine than it could possibly burn, so it flooded out all over the engine and caught fire.

Dump the Teacher

One of Kenting's A-26s was ready for the next season and my job was to manage the duo of the newly minted Ontario Tracker and Kenting's A-26. I would also be teaching Bill Nash the techniques of Fire Bombing. It was appropriate for the airplanes to be based in Sudbury, the centre of the sulfur-saturated scenery. Prior to going to the base, Kenting had a verbal understanding with the forestry department that I would be teaching the use of One Strike. That concept necessitated that both airplanes would receive immediate dispatch to every reported fire. Sudbury is a heavy fire region so we weren't short of targets.

I was completely floored by what happened as soon as the action began. Contrary to Kenting's understanding, the Tracker was sent to a fire all by itself even though the Kenting A-26 was supposed to be dispatched along with it. If time meant anything to the department while fighting a fire, I could not imagine why a single airplane would go back and forth to a fire, when the addition of second aircraft would shift the attack so much more in our favour.

In my naiveté, I didn't realize that the politics of destroying the Tracker experiment had already begun. Teaching these people about One Strike and good fire fighting tactics with the use of long-term retardant was purely incidental to the skullduggery of the politics immediately in progress.

I called Frank Smith, the General Manager of Kenting in Toronto, and asked why our A-26 wasn't being dispatched along with the Tracker. He didn't know but said he would ask Bill Foster to honour our agreement and dispatch our A-26 along with the Tracker. "Yes, sorry for the oversight," dispatch tactfully said, "we will do that." An order came through to Sudbury to dispatch them both. For a time, I had control over the use of both airplanes and we achieved spectacular results. Orders must have come from headquarters to dispatch us early and, surprisingly, that, in fact happened. We were sent early to a succession of fires. Each time we achieved One Strike I marked our success on the base blackboard. The department base personnel were there to observe. We were sent early enough to achieve One Strike on thirty-five fires in a row and we could have kept up that kind of success all summer. I suppose that those kinds of results must have been extremely embarrassing to people in the field because early dispatch soon changed. Surprisingly, we suddenly found that a Beaver aircraft would be at every fire dropping water long ahead of our arrival. The most powerful tactic in shooting down the Tracker fleet was underway: dispatching the land-based bombers late to out-of-control fires.

Tom Cook was head of the Ontario Department of Lands and Forests aviation department headquartered in Sault St. Marie. Tom was about five foot eight and always wore an immaculately tailored suit. He flew a PBY during the war and was credited with sinking a German submarine. He pretended to support Bill Foster fully, but from his conversations it wasn't hard to see that he suspected the Tracker would infringe on his float-plane empire. He had retired from flying and was head of the float-plane operation. On a visit to his operation in Sault St. Marie, I was dumfounded at the size and décor of his office. It was the size of my entire house and was tastefully decorated with expensive furniture and a conservatory full of plants.

Nothing was too good for the department and Tom bragged about his lavish spending habits. He and Bill Foster were the individuals negotiating the contracts with Kenting. One day the two of them had informed Frank Smith the manager of Kenting and me in an outdoor, street-briefing that Kenting would be managing the entire Ontario Tracker fleet. Frank and I often discussed the project. Frank was of the opinion that Bill and Tom's word could be accepted at face value. I was firmly of the opinion that Kenting would never get to operate the fleet. The Department of Lands and Forests were picking our brains so they could operate the fleet themselves as part of their whole operation. It wasn't hard to know of their motives when the Tracker came out of their hangar painted in their colours, and any time we discussed contract, it was done while we went for a walk out on the street. There were never any witnesses to the conversations between the top people in the Ontario Department of Lands and Forests and Kenting.

My suspicions were correct. The Department of Land's and Forests had no use for the A-26 after that first season and would not use it the following summer. Business and politics are a ruthless game. People are used in the machinations of political and business ambitions. Kenting's usefulness was over, so they were dumped. The Ontario Department of Lands and Forests went on to operate the fleet of Trackers on their own as part of their large-scale aviation department.

I named the effort to introduce land-based bombers into Ontario as the *Charge of the Light Brigade,* after the ill-fated British cavalry charge led by Lord Cardigan against Russian forces during the Battle of Balaclava on the 25 of October, 1854 in the Crimean War. The problem with the charge was that the Russians had cannons on three sides of the attack and were able to decimate the English, as Alfred Lord Tennyson memorialized in his famous poem *The Charge of the Light Brigade.* One of the lines described the enemy as having "cannons all around." There certainly were attacks from all directions toward the land-based bomber experiment in lake country Ontario. Everyone in the field was against it and fired all their cannons to sabotage the experiment. They were remarkably successful in proving to themselves that dropping water was superior to using long-term retardant.

Reproduced courtesy of Jean Barbaud

Douglas A-26 - Invader

Chapter Fourteen
Flying the A-26 for Kenting

The only time you have too much fuel is when you're on fire. Anonymous

Dispatch by the Fire Boss

I grew up, so to speak, with the development of the One Strike concept of using the Fire Bomber. I was used to flying on initial attack actions in British Columbia and for the CDF in California. It's what I had taught in Ontario for the use of the Tracker. The results spoke for themselves: the only way to use the airplane was as an initial attack weapon. The amount of retardant a couple of A-26s could deliver to the early-discovered fire size gave the bomber a huge advantage for early containment. I could not imagine anyone doing anything else with the airplane.

To my complete astonishment, at the first pre-season briefing in Alberta, I was to discover that Fire Bombers were not used in initial attack. Part of our pre-season briefing came from the fire crews who would be on the ground performing their initial attack. They informed the bomber crews that we would be called if they thought they needed us. I couldn't believe what I was hearing. Why weren't the airplanes used in initial attack when they had such a huge advantage at a small fire?

That first season in Alberta should have taught me the humbling lesson that I was only an airplane driver and the politics of Fire Bombing was none of my business. In truth, I never did learn to keep my mouth shut and just fly the airplane. I spoke up a few times and thought afterward I could be in trouble with the higher-ups. But it didn't happen. It seemed so wrong not to use such an effective weapon to its best advantage. Perhaps it has all changed since then.

The problem with holding the bombers back from a small fire and letting the few men on the ground have their go at controlling it is that the people on the ground do not like to admit having failed at their job.

The logic of "escalation of effort" is that all fires are small at discovery so an appropriate sized crew should be able to extinguish it (small fire = small effort). It makes sense and is a workable concept in a low hazard. But it becomes irresponsible folly in high or extreme hazards when the fire can become explosive all too quickly. As the fire increases in size, additional helicopters with more men are sent to assist (larger fire = more effort). Usually, the fire crew on the ground will hold out to the very last second before admitting they can't handle their mission and need more help. They wait until the situation gets out of control and only then will they call in the bombers as a last resort.

At this point the fire to retardant ratio has completely reversed. Whereas the bomber carried more than enough retardant for containment in an early dispatch to a small fire, the bomber now arrives with a drop in the bucket to a fire that is a raging inferno. The bomber has become virtually useless for containment. The airplane then becomes relegated to a support action. Unless there is property to protect, in most cases the bomber should have stayed home.

Contrary to all of the initial attack actions I flew on in British Columbia and California to a small fire, every fire I went to in Alberta was big and growing fast. It was so hard to fly my bomber and keep my mouth shut when it was so painfully obvious that an initial attack a few hours earlier could have achieved brilliant results.

Fort McMurray

Fort McMurray, situated 270 miles northeast of Edmonton, has a humid continental climate which supports a vast area of valuable forest. The city sits in a river valley at the confluence of the Athabasca and Clearwater rivers, which flow north into Great Slave Lake and then via the McKenzie river to the Arctic Ocean. Fort McMurray is Canada's gold rush city, except that the current rush isn't about the metal, it's about black gold: oil. The city is at the south end of one of the world's greatest oil reserves, the Alberta Oil Sands, containing 171.8 billion barrels of oil, a reserve second only to the reserves in Saudi Arabia that contain 264.2 billion barrels. To exploit such riches, the city continues to grow at a phenomenal rate, with several mega oil-separating plants in operation, more under construction and many more in the planning stages. Alberta is currently exporting 1.51 million barrels per day to the United States, which makes up fifteen percent of US crude oil imports, a figure which will ramp up considerably over the years as the new cracking plants come into production.

Alberta now factors significantly into US plans for "safe" oil. Oil sands production is sent south by pipeline to US refineries, a safe mode of delivery independent of vulnerable oil tankers or the volatile politics of the Middle East. It appears that a time will come in the not-too-distant future when US oil supplies will be entirely secure within the continent of North America.

Fort McMurray is a great place for bomber crews as the city is one big boom town with plenty of action. Pay scales for the plant workers reflect the shortage of skilled labour and the boom-town mentality has women driving the huge Caterpillar trucks used to haul the oil-soaked sand earning far more than we did flying our bombers.

The city is also famous for another reason: the area has giant, vampire mosquitoes that easily suck a pint of blood at one sitting. Swatting a filled one on your arm or leg may have your friends calling an ambulance, thinking you've sprung a leak somewhere and are bleeding to death.

This particular season was off to a great start. In fact, we were called to action in late April because an early fire season was well under way. Early fire seasons are common to the flat lands and deciduous forests of central and eastern Canada and the United States. Dry leaves and dry grass are the fire carriers before the new green grass acts as an inhibitor and virtually eliminates this hazard. Lightning had started a multitude of new fires in this district, and were fanned by high, gusty winds. We started flying on the first of May and the action was continuous for the next two weeks. The weather continued hot and dry and it looked like we had the makings of a great summer.

Among the base personnel was an observant, young farmer who now worked for the forest service. Roy* was about five foot ten, had light brown hair and wore the dull khaki uniform of the forest service. His sparkling blue eyes let it be known that he was in charge and all would work as it should. In charge of mixing and loading the retardant, Roy's farmer resourcefulness was apparent in the way he ran the base. Little escaped his attention. In the midst of all the intense flying, Roy uttered a highly unusual statement:

"We're going to have a very wet season. There won't be many fires."

"Come on, Roy," I said, "fires are going all over the place and we've been flying steadily for the past two weeks. It's hot and dry and it doesn't look like we're going to stop."

"Linc, the beavers know that it's going to be a very wet season."

Up until now, Roy had shown down-to-earth common sense, great organizing ability, and what I thought was a purely scientific mind. But this was a new twist I hadn't suspected.

"Okay, Roy, sounds like a lot of BS to me but what magic fairy has told the beavers that it's going to be a wet season? What do the beavers know that we don't know and how do you know the beavers know it?"

"The beavers are cutting their big logs well up on the sides of streams and rivers," he said "and before too long, the water level will be up where they can float these big logs with no problem because that's where the water level will be."

"Ya gotta prove that one to me, Roy, sounds like a crock to me."

In the next few days we got a short break and Roy drove the pilots out to a stream that wasn't too far away.

"See where the beavers are cutting the big trees? It's almost at the top of this creek bank."

What Roy said was true. They were cutting well up from the existing level of the water. The creek would have had to rise six to eight feet to be near their logs.

Somehow the universe had given the beavers a message about the weather that was denied to mere mortal meteorologists. In the next few days it began to rain and rain and rain, not in small showers, but in tropical downpours. So far the beavers were off to a great start.

These unending avalanches of water eliminated our fires as fast as a hurricane taking off roof tops. We were starting to believe what Roy had said about the weather so we resigned ourselves to spending a wet season in Fort McMurray. We could handle that. It was an excellent town for the forest service to forget about us.

It seemed, however, that the forest service had different ideas. They couldn't let the boys have a good time while they're sitting around doing nothing. They deemed it best that we should be miserable in a miserable place while sitting around doing nothing, so we were sent off to High Level.

Exile to High Level

High Level is Alberta's most northern base. If it's going to be wet, this is where it likes to do it. High Level, a million mile trip up Highway 35 from Edmonton, is a sawmill town of a few thousand people totally surrounded by forest. As isolated as it is, the town, nevertheless, has bragging rights: it boasts of having the largest woodpile in the world. I can readily testify to that claim since I have seen many a woodpile in my bomber base travels. But this sawmill and woodpile were special. As pine and spruce trees are milled into lumber they release the intoxicating scent of pine, which drifted over the entire community. As pleasant as that was, it was small comfort to our misery. In reality, most of the province was wet that summer. The various forest districts didn't share their airplanes and when some districts had a bit of flying, they didn't invite us to come and help. We heard about all the flying time that the other districts were getting and all we did was sit, bitch and detest being there.

Dispatches occurred occasionally. One in particular gave me some pucker-factor for awhile.

The Tire is on Fire

One day shortly after takeoff as I was heading northbound to a fire, I get a call on the radio:

"Tanker Two Eight, I have received a report from Canadian Airlines Flight____. There are large pieces of rubber on the runway. You were the last aircraft to take off. Would you check your landing gear for possibly having shed some rubber?"

"Roger, High Level."

I was at altitude and cruise speed so I had to slow down to lower the gear. After I slowed the airplane down and dropped the gear, I checked the left tire. It was on fire. *Well goodness me — look at that —* yes indeed, it was on fire.

"High Level, this is Tanker Two Eight."

"Go ahead, Tanker Two Eight."

"Yeah, it was me who shed the rubber off my left tire and I've got a fire. I'll let you know what I'll be doing."

"Roger, Two Eight. Will you be coming back here and do you want us to standby with fire equipment?"

"I'll let you know in a minute, High Level."

Approximately the lower quarter of the tire was burning. It was hard to believe that shedding some rubber from a tire generated enough heat to light the tire on fire. I was watching it burn, disbelieving and spellbound. Yup, it was burning all right. *Now what? What do I do with a tire that's on fire? I couldn't hit it with the fire extinguisher and there was no way I was putting it back inside the nacelle.* The aircraft manual dealt with all kinds of gear emergencies, but whoever wrote it forgot to mention flaming tires. As I was watching, I saw that the slipstream was slowly blowing the fire out. After a few minutes, the fire seemed to be completely out. Hooray for that.

I'm guessing the tire caught fire as it shed rubber and once it was retracted inside the nacelle, it was in a warm, sheltered environment, perfect for the fire to spread. I had no idea as to whether or not the fire had done any damage inside the nacelle. All I could do was to keep an eye on it.

As the rubber tore away, it sheared off the left hydraulic line to the brakes and the hydraulic fluid was all pumped overboard. I now realized I could no longer raise or lower the gear. But that was not a problem with the gear, as it was down and would stay down. The more ominous problem was not having any brakes, nor would I be able to steer the airplane. The A-26 doesn't have nose wheel steering; it's steered with differential brake. The pilot applies the brake for whichever way he wants to turn. The left brake causes the nose wheel to castor left and the turn results. The same is true for the right turn. Brakes are absolutely essential for controlling an A-26 on the ground. I realized that after I landed, I would be in an airplane which was totally out of my control, but with one remaining option – I could stop using the emergency air brake.

I took consolation from the appearance of the tire. It looked solid and intact and should be able to take a landing. The fire was out, so, with the gear hanging, I would have to go somewhere to do an emergency landing. With only one runway at High Level and trees on both sides of the runway, it was not a good place to land without brakes, so I elected to go to the Municipal Airport in Edmonton. There are several runways with plenty of clear space and at least I wouldn't be running into any trees. While the airport was fairly large, it was nevertheless in the middle of the city, and it was fenced all around. At the time I didn't think I might run into something else.

"High Level, this is Two Eight."

"Roger, Tanker Two Eight, will you be needing assistance?"

"Negative, High Level. The fire is out and I'll be going to Edmonton."

"Roger Tanker Two Eight, let us know if we can be of further assistance."

It was a slow, shaky trip because the hanging gear, along with their doors, set up considerable turbulence around the airplane and severely restricted my speed. I told Edmonton Tower of my problem and they ordered emergency fire trucks to stand by. By slowing the airplane down to as slow as it could fly with full flap down, I was committed to landing. There would be no go-around. As I touched down I immediately cut the fuel and ignition to the engines. However, the A-26 is such a clean airplane that it has very little drag as it rolls along in the level attitude. While the propellers had stopped turning, I didn't feel that I was slowing even slightly. I think the airplane would have continued to coast off the end of a twenty-five-thousand foot runway.

It was time for the emergency brake. I turned the predominantly displayed red handle to fire its shot of compressed air to the brakes. The air blast locked the right wheel just long enough to turn the airplane about forty-five degrees to the right. The rest of the air rushed out of the broken left brake line and I realized I had no further applications of brake.

I was now charging across the infields between the runways. Out front, I saw light airplanes that were in the process of running-up flee helter-skelter out of my way. I became the falcon scattering the flock of pigeons. On my left side, not more than about forty feet away, a fire truck with a fluid reservoir the size of an oil tanker was keeping pace and pointing a cyclopean fire nozzle right at me. From my perspective that mondo nozzle looked to be about six feet wide and about six inches away from my face. All I could see were the separator vanes inside that could spread a torrent of high-pressure foam across the entire airport. If he had turned that thing on, my injured little airplane would have been buried in foam and I would have been blasted right out of the cockpit. Maybe that was the idea: If I wasn't in the cockpit, I couldn't catch fire. He was both a comforting and intimidating sight.

Getting turned to one side and running through the green infields was the best thing that could have happened. The grass and softer surface was slowing me down, but I was still travelling far too quickly to remain on the airport property. After I had charged across all the taxiways and crossed over all the runways, I could see that I would leave familiar territory to blitz on to Kingsway Avenue to mingle with the cars, buses, trucks and terrified pedestrians. I was out of options. I had nothing left to do but quietly sit and watch. With about a hundred yards to go, the airplane began to bog down quickly in the soft soil and grass at the outer edge of the airport. The airplane, and I as a most anxious observer, finally stopped about ten feet away from the fence separating me from the street.

I am extremely thankful that the pilot of the 737 called in to report the rubber on the runway. If I had continued flying with the wheels up, the left tire would have become a ball of fire and ignited the fuel tank. In a short time the wing spar would have melted and the wing would have folded. I can only speculate that I would have seen the fire on time. As it was, the worst that came of it was having to change a tire, repairing the hydraulic line, and going back to High Level.

Finishing off the Summer

There was little memorable about the isolation of this northern base, but there were a few events which made interesting diversions.

The High Level airport often had a disturbing little surprise. The mountains were about seventy miles away so it was hard to figure out what caused an almost daily wind shear on the final approach for landing heading southbound. A wind from one direction with very little vertical separation to a wind from a different direction is a wind shear. An aircraft suddenly flying from one zone into the other can experience heavy turbulence or large changes of airspeed depending on the direction and strength of the winds. In this case there was an instant airspeed loss of anywhere from twenty to thirty knots somewhere below about 300 feet.

The tower operator always warned that it was there, but it was hard to discipline myself to approach the runway with about twenty to twenty-five knots extra airspeed, since at the higher speed, it was easy to get the impression that I'd run off the end of the runway. Nevertheless, when the tower called it, there was no mistake: the wind shear was there and the approach had to be faster. I was always anxious on my high-speed final until the predicted airspeed loss would hit. Then I could relax and go in for a normal airspeed approach and landing.

Perhaps as some kind of apology for the isolation of this base, the forest service decided that the bomber crew should see the natural gas flare pit, about thirty miles to the north. A helicopter was chartered and we were treated with a ride to a wilderness spectacular. At some distant time, natural gas began seeping out of the ground at this site. The gas had ignited, most likely by lightning, and has been burning for hundreds, or perhaps thousands of years. The pit was about forty to fifty feet wide and about ten feet deep. A distinct hissing sound could be heard as the gas erupted into flames about fifteen to twenty feet high. From more than one hundred feet away we felt intense, radiant heat, but I had the impression that the fire may have been considerably bigger and hotter at some time in the past – there were no trees for at least two hundred feet all around the pit. The oil industry is aware that as the gas leaves the gas-bearing strata below the pressure drops, so the fire may have slowly diminished over time. I wondered if the province had any plans to tap this gas, or to build a road into this unique natural fire for all to see.

Swallows are to the North what geckoes are to the tropics: they eat copious amounts of flies and mosquitoes. The dark blue and orange-red barn swallows had built a lineup of tan-coloured clay nests under an eve of the maintenance building and the time came for the new hatch to leave their comfortable home to fend for themselves. Amazingly, the young chicks hopped out of the nests and flew away on their very first attempt to begin their adult life of ridding the skies of our blood-sucking pests. However, five of the many dozens of chicks didn't get their wings on the first try. We found them sitting on the ground, apparently not knowing what to do next.

Time for flying lessons. After a quick discussion, we pilots and engineers took all five over to a soft lawn and tossed each one in turn high up above our heads. Each little swallow made a short flight before landing in the soft grass. We tossed them again and again. With every toss, we were delighted to observe that each one flew a little farther before they landed softly. Our flying lessons were getting results. Four of the chicks continued flying after the fifth launch. They flapped their wings as they had done every other trip but on flight five they just skimmed the grass before they climbed away to our cheers to join their anxious parents circling and chirping overhead.

One didn't make it. The little guy seemed weak and exhausted before his lessons even began. Hoping he would pull through, we set him on a branch of a low tree and tried to push flies down his throat, just as we had seen the parents do. Sadly, it didn't work. Like all wild species, it's survival of the fittest. Swallows are one of my most admired birds for their streamlined beauty and incredible flying maneuverability. We felt a great pride that we saved the brave little four.

We stayed in touch with Roy at Fort McMurray to see if Roy's observation about the beavers was correct. We really didn't have to. It rained so much that every creek and stream in the country was overflowing. Roy's beavers were right. They could have floated those logs anywhere they wanted in the entire province.

Singing in the rain with the beavers, day after day. High Level, Alberta

It's not hard to know how the weather will be in the high or middle latitudes of Canada. The jet stream determines everything. It's literally a weather wall. Sunny skies and dry, warm weather lie on the south side of the jet stream and rainy weather passes to the north. That summer, the daily weather map told us the story: the jet stream was far to the south of Hay River. We were on the wrong side. All of the cold, moist air from the Pacific, the Gulf of Alaska and the Arctic passed over us and one weather system after another dumped exuberant, endless amounts of rain. The unfortunate thing (depending on which side you're on) is that the jet stream system can remain stable for months at a time. As much as we tried to coax it mentally to swing north and bring us some warm, dry air, it didn't twitch an inch. It remained stable for the entire summer. We were happy to finish the season and leave the rain behind.

Chapter Fifteen
Flying the A-26 for Conair

It's always a good idea to keep the pointy end going forward as much as possible. Anonymous

I started flying the A-26 for Conair Aviation in April of 1974 and flew it until I transferred to the DC-6 in 1978. Conair had a beautiful fleet of A-26s. They were very well maintained and I didn't have any mechanical problems with the ones that I flew during my four years in the seat.

Conair Aviation A-26. Photo by author

During the summer of 1975 I was based in Williams Lake, a small city of about 10,000 sitting on a two thousand-foot-high plateau. The area to the north and east is covered in the heavy pine forest typical of British Columbia. The area was open to the west but the real surprise

came the day I drove down into the deep Fraser Canyon a few miles away. Up top, the
day was cool, but on entering the canyon, the temperature had climbed by several degrees and I was in the grassland and sage brush of a desert. Farther to the west, are the broad, grassy plains of the Chilcotin.

The story goes that during the War, five Wildcats, unable to find their aircraft carrier in Pacific Ocean off the coast of British Columbia, turned and headed east.

They broke out into clear skies and the grassy, smooth plains of the Chilcotin. All five landed safely. Parked in a neat row for a number of years, they were finally removed. Like the many stories of lost and missing aircraft between the chain of airports leading to Alaska, this story is persistent among the local people. I have tried to check its validity but have found nothing.

This was a different kind of summer, not for the amount of flying we did, which wasn't much, but for the chance to play golf. Williams Lake has an excellent golf course and when we were on Blue Standby – twenty minutes to be in the airplane from a call – we were allowed to carry a forest service radio on our golf carts so we could respond to a dispatch.

Conveniently, the golf course and the airplane were exactly twenty minutes apart, so we spent the summer golfing almost every day.

I decided to get serious and learn golf, so I took eighteen lessons over the course of the summer. George and I were based together that summer and he was an inveterate, low-handicap golfer.

Most days during the week, we would hit 300 practice balls and then play eighteen holes. I discovered that golf is deceptively the toughest sport there is. It takes an infinite amount of practice to teach the body to make a consistent swing. I had always put my heart into every physical sport I did, whether skiing, tennis, squash, racquet ball or high board diving. Putting more physical effort into these sports generally resulted in better performance. Golf wasn't like that. Pushing harder in golf didn't help a bit; I just went further out of control. The slightest nuance of muscle difference somewhere in the body affected the swing and would send the ball off on a trip of its own. Golf is very much a mind-over-body sport. The mind has to put every body muscle into quiet disciplined behaviour to get decent results. Once the body is under masterful control, more effort can be gradually added for longer shots. And, miracle of all miracles, it's actually possible to call the shot. I had finally acquired enough control over that exasperating, diabolical, little white ball to call a straight shot, a slice or a hook. I also discovered something else: if you want to stay sharp, you practice constantly. It's like instrument flying – do it or lose it. Now I know how Tiger Woods does it.

We'll Switch the Run

One windy day that summer, I was on a fire action not too far from our base with a couple of other A-26s. A slowly-expanding fire was about halfway down a fairly steep river gulley that dropped about 1,500 feet to the valley below. The fire had spread to several acres in size, but it looked like our sustained delivery could quickly sew it up. The first action was across the head and that was where Birddog directed me to drop my first load. I made the run by entering the gulley some distance from the fire and flying down it to the head. It was a straightforward run, extremely bumpy, but not too unusual. The Birddog then requested more runs across the head.

When my turn came for the next drop, my instructions were to drop down the right flank of the fire at about a forty-five degree angle to the head. A previous load had gone down the other flank at about the same angle because the gulley was too narrow to come straight down the fire side.

The wind was blowing across the top of the densely-treed plateau. The smoke was fairly diffuse, so whether or not the wind up top was tumbling down into the valley was hard to tell. My previous run down the gulley was bumpy but there were no indications of a downdraft. The bomber ahead of me had flown over the ridge with no problem. It looked like a normal run downhill but there was caution on my mind. It didn't look good. I wasn't taking any chances so I started over the ridge with extra airspeed and a little extra altitude. It wouldn't be a long run downhill so I would be dropping at only a slightly higher airspeed than normal. That type of compensation was not unusual. The retardant could take a fair bit of over-speed on the drop and not be broken up too badly. Each airplane has its ideal drop speed, but the retardant is cohesive enough that drops can be made at higher speeds yet still make an effective pattern on the ground.

As soon as I dropped over the ridge, a flush of ghastly fear came over me. Terror would be a better word. *This can't be happening*, I thought. I broke instantly into a white-hot sweat. I felt I was falling instead of flying. I immediately lost airspeed and it seemed as if nothing was holding the airplane up. It wasn't stalled, the engines were running, but they didn't seem to be taking me anywhere. All I could feel was the grip of a mighty hand pushing me straight down. I didn't know how close I was to the stall and it was best that I didn't. A-26s don't take well to slow airspeeds with full flap down. For an instant, I saw myself in the TBM in California when it fell out of the sky. *My God, it's going to happen.* I had fallen at least a thousand feet, and there was only a little way to go to hit bottom and I was rapidly heading for it. I knew I would die in a matter of a few seconds. What had gone wrong? I had made allowances for a downdraft. Why this huge drop? I had nowhere to go.

Then just as suddenly, the fall stopped a few hundred feet from the river at the bottom. I began flying again. Birddog called:

"Tanker Two Two, that didn't look too good. Were you having trouble? You didn't drop your load."

As soon as I realized I was back in control again, I collected my thoughts and responded to Birddog.

"I got a big downdraft, Birddog. I don't think we can do these runs going over the ridge."

A-26 drop, courtesy British Columbia Forest Service.

"Roger, Two Two, we'll switch to laying loads parallel to the ridge and work our way down the flanks. Are you okay to do your drop on the right flank just below the retardant?"

Other than his brief question, Birddog didn't seem to be aware of my life-threatening plunge. While I was still recovering, his voice was quite matter-of-fact as he simply carried on with new instructions for the attack.

"Roger, Birddog."

We continued working that fire. The turbulence tossed me all over the sky, but we worked for the rest of the day with no more problems. The afternoon was so typical of many other fire situations. I entered a severe downdraft when it was least expected, and there were no more for the rest of the day when they were expected.

I analyzed my run over and over again. What could have I or should have I done differently? The same answer came up as when I almost bought the farm in the TBM. Nothing. I had always been right in planning all my runs, with plenty of safe margin. Now it strikes me that I only got away with the TBM and this event because my addition of airspeed and altitude was just on the edge of being right enough to avoid catastrophe. An undeniable and ominous realization had just landed on me.

In spite of all your planning and bombing run allowances, the unexpected will happen to you, Linc. Just hope one won't come along that will get you.

I don't know if all pilots experience the same emotion when they "come close." I could have crashed and died, but I didn't. Someone was looking after me, and I believed then, as I do now, my time hadn't arrived yet. I had done so many run-of-the-mill drops and now I had been given another terrifying surprise. When the flush of fear was over and I was back in control again, I thought about why I made no effort at self-preservation whatsoever. I didn't add power and I didn't drop the load. Now I thought about my first brush with death in the TBM when the same thing happened, and the fact that Tracker pilots went in with power on and a full load. In my out-of-control plunge toward the trees, there was only one thought and it was overpowering: *You are going to die.* I sat transfixed with immobilizing fear, waiting for it to happen.

In spite of those moments or terror, I was ready to go again right after the event. There was no fear about flying the airplane or about what I was doing. I didn't forget; I made a mental note that I must never let up on my planning, but then it was back in the saddle. The close call was soon put out of mind.

How many times had a pilot been in just such a situation and recovery didn't happen? Unfortunately, pilots were getting killed with distressing, almost predictable frequency. Not a single year passed without fatalities in Canada and the USA. I don't recall if it was that year, or a year earlier that Conair lost six of its workforce of sixty pilots in one season. Like pilots in war, we would deliberate these crashes in detail over our ritual beers in the evening, toast our fallen comrades and fly again the next day as if these fatalities had never happened. Does this cavalier attitude make people careless and contribute to the fatalities, or was our sometimes frivolous behaviour a coping mechanism?

Abbotsford Tanker Base

Abbotsford was a highly desirable base that normally gave considerable flying. The beautiful, pristine city, the berry capital of Canada, sits in the shadow of Mount Baker, only a short distance away in the USA. This magnificent peak, named after Captain Cook's First Mate, remains snow-capped winter and summer, a brilliant sight all year round. Occasionally, puffs of steam rise from its hot springs. At 13,000 feet, it's a perfect navigational landmark. Abbotsford is Conair's home base and we did our spring training in this picturesque setting. A large airport was intentionally located in Abbotsford as an alternate to Vancouver International because it normally remains open during the dismal weather and fogs that afflict Vancouver during the winter.

The summer climate is warm and pleasant. During our training we spent as much time over Bellingham in Washington as we did over Abbotsford. We did our instrument holding patterns to the accommodating voice identification at the Bellingham WA, VOR (Very high frequency omni-range). VOR facilities used to be identified with Morse code dots and dashes but that was changed to voice identifiers when the use of Morse code was discontinued. As an example, Seattle VOR would have the voice identifier "Seattle VOR." Someone with a sense of humour changed the Bellingham VOR voice identification to "Bellingham VOR...eh! for the benefit of us frequent Canadian users.

Abbotsford was a great base for dispatches both east and west and on many occasions, when USFS resources were taxed to the limit, south into the state of Washington. I liked the approach that the USFS had with our bombers. Their Lead Plane would simply inform our Birddog of where they wanted the action and we would be left to work on our own as we normally did. The USFS was pleased with our results and used us when the occasion warranted.

Holding down that bomber base provided an opportunity to fly in the Abbotsford Air Show, at one time the third largest air show in the world. We weren't part of the show by design. On each of the two seasons I spent in Abbotsford, we were conveniently dispatched during the show. An accommodation was made with the Air Show Committee for just such a contingency. If a dispatch for us arose, the next act was put on hold for the few minutes and we then became the Fire Bombing dispatch narration. We were also slotted into the show when we came back. It was fun, but we didn't get the adulation from the ladies that they showered on the Blue Angels.

Chapter Sixteen
The S2-F Tracker – The Duplicitous Toy

Gravity is not just a good idea. It's the law and it's not subject to repeal.
Anonymous

The Tracker as a Fire Bomber has always held a special interest for me. Being invited to consult on the very first conversion meant I wanted to see what the future held for this airplane. The initial conversion was for the flatlands of Ontario. Would other companies follow the example and create conversions for mountain bombing?

My sessions with Bob Fowler on the S2-F in 1971 determined that the pitch-up characteristics of the Tracker were not significant or severe enough to prevent it from being a safe Fire Bomber. A proper amount of stick forward at the time of pitch-up would keep the g-forces within limits through a satisfactory range of bombing speeds.

The visibility forward and to the sides is perfectly adequate for the job and the airplane can descend steep slopes without picking up excessive speeds. The excellent drop patterns from the tank further verified the airplane's suitability as a Fire Bomber. In terms of visibility, handling around fires and the ability to get into and out of tight places, it was more than the equivalent of the A-26.

With these satisfactory assessments, the Ontario Department of Lands and Forests decided to go ahead with its land-based bomber experiment. Seven airplanes would be converted by Field Aviation, beginning in 1972. Because I was involved with the project from the very beginning, I was highly interested in whether or not they used them in initial attack, and how well float-plane pilots and others who had no bombing experience would handle the airplane.

Other operators began the conversion of the S2-F to a Fire Bomber and the California Department of Forestry acquired their first S2-Fs from Hemet Valley Flying service in 1973. At the same time, the Province of Saskachewan's Northern Air Operations began receiving their six Trackers, which had been converted to bombers by Field Aviation. The flood of S2-F conversions had begun. In 1978, Conair Aviation launched its Firecat, to be later updated in 1988 to the Turbo Firecat. To date, Conair has built thirty-five conversions, with fourteen Firecats and six Turbocats going to the Securité Civilé in France. The Marsh Aviation Turbo-Tracker S2-F3 came along in 1991, with the company building twenty-three conversions for the CDF to date. Over seventy S2-Fs having been converted to Fire Bombers, both piston- and turbine-powered. This is a remarkable testimony as to the desirability of the Tracker as a Fire Bomber.

Conair Trackers at Smithers Tanker Base. Photo by author

**S2-F Tracker. Photo courtesy
British Columbia Forest Service**

Every pilot who has tossed the airplane around a little bit knows it's light on the controls and has spectacular turn performance. It has excellent maneuverability both loaded and empty. Simply put, it's a pleasure to fly. Consequently, the fabulous handling throughout its performance range can lull the pilot into thinking nothing can harm him in this airplane. It flies so lightly and nimbly, a pilot feels he can do no wrong with this delightful plaything. I had seen Conair's President, Barry Marsden, do a demonstration with the airplane at Abbotsford. It was truly impressive to see how tightly the airplane would turn. The entire show at Abbotsford was done in the infield inside the boundary of the runways. As I watched, my thoughts were with Barry.

Surely Barry must have known that he was like a man walking on a tight rope in a howling wind during the entire time of his performance. I sincerely hoped he could pull it off without mishap. There wasn't a slip; the performance was flawless and spectacular. But that was Barry Marsden: he has exceptional flying ability.

The first Tracker conversions to Fire Bombers had a stick shaker and a warning horn to warn of an impending stall. It activated approximately ten percent above the stall. In normal flight or in light or no g-turns, it gave sufficient warning for the pilot to take corrective action. Pulling a little g in a steeply banked turn (sixty degrees or more), however, will demonstrate to the pilot that the stick shaker, the warning horn and the stall may all happen together – or there may be no alert from the stick shaker or warning horn at all. The system was unreliable at over sixty degrees of bank. And once in a stall, everything happens so quickly there is no time to take recovery measures.

To fly the Tracker safely, the pilot must experience the airplane's vicious and unforgiving side. The airplane goes from perfectly controlled flight to an airplane completely out of control virtually instantly. There is no period of compromise between the two.

Unfortunately, compromise is not in the Tracker's nature. She is your willing and accommodating mistress as long as you play by her rules, but for want of one knot of airspeed, she will turn her terrible suicidal wrath upon you as if you had betrayed some sacred trust. She will destroy herself and you as punishment for your indiscretion. The airplane reveals its dark side, a place where you never want to go. There is no recovery at low altitude.

Pilots who have bombed with the airplane in level terrain (Ontario and Saskatchewan) may not have known about this lack of stall warning above sixty degrees of bank and have never, in reality, had the need to go there. The pilot could confidently fly at comfortable speeds knowing he would not be encountering the hazards of mountain flying. It was highly unlikely that unpredictable or unforeseen turbulence or downdrafts would ever overtake his airplane.

To drop on level ground, pilots are not required to do very tight turns or pull g to line up for a target. The airplane can be flown very leisurely to the final run for bombing. There is no requirement for "extreme" handling. This is borne out by the fact there have been no Tracker crashes while Fire Bombing in these two provinces.

I was watching the progress of the Ontario experiment when a Tracker crashed in California in 1978. To that point, I wasn't concerned that there may either be something wrong with the way the pilots handled the airplane or the California winds had anything to do with it. There were two crashes in 1978, one in California and one of Conair's Trackers in British Columbia. The one in British Columbia really caught my attention after seeing the photo of it pointing straight down a few feet from the ground.

No amount of verbal description can adequately disclose what the photograph actually shows: a demoralizing portrait of the airplane and pilot caught in a final act.

Tracker demonstration gone tragically wrong.
Photo courtesy Dick Jordan

I know the Tracker's reaction when it stalls and there weren't too many places to look for the cause of this crash. The pilot was doing a demonstration with the airplane at Castlegar in British Columbia. He was doing an extremely tight air show, keeping the airplane within the perimeter of the airport, just in front of the crowd.

I could only imagine that the pilot at Castlegar was trying to imitate Barry. My own assessment of the situation was that at some point one of two things happened: he either pulled too much g and high speed stalled, or he was still in a safe flying range close to the stall when he crossed his own slipstream. That turbulent air of the slipstream could be enough to detach the airflow over his own wing. Either way, the airplane's unforgiving nature became all too apparent.

It was immediately after the Tracker began its duties in the mountains of Canada, the USA, most notably California, and France, that its uncompromising nature began taking pilots to their death.

Beginning in 1976, Trackers were crashing in the mountain environment where steep, g pulling turns were required in the performance of their duties. Pilots were either not aware of the flight regimen they should avoid or they relied on stall warnings that would never trigger.

In mountain flying, another deadly factor is ever present. Mountain winds have their own dark side to throw at the airplane. Slowing down to do a power-off stall is not the only configuration that will induce an airplane to stall. The smooth air flowing over the wing could be forced to break away if the airplane is close to stalling and is suddenly jolted by turbulence. Other factors like a sudden downdraft, sudden updraft, or the onset of an instant tailwind can knock off enough airspeed in any attitude to take the airplane from a safe configuration to one where the airplane has completely stalled.

A Deadly Mistress

The first of Conair's Tracker crashes occurred in 1978 to the pilot doing a demonstration at Castlegar airport in British Columbia. The other two fatal Conair crashes involved a stall/spin into the ground during a fire action. Accident report comments include:

"Aircraft struck the ground while spinning to the right."

"The aircraft encountered a stall/spin situation – the throttles were not closed and the retardant load was not jettisoned."

What is apparent in both of these cases is the sudden onset of the stall and spin and the inability of the pilot to take any corrective action, not even cutting the throttles or dumping the load. I could easily understand this immobility after my own close calls.

The first California Department of Forestry crash occurred in 1976 with the latest one occurring in 2001. The series of crashes is summarized by Walt Darran, himself a Tracker pilot. His comments are his personal opinion only and are not the official report of the California Department of Forestry (CAL FIRE):

Seven of the twelve fatal S2A accidents (eight of the thirteen pilot fatalities,) were attributed to LOCIF (Loss of Control in Flight.) Three others appear to be a subset, CFIT (Controlled Flight into Terrain) but were possibly LOCIF. From discussions and debriefs, it appears that there have been numerous other occurrences of LOCIF that have resulted in satisfactory recoveries.

From 1985 to 2005, France has lost four piston-powered Conair Firecats and three Conair Turbo Firecats. Since the Trackers first came into service as Fire Bombers there have been twenty-two crashes, almost a third of the total conversions. With the exception of the mid-air collision between two Trackers in California in 2001 and one non-fatal crash of a Tracker in France, the accidents are attributed to LOCIF or CFIT.

Loss of Control in Flight in these instances means the airplane is no longer under the control of the pilot. In the British Columbia crashes, the Birddog witnesses were able to state the airplanes crashed while in a spin. The cause of loss of control can be attributed to either the pilot's mishandling of the airplane resulting in a stall, or the airplane was victim to a sudden downdraft, rotor wind or tailwind that caused the stall. Walt Darran's statement is consistent with my own experience in California. I only need to recall my forty-five knot loss of airspeed over the city of Ukiah due to a sudden onset of a tailwind. I can only speculate about the result had the same thing happened in a Tracker. I had many other instances of large airspeed losses; some I had allowed for, while others came as a complete surprise.

Controlled flight into terrain remains a mystery since there are no "Black Boxes" (Flight Data Recorders) to record pilot conversations or what the airplane was doing prior to the crash. My experience over Ukiah and the downdraft plunge down a mountain where I thought death was certain could both be labeled as controlled flight. I was neither stalled or in a spin in any of my "close calls," but I was being carried into the ground by factors beyond my control. I was in control of the airplane but not in control of where I was going. I was lucky to escape, but if a crash had occurred in either of these events, it would have been seen as "Controlled Flight into Terrain."

What appears to be glaringly obvious about the crashes is the possibility of the pilots being unaware of the airplane's vicious stall characteristics. If they did, it seems inconceivable they would have allowed themselves to even get close to this situation – unless they didn't know how close they were and unless they were oblivious to the unpredictable winds that mountain flying would throw at them.

Death on a Sunny Afternoon

On a July afternoon in the high mountains of Eastern British Columbia, four pilots flying the S2-F were flying support action on fairly quiet fire on the side of a steep mountain. It was a fire strictly worked by men on the ground as it was impossible to get equipment such as bulldozers up the steep slope. The men had the fire largely contained with a hand line but had requested a line of retardant around the fire as insurance. A line of retardant had already been laid across the head and down both sides of the flanks almost to the base. Two bombers had just dropped and three Trackers were in the air waiting for their instructions from the Birddog. The first airplane in line got his directions.

"Number Six One, I want you to string drop down the left side. Join up with what's there and that should take your load down to the base."

"Join up and go down the left side – got that, Birddog."

"That's roger, Six One. You're cleared for your run."

The fire was in a ravine surrounded by high ridges on three sides. Once the load was dropped, escape was easy: just fly straight out into a wide open valley. Getting at the fire was quite a bit more difficult. It could be approached in two ways, either to fly straight over the ridge aiming at a point that should put the airplane on the correct line to get down the flank, or to enter the bowl from the valley side and do a steep turn within the bowl to line up on final.

Aiming to go straight over the top of the ridge was difficult, presenting a number of problems. A couple of landmarks must be selected that would put the airplane on the correct line. One landmark must be at the top of the ridge and another landmark is needed on the far side of the valley. Two points for lineup are necessary to assure the pilot that his heading is just right to accurately pass over that small path far down below where he's going to put the load. After going over the ridge, the nose must be pushed down at a very steep angle to bring the target in sight and to make the descent rapid enough to get down to drop altitude. Also, long, steep descents usually result in too high a speed for comfortable, safe dropping. With the base of the fire being a few thousand feet down the slope, this approach was too much of a challenge. No one was using it.

There was also an invisible prevailing westerly wind spilling over the top.

Entering the bowl from the valley side was the better of the two options. The target could be seen during the entire turn in the bowl and a steep turn to final could be made at an altitude much closer to the fire. This method was commonly used as it provided a short final run to the target which keeps speeds in the safe dropping range.

Six One went out into the valley, turned around, and entered the bowl on one side. He flew a perfectly executed steep turn, made a few quick adjustments to straighten up for his line on final and dropped the load.

"Bull's eye, Six One, return and stay. I'll let you know if I need you back."

"Roger, Bird dog."

"Did you see that drop, Six Four?"

Six Four was flown by Dave Raymond,* a seven year veteran on Fire Bombers. He knew his airplane and was an aggressive, accurate pilot. He could put his airplane anywhere the Birddog requested it and put the load precisely on target. It was his turn next. He had already been on this fire and had put a load higher up on the flank on an earlier run, and he was familiar with the area.

"Roger, Bird dog."

"I want your string drop down the opposite flank. You should get down to the base the same as Six One."

"String drop on the opposite side to Six One – okay, I've got it."

"Roger, Six Four, you're cleared for your run."

His acceptance of the instructions would be the last words of Dave Raymond's life. The Birddog and Tanker Six Eight flying above, waiting for his turn, witnessed the scene. Dave went into the bowl making a steep turn exactly the same as Six One. Just before it was time to turn to final the airplane rolled over, pointed straight down and crashed into the trees. It went up in a billowing cloud of fire.

What could possibly have gone wrong? There were several loads put on the fire with Dave and other pilots following the same kind of approaches. Why had this one sent Dave to his death?

Dave was an accomplished pilot who flew the airplane to its limits. Dave loved the airplane, often stating that it was a dream of an airplane to fly. While in the steep turn, all was going well, close to stall speed, but no problem since he was making the turn slow enough that he wouldn't exceed drop limit speeds on the way down. It was common practice. But something went wrong. The airplane had stalled, rolled over on its back and pointed straight down at the trees a few hundred feet below. From that position to the time he entered the trees was only a matter of a few seconds.

Dave had no time to react. There was no transmission saying "I'm in trouble." There was no time to drop the load or even pull back on the throttle. He went in at close to full power. When he rolled over there was an instant hot flush of terror that paralyzed his entire body. He was in a position where he knew he faced certain death. Something happens with the mind when it's suddenly confronted with death. It goes into hyper-speed, changing normal time to ultra-slow motion. Soldiers in Vietnam who have suddenly fallen victim to an ambush describe seeing the bullets fired at them going by in slow motion. They are seen as big as baseballs slowly passing by.

Dave's mind was put into ultra-slow motion. Death was an infinity away. His entire life was presented as a panorama before him. He had time to reflect on the successes and failures of his life. He had time to wish time itself into reverse. He should have the right to do what Superman did: spin time backwards to prevent the death of Lois Lane. He would only back up time for thirty seconds and make a miniscule adjustment to his airspeed. It could not be denied him. It was such a small request. But Dave was not Superman.

The mighty Ponderosa Pine and Douglas Fir trees rose up to begin touching his airplane; gently at first. An upper branch silently brushed the windshield like a feather duster flitting across a precious vase. The windshield deflected more branches like a hiker gently pushing aside leafy branches leaning across a trail. Then a heavy branch several inches in diameter caved in the windshield centre post and the windshield turned opaque as it disintegrated into a million fragments that floated slowly toward his face.

The bigger branches now tore into the wings, spilling the volatile fuel to be ignited by the roaring engines. All was silent; he heard nothing of this destruction. He opened his mouth to scream but nothing came out. His throat was shut. Halfway down the canopy, he had but one more second to live. A ball of fire enveloped his airplane in the endless time it took for the ground to rise up and crush his cockpit. Then it was over. He could not reverse time and go back to start his run again, this time with more speed. He could not beg the Fates for a second chance. Events conspired against him and time dispassionately ticked off the irreversible.

Watching from above, the pilots of Birddog and Tanker Six Eight gasped in disbelief at the scene. They could only wonder why a man with Dave's ability should go in when everyone else making the same runs were perfectly fine.

Dave fell in the line of duty the same as a fighter pilot who falls to the enemy. There was no time to mourn. Now, there was a new fire to contend with, and new plans were made for another bomber attack. Six Eight was directed to drop the first load on Dave's cremation pyre. The pilots would send their condolences to Dave's family, toast Dave with pints of ale that night and fly again the next day.

The forest service and the company would dissect the accident to discover the cause. What went wrong? There was no obvious answer. Everyone else made the same run, no one had a problem. Why Dave?

Every bomber pilot knows that the cause can be laid down to a few events. There was a westerly wind spilling over the ridge above the fire. Did Dave not make enough allowance for the possibility of a downdraft or a sudden tailwind? Either one, if a bit too strong for the speed he was carrying, could cause a stall. Was his steep turn too tight? Dave flew to the edges. Was he cutting it a bit too fine? Did Dave make an error in judgment, or was he just unlucky? Perhaps Dave did carry extra airspeed on entering his run. If he did, it wasn't enough. None of the pilots that flew on that fire during the day had called airspeed losses.

We cannot see the wind that may take us to an untimely death. We must outguess it and stay on the safe side. We must do things that are sometimes counterintuitive: fly at higher than normal airspeeds just prior to a descent where we should be picking up speed. We must presume the worst and get it right every time. We can only get it wrong once.

The accident report will say: "The aircraft struck the ground while spinning."

The Stall Margin Indicator (SMI)

It was no secret that the military stall warning indicator system on the S2-F did not provide the pilot with the proper indications at high angles of bank. A logical question then became: what does a pilot need in terms of instruments or other aids that will prevent him from ever going there?

To make the flight regime of the airplane better known to the pilot, Conair in co-operation with the Rosemount Instruments developed their Stall Margin Indicator in 1990 (SMI). A wind vane on the side of the fuselage of the Tracker provided the input for four configuration parameters of the airplane. A computer measured how close the airplane was to the stall by integrating the conditions of the landing gear, the manifold pressure (power), the flap and the angle of attack. A needle on the SMI instrument showed the pilot how close he was to the stall. The pilot now had a visual indication of how close he was to the condition that must never be allowed to happen. There was no guesswork about the safety of any flight configuration.

Even though I wasn't flying the Tracker, Conair gave me the opportunity to have a demonstration flight in the Conair Turbo Tracker. As we went through the entire flight regime which we would encounter while bombing, we could see what each change in our flight configuration did to the SMI indicator. Whether turning, dropping flap, changing the power, or pulling a bit of g, the pilot immediately knew if he was getting too close to the forbidden range. It was a magic translation of what went on outside to the inside, where the pilot could see it. One thought immediately came to mind: all Fire Bombing aircraft should have this feature. This instrument took its indications from the invisible air and turned them into a picture. As long as there were no surprises on a bombing run, the instrument became the Fairy that sprinkled green pixie dust to show safe air.

I spoke to a number of Tracker pilots who had flown with and without the SMI and the comments were not an unexpected revelation:

"Before I got it, I never knew how close I came."

"Flying without the SMI is like flying with your eyes shut."

"It's my primary instrument; I don't need an airspeed indicator."

"Now I can see my "happy zone", I can throw away the airspeed indicator."

"There's just no comparison between before and after. Now I know what the airplane is doing."

The system was immediately installed on all of Conair's Trackers. They have had no fatalities since. In 1990 it was also sold to California and France.

Tracker crashes have occurred since 1990, but every pilot who Fire Bombs in the

mountains will have found out the same thing that I did: we fly in the boundary layer where capricious mountain winds will throw the unexpected at us at any time.

The SMI shows the pilot flying condition in the present; it does not tell him what he will encounter where's he's going. Mountain air currents are full of hazards, and unfortunately the hazards are invisible. There is one more and final protection for the Tracker pilot: become a defensive driver and assume the worst before every run.

I have known some extremely capable pilots who met their death in a Tracker. They were my friends. These men were professionals, exceptional pilots who never should have died in this occupation. Yet they did. These individuals never had the advantage of the SMI. Like the pilots I spoke to with Conair, they may have flown at low airspeeds close to the edge of disaster, feeling comfortable and confident, not knowing just how close they were. They were indeed flying with their eyes shut. One day these friends flew one knot too slow.

The dangers will never go away, but an SMI/AOA indicator at least gives the pilot indispensable knowledge that immeasurably contributes to his safety.

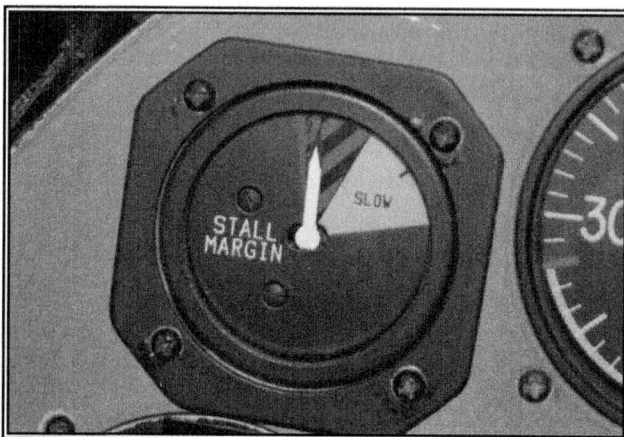

Stall Margin Indicator (SMI) Instrument.

The New Tracker

In the early 1970s, the California Department of Forestry (CAL FIRE) acquired a fleet of piston-powered S-2F1 Trackers from the US Navy. Given the CAL FIRE initial attack philosophy, they proved to be very successful as Fire Bombers. The state's twenty-three plane fleet has been upgraded to the better-performing, turbine-powered S-2F3 models during the nineties. Grumman literally rebuilt the airplane to accommodate new, longer nuclear torpedoes. In this process they added three feet to the wingspan, thirteen inches to the length of the fuselage and five feet to the horizontal stabilizer. Recognizing the need for a better-performing, safer airplane, more vortex generators and a "stall strip" radically changed the airplane's stall characteristics. Grumman Aircraft and Marsh Aviation must be given full credit for nothing short of a marvelous transformation from what had been a killer. The "new" Tracker was no longer the scorpion waiting to sting the pilot fatally who was slightly errant with his airspeed. It gives adequate stall warning of an impending, gentle, controllable stall.

The Marsh Aviation conversion is powered by the Garrett TPE-331 GR turbine engine developing 3520 shaft horsepower for takeoff and 3300 continuous shaft horsepower. The S-2F3 carries 1200 US gallons of retardant dispensed from a constant-flow, variable-quantity dropping system. This type of retardant tank with its continuous flow greatly reduces the "barn door" effect which led to some less-than-pleasant pitch-up characteristics on some aircraft.

Jim Barnes evaluated the airplane's suitability as a Fire Bomber and gave it top marks. Bob Forbes, who is currently flying one, couldn't have been more lavish in his praise about the safety of the airplane. I was interested in hearing a before (S-2F1) and after (S-2F3) comparison from Jim, Bob and Joe Satrapa. They were unanimous in their comments about the S-2F3 being an entirely different airplane than the S-2F1. The 3 has none of the nasty stall characteristics of the 1, and the airplane's SMI instrument is strategically placed for heads-up viewing on the forward glare panel. As the pilots enthusiastically indicated: "Just keep the needle in the yellow range and the entire run can be done without having to look down at the airspeed indicator."

With an excellent power-to-weight ratio, the airplane is a joy to fly. Its superb maneuverability, power and speed understandably make it a safe and delightful place for the career bomber pilot. It's an ideal initial attack airplane.

CAL FIRE Tracker S-2F3. Photo courtesy Bob Fish

**S-2F3 panel with the SMI located next to the centre post.
Photo courtesy Lee Monson**

Reproduced courtesy of Jean Barbaud

Douglas — DC-6B

Chapter Seventeen
Deciding to fly the DC-6

If you push the stick forward, the houses get bigger.
If you pull the stick back, they get smaller;
unless you pull the stick all the way back,
then they get bigger again. Anonymous

In the early seventies, Conair started acquiring the DC-6B. I had watched them in action for several years and I was anxious to get into the giant of the fleet as I had never flown a four-engined airplane. The DC-6 was a beautiful bird. Pilots were speaking highly of it and I wanted to upgrade. The pay was better and the Six got plenty of work. However, I was of two minds about getting checked out in the airplane: I wanted to fly it, but for my safety, only as a captain. In that seat I knew I could look after myself and the First Officer (F/O) as well. Unfortunately, I was going to have to be somebody else's F/O until I could get a bird of my own. And I didn't like the idea one whit.

The Captain - F/O Relationship

At the time of my training on the DC-6, the captain of the airplane was designated as God. He had the final word about everything that happened with the airplane. Presumably he had the experience and wisdom to fly safely and would react properly in any emergency. We were being trained as future captains, but we had to do our penance as F/Os until we had the experience and the proficiency on the airplane to move to the left seat. The captain's word was law, and as F/Os, we were given the impression that we were on board merely to obey the captain's commands. A particular point was continually emphasized and it stuck out in my mind as extremely counterproductive given the hazards of this business: "The captain is the final authority." It sounded like we were there to move some controls when the captain asked for it. Otherwise we could be redundant.

It was not too surprising that this approach to our training gave license to some of the captains to fly "one man" airplanes. Did we have any input if the captain was doing something stupid? If we were low on the glide path and about to fly into the ground on an ILS approach to limits, could we say something? Could we react if the captain didn't? I thought about these things because I knew of situations where the captain of the aircraft took the flight to disaster while the rest of the crew, who knew better, just looked on.

The entire world saw the events that led up to the horrific crash at Tenerife in the Canary Islands. In dense fog, the captain of a KLM 747 started into the takeoff roll without having received a takeoff clearance. The crew knew they had not received a clearance for takeoff but were too intimidated to question or tell the captain. The crash into a United Airlines 747 that was back-tracking up the same runway resulted in the deaths of over five hundred people. Nevertheless, in the 1970s it was still standard practice for the captain to be exalted as infallible, and it made for a very uncomfortable situation for many crews. Certain captains took their position quite literally: only they could navigate the perilous skies safely. The rest of the crew were mere appendages, fit only to obey their commands.

If a captain was crew-minded and would admit that he was prone to making a mistake like anyone else, he would ask for and expect crew input if he was doing something which might endanger the flight. In later years, as I approached retirement, I realized that having a proficient F/O had many advantages. If I lost one of my marbles, a sharp F/O would pick it up and put it back in the bag. That type of crew co-operation has now become standard airline procedure. All crews on airlines today monitor each other so as not to get into untenable situations.

I didn't realize it was not Conair practice, but I was under the impression that my captain would be evaluating me and writing reports on my proficiency and hence would determine my future with the company. I also thought that only the very best pilots showing the greatest talent would graduate as captains, that these were talented men put in the left seat because of superior ability. My impression of the supposedly superior ability in the left seat left me as a very intimidated F/O not knowing what to expect in the near future.

When I began the course, I didn't know who would be my first captain. I had far more Fire Bombing experience than many of the people who were DC-6 captains since I had already flown Fire Bombers for many years in the Stearman, the TBM, the Tracker, the B-26 and the F7F.

Whether a pilot lives or dies in this business is up to his own professionalism. If he figures every run right, he gets to fly another day. Two airplanes had fallen out from under me, and each time, I was only a few seconds away from certain death in the trees. Each of those incidents taught me more about how hazardous this business was and I didn't want some incompetent to set me up for number three.

If I was going to be killed I would do it to myself; I didn't want to be someone else's mistake. I had seen many men die. It's an unpleasant reality of Fire Bombing. Conair had lost a DC-6, with the death of three people. Furthermore, I made it my business to know the cause of every crash. None of the crashes should ever have happened, but they did. I was determined it wasn't going to happen to me. I always believed that if the airplane didn't let me down with an engine failure in the wrong place, I would live and survive the occupation that I loved so much. I had learned what it took to plan and safely execute the final run, put the load on target and escape the area. I had studied this business with a microscope and my third "how to" book on flying Fire Bombers, *Air Attack on Forest Fires,* was teaching others what I had learned. Twelve years of painstaking work went into it and every sentence detailed the essentials for survival.

I had seen too much pilot error to enter the right seat lightly and didn't like the idea of sitting in the right seat with some of the company's pilots. I had already heard stories about captains that were flying "one man" airplanes and I knew a few of them were not great examples of Fire Bombing proficiency. Like it or not, the airplane was theirs; the F/O was there to reach controls that the captain couldn't reach himself. When the captain made a command, the F/O obeyed his orders (no input wanted, just do as the captain says). If he decided that he wanted to fly straight into the mountain ahead at dry power and asked for dry power, dry power it was. It was the captain's order and the F/O didn't question the captain's orders.

When I did finally decide to fly the DC-6, I came up with a strategy for survival. I would do my job as the F/O and keep an eye on what the captain was doing as well. I could sit it out until I became a captain, but if my captain was leading me to disaster, I would not sit around and wait for it to happen. As it turned out, my first captain shattered my every thought about what this supremely qualified man should be. As if to justify my intense trepidation about wanting to fly the Six, I was soon to get the biggest shock of my flying life.

The DC-6B

Originally intended as a military transport aircraft, the DC-6 was a product of the Douglas Aircraft Company. Other models were quickly developed to compete with the Lockheed Constellation in the long-range transport market and 700 were built from 1946 to 1958. The model used by Conair was the Airliner version, the DC-6B. As an airliner, it carried about 100 passengers and had a gross takeoff weight of 107,000 pounds.

The DC-6 carried 2500 imperial gallons of retardant (about 3000 US gallons) that was dropped from twelve doors from an external tank. It carried an effective load for One Strike and could lay substantial lines on a support action, so it made the airplane a desirable item for any forest service. The company had contracts in British Columbia, Alberta, the Yukon and the Northwest Territories. When the occasion arose, we also got invited to assist in actions in Montana, Washington and Oregon.

I joined the six-week course and put my heart into it. The course covered all of the airplane systems like the electrics, the high pressure hydraulic system and what it operated, the fire detection system, engine feathering system and all about the wonderful Pratt and Whitney engine, the eighteen cylinder CB-16 R2800. The engine normally cranked out 2000 horsepower, but it could be flogged with water injection to give an extra 400 horsepower for takeoff. It was almost like hanging on a fifth engine for takeoff.

Taking most of a tabletop, a formidable-looking device awaited an explanation. The instructor pointed his little stick at it and proudly proclaimed that this was a Stromberg Injection carburetor. It was a revelation for me. I had never seen such a massive, complicated device designed with only purpose: to squirt fuel into the engine. That carburetor was not only bigger than the one in my car, it was bigger than the entire engine. The instructor delighted in taking endless hours to point out the various channels, shown in cut away sections, for fuel and air and how it efficiently regulated itself to feed fuel to the engine at all altitudes. And there was one other important point: if it was cold and damp outside, we could send hot air into it to keep nice and comfortable and from icing up. *Good*, I thought, *that's all I needed to know: two controls worked that threatening pile of iron.* Hot air kept the ice out and the mixture control lever either allowed fuel into the carburetor or shut it off. Otherwise, there was nothing I could do (other than shut the fuel off) if it decided to run amok as it did on the A-26. Nevertheless, I had to memorize a head-full of otherwise useless information about that menacing looking apparition in order to pass the aircraft systems exam.

Fuel Management

We also learned about fuel management. On large, long-range airplanes all the fuel is carried in the wings and for very good reason. The idea is to put as sizable a portion as possible of the total weight of the aircraft in the wings. It's very simple logic: the lift comes from the wings, not the fuselage, so it makes sense to put the load where the lift is. A simple thought experiment (Einstein did thought experiments all the time) to illustrate the point is to imagine two bricks at the centre of a wooden yardstick. Lift the tips of the stick and see the outlandish bend of the stick as you get the bricks off the ground. If the stick will take it, bounce it a few times to simulate air turbulence. That's how the wings of the airplane behave if there is excessive weight in the fuselage and very little out where the lift is coming from.

Now take each brick and place it midway between the centre of the stick and the tips. (If you want a wooden yard stick and the bricks, they have them at Home Depot.) Lift the tips and see the enormous difference in how much the stick bends. The load is now being supported at the location of the lift and the wings can carry the load with a minimum amount of flexing. Therefore, the practice on any heavy airplane is to carry as much of the fuel load as possible out toward the wing tips. The fuel is used from the tanks closest to the fuselage first and then outboard in sequence. The fuel furthest out is used last.

To make sure that empty wings aren't lifting the maximum load of retardant centred in the fuselage, each airplane mandates a minimum weight of fuel to be carried. When fuel is burned down to this minimum, the airplane must land and be refueled. Good fuel management assures that it's carried in the most outboard tanks, critical to the safe operation of the airplane.

In the normal regime of Fire Bombing, we would carry about five to six hours of fuel in the DC-6. This kept wing loading well within the safe operating range. If we flew for an hour or two and the action was over, re-fueling restored peace of mind to the pilots and kept the airplane happy.

The Gentle Lady

All Fire Bombing activities were to be conducted in daylight and in good weather, so as a result of this one-dimensional approach, the DC-6s that we would be flying as Fire Bombers had been given a thorough going-over to remove all of the systems on the airplane we wouldn't need in a VFR (Visual Flight Rules) operation. It was contradictory to say the least: we had to be instrument-qualified on the airplane to be able to ferry ourselves to virtually anywhere. We didn't do bombing trips on instruments, but we certainly travelled around the country in all types of weather. The main reason for the gutting of the airplane was to make it lighter. Unfortunately, all of the systems that would make long-distance flight more comfortable were ruthlessly removed, including the insulation, the anti-icing system, the cabin pressurization, the autopilot and, incomprehensibly, the toilet.

On some trips I encountered a fair bit of ice, so wing and tail anti-icing would have made life a lot less anxious. On one particular trip across the country, the pitot head supports looked like they had accumulated about five inches of ice. Of course, this same amount of ice accumulated to the leading surfaces all over the airplane. It was loaded. We knew we were gathering a fair bit of ice when we heard the loud staccato of ice chunks hitting the fuselage as they were being flung off the propellers. All that the great bird did was slowly lose airspeed. Once in warmer temperatures, it all came off in great sheets. That marvelous airplane could carry enough ice to build the Swedish Ice Hotel.

It was as beautiful an airplane to fly as it was to look at. The airplane was a mature lady, one to take to an expensive club to dine and then dance closely embraced. She had a long, graceful fuselage with nothing protruding to trouble the eye or cause unnecessary drag. She had the distinctive Douglas vertical stabilizer also easily recognized on the DC-4 and DC-7. Of all the bombers that I flew, the sound of the DC-6 had its own special character. The eighteen exhausts were collected into one collector ring and exhausted out of a single pipe. It produced a deep, throaty rumble that was unmistakably a DC-6. I never tired of it.

DC-6 — The gentle lady. Photo by author

The airplane is completely predictable — she serves her crew faithfully through her entire flight regime. She springs no surprises and if she is brought close to the stall, she begins to shake gently as if she is waking the pilot from a random daydream. If the pilot persists in his folly, she will make her gestures ever more emphatic telling the pilot that he must restore the airplane to normal flight. All the while she is incredibly forgiving. She waits for his response and will reciprocate immediately to the pilot's corrective input. She was built to fly her crew and her passengers safely and performed her duty flawlessly over the years.

I would have liked the controls to be a bit lighter, but she was designed with the input of the latest aeronautical design criteria at the time. The airplane could be turned in a remarkably small radius, quite a surprise for an airplane of this size. The Six didn't have the power for the great rates of climb now possible with the newer turbine aircraft, but was a steady partner that you could place wherever you wanted around a fire. Donald Douglas would have been surprised at what we did with the airplane.

Russian Roulette for the Hourly Pay

A great deal of our pay came from flying hours. We got a base pay and an hourly flying pay, but since the flying pay made up most of our season's earnings, we didn't like to miss a minute of it. On sustained actions, I usually kept flying and only stopped to fuel when it was absolutely necessary. There isn't a pilot flying a Fire Bomber that hasn't landed with little more than fumes left in the tanks. Burning the fuel weight down to well below minimums provides an immediate performance benefit to the pilot. As the airplane lightens, performance improves, the climb rate is better, the airplane turns tighter, it feels lighter and it's a more pleasant airplane to fly. Like some sins, it feels good. While the crew basks in the delight of a better-performing airplane, in silence, the airplane knows that her integrity has been violated once again and that one day her wing joints may catastrophically fail from metal fatigue. Metal fatigue is an insidious, creeping disease where the metal slowly weakens and microscopic cracks begin, often with no visible sign. Then one day under the final stress, it lets go. Airplane and crew will suffer the terrible punishment from breaking the rules just one time too often. I have committed this sin so many times myself: I've had a full load of retardant in the fuselage tank, and other than the engines, virtually no significant weight out in the wings. The DC-6 is a very strong airplane. I got away with it.

The Stowaway Compartment

On one side of the bay where the nose wheel is retracted, there is a box-like compartment about six feet long and about two feet wide that is separated from the nose gear bay itself by a wall. The wall is high enough (about a foot and a half) to hide a person completely. A stowaway could crawl in there and be completely hidden. The DC-6s regularly operated from Hong Kong to Sidney, Australia. A pilot who had flown with Canadian Pacific Airlines related the story that this space would be sold to a Chinese who wanted to enter Australia illegally. The person would be sneaked into the space to wait for his long ride. Tragically for the stowaway, the DC-6 would climb to about 30,000 feet and remain there for the several hours it took to make the flight. At that altitude, the temperature is a constant sixty-seven degrees Fahrenheit below zero (-55 °C) and to compound the stowaway's plight, the air is thin enough for person to die from lack of oxygen. No one would know about the person's presence in Australia. He would be dead and frozen stiff. Eventually the body would thaw out and after a few days, the smell would alert people to begin looking.

Is this story true? Very likely. FAA spokesman Ian Gregor said in 2007, that since 1947, there have been 74 known airplane stowaway attempts worldwide. Only 14 of the individuals survived.

Flight Training

When our ground school was finally finished, it was time to fly the airplane. All of the aspiring DC-6 pilots took their training in the left seat. We supposedly had the qualifications to be there one day, so that's where our Six flying began.

We had one familiarization flight where we sat in the right seat and had a brief turn at flying the airplane VFR. Several of the trainees went up for this trip, so each man's turn to gain a bit of a feel for the Six was quite short. After this trip, it would be serious training.

Learning to start the CB-16 R-2800s on the DC-6 was a three-fingered waltz. The right hand reached up to the roof where the starter switches were and the captain called for the F/O to "select three." We started number three first because the hydraulic pumps were on number two and number three engines. The thumb pressed and continuously held a safety release switch while the forefinger turned the starter on the selected engine. Once the mandatory twelve blades had gone by, the index finger tickled the primer switch. It was a thumb-and-two-fingered affair. Tickling the primer switch meant that the pilot gave it small "on" movements to squirt raw fuel into the cylinder from a fuel injection system. Once the engine started firing, the primer switch was held on steady until the engine ran at about 1000 RPM. Engaging the carburetor to start the engine was not advisable, as it poured far too much fuel into the engine for start purposes. Once the RPM had stabilized on the primer switch, the mixture was brought to full rich and the carburetor took over the fuel supply to the engine. The same procedure was repeated on each of the engines.

Running through the engine checks on run-up was not too different from what I had been used to on the A-26. Once the run-up was complete and we were ready for takeoff, the captain briefed the F/O on takeoff and emergency procedures that might occur during takeoff.

Arming for Takeoff

We can easily miss executing life-and-death items if it means total reliance on what we may think is our infallible memory. Meticulously following the check lists eliminates that problem. It's a zero tolerance item; each item is read by one crew member and carried out by the other. One of the items on a Fire Bomber's takeoff check list is the arming of the drop system. I always set up the drop to have the entire load go with one press of the drop button. On the DC-6 we could drop singles, two, four, or six at a time, or the entire load of twelve doors. If we had to drop load in the takeoff configuration because of an engine failure emergency, company check pilots suggested that we drop only enough to get down to landing weight. The idea was that there would be less of a mess to clean up on the ground and less retardant would be wasted. I ignored that suggestion since it wasn't a company regulation. We could do what we thought best.

If it looked like I wasn't going to get into the air in the latter part of a takeoff run, or I had an engine failure at the wrong time, I didn't want to complicate my actions by additionally thinking about how much load I had to get out and how much should be saved. I didn't fancy the idea of me and what was left of the airplane being part of the ground cleanup. Dropping the entire load and dealing with a much lighter airplane made it far easier to deal with an engine failure. The three remaining engines would have adequate power to climb to circuit height and go around for a landing.

It was just as important to disarm the drop system with the post-takeoff check list. Accidentally hitting the drop button at cruise speed could be disastrous. This could very well be what happened to an A-26 flying out of Calgary, Alberta heading westbound into the mountains, at altitude and at cruise airspeed. A witness who just happened to be looking at the airplane flying overhead reported he saw retardant coming out of the aircraft just as the wings came off. The pitch-up increases with speed and a drop at the A-26 cruise speed of 220 knots would have caused g-forces that far exceeded the strength of the airplane. The witness was quite sure of the sequence of events, the retardant coming out and then the wings coming off. The pilot had admitted to others that it was indeed his habit to leave the arming switch "on" at all times. Why he would chose to do that is a mystery if he was aware of the exponential climb of load-dropping g-forces with increased speed. But he was new at the business and it appeared he had not yet learned all that he needed to know.

Leaving the arming switch on during cruise flight doesn't seem like it could be anything dangerous. If the pilot doesn't press the button, all is fine. But it is such a fine line. On the DC-6, the drop button is within inches of the hand on the control wheel. And just to add an additional possibility for error, the mike button for radio transmission is directly on the opposite side of the control wheel from the drop button. More than once, pilots have dropped part of a load either before or after completing a bombing run. The pilot wanted to say something to the Birddog and hit the drop button instead of the radio transmit button. I did it myself once. All I ever needed as a reminder that arming for takeoff was a good idea was the jettisoning of my load out of a TBM over Ukiah, California. Thinking about arming for load jettison when it's absolutely needed it is too late. All systems have to be an instant "go" for possible emergencies.

Pre-Takeoff Briefing

From memory, the captain goes through the takeoff procedure and the F/O acknowledges. During training, the check pilot sits in the right seat and he calls out the procedure. The airplane is lined up on the runway and the parking brakes are set.

Captain to the F/O:

"Set thirty inches of power and check that all instruments are reading normally. Call any malfunctions."

"This will be a standard wet-power takeoff."

"I will call for dry power. You will call "water in" (right — F/O will call for engines # 3 and 4) and I will call "water in" (left — captain will call for engines #1 and 2).

Dry power on the DC-6 is fifty-three inches of manifold pressure (MP). The water injection comes in at about thirty-five inches of MP. The Captain only calls for "dry power" at this time because it's not safe to call for wet power on the engines until the water injection is actually flowing.

As the power is advanced and both the captain and the F/O call "water in," it becomes safe for the captain to call "wet power." Wet power is fifty-nine inches of MP. Water injection provides the cooling the engine needs at these high power settings. It also de-riches (cuts out) the extra amount of fuel that was used for cooling. With de-richment, a proper fuel/air ratio can be maintained at a higher MP setting. This allows pushing the throttles up the extra six inches of MP, getting 400 more horsepower out of each engine.

"You will call 'sixty knots.'" This call is made because the captain can now take his hand off the nose wheel steering and begin steering the airplane with the rudder "V1", "V2", and "positive rate of climb."

"V1" speed is usually about ninety knots and "V2"speed is about 110 knots. But both of these depend on how heavy the airplane is. V1 is the speed at which, in the event of an engine failure, the airplane can safely stop on the runway. V2 is the rotation speed for takeoff, the airplane is committed to fly. The positive rate of climb call is asking the F/O to call out that the instruments confirm that the airplane is indeed climbing. While it's not too significant a call in VFR conditions, it's a vital call if instrument conditions are entered immediately after takeoff; everybody wants to be sure the airplane is indeed going up.

"Any malfunction affecting safely prior to V1 I will reject the takeoff. After V1, we will continue the takeoff. I will call the Phase One items for you to complete."

"I will call for the emergency check list for you to review and complete."

"Any questions?"

The F/O nods approval and the throttles are advanced for takeoff.

Completing the Check-out

Check pilot instructors all attend the same Attila-the-Hun student-killer school, whose primary mission in life was to make life extremely difficult for us new trainees. During training, he's had the opportunity to size up each timid student to know when he will decide on suicide instead of finishing the check-out. The idea was to eliminate the marginal pilot who couldn't handle a heavy workload under adverse conditions. Once each flight began, there were no breaks in the pace of emergency procedures which the instructor threw at us. One knot after passing through V1, he cut an engine. We couldn't be sneaky and cut the power and stay on the runway. Once past V1 we were committed to fly. We had to deal with establishing the airplane into a climb with reduced power and everything hanging down. Once we dealt with that, he tossed a fire or hydraulic or electrical failure at us. Then there was another engine failure with a fire thrown in just to keep things interesting.

We'd have a couple of trips dealing with every conceivable emergency. Some he mercifully tossed in only one at a time. Then the instructor's barbarous, student-killer training compels him to go for the throat. There were engine failures with fires compounded with electrical, hydraulic, propeller and gear failures all at the same time. These instructor pilots never liked to see us get bored. All of these procedures were done VFR to begin with to allow us to get the feel of the airplane.

We got one more fun procedure while we could still see, a two-engine circuit and landing. An empty DC-6 on two engines has the performance of a slug crossing dry concrete. It would never stay in the air at full gross weight.

The rest of our check-out trips were all done "under the hood." It meant shields were put up that prevented us from seeing outside. With no grasp of reality left for us to cling to, the instructor was free to "emergency" every man to the breaking point. We first flew all of our instrument procedures, holds, vectored approaches, ILS approaches and emergencies on four engines. One engine was then cut and we sweated through it all again on three engines.

When we had flown the required procedures and training time, it was time for the nerve-wracking "check-ride" with an examiner. Being sent on a check-ride is like being sent on a trip through a mine field. Making the ride meant not stepping on a mine. It was a make-it or break-it, exhausting two hours. When it was over and the examiner said he was going to let you fly but only under the condition that you must never go near the edges, you kiss the man and then break into hysterical crying.

We certainly didn't have the finesse on instruments that airline pilots have, but we were good enough on instruments to please the Department of Transport and to be able to get from A to B in bad weather. It's a "tons-of-sweat" six weeks and a tortuous instrument ride with the executioner. Fifty percent of my course made it. When the endorsements were finally put on the survivor's licenses, we headed for the Aldergrove Fox and Hounds pub to celebrate our successes.

Chapter Eighteen
Duties of the F/O

Pilot "Squawk": Something loose in cockpit.
Maintenance fix: Something tightened in cockpit.
Quantas Airlines

I was now assigned my first captain. We did a Spruce Budworm spray project in Eastern Canada and I was informed that before I would go bombing, I would act as the F/O for a captain by the name of Paul Severn*. I had heard that Paul had flown F-4 Phantoms in Vietnam. To my mind, it would take a very capable pilot to fly combat missions and survive. Perhaps all my imagined fears about getting an incompetent captain were overblown.

Becoming Acquainted

Paul was about five foot seven inches tall, had light brown hair and wore a great-looking, brown leather jacket. He had worked for the company a few years, had flown as an F/O on the DC-6 and trained earlier as captain, but we had not met before. We shook hands and he began to talk about his vast experience on what seemed like a hundred different airplanes. Two that stuck in my mind were the F-100 Super Sabre and the F-4 Phantom. It seemed like he also had thousands of hours of four-engined time on a variety of big airplanes. I listened and tried to evaluate if he really had done everything he claimed, as he had the reputation for telling Texas-sized tall stories. He looked like he was in his early fifties and I asked where he might have acquired all this experience. He told me he had been in the USAF, so I supposed it was possible.

As we talked, I was beginning to detect a rather inflated ego, nothing too unusual. Otherwise, he seemed to be a perfectly rational and reasonable person. He was easy to engage in conversation and we talked about our imminent job, the Budworm Spray that we would be doing in Newfoundland.

The next day, when it was time to head east, I noticed that Paul had checked the weather and done the flight planning well before I arrived at the Abbotsford airport. He had also done the complete flight planning sheet and ordered the amount of fuel that we would be needing for the long, thirteen hour flight. I expected to be helping him with the planning but he had done it all himself. He also informed me that I would do the things he asked me to do and nothing more.

When we got into the airplane, he imperiously called out the check lists and told me which items he wanted me to do. In a matter of minutes I discovered that Paul was the exalted captain. The airplane was his, he was totally in charge and I would do only those things that he specifically ordered me to do. I was in the airplane to reach the controls that he couldn't reach for himself.

A scary thing happens when an ego is given a uniform, stripes on the shoulders and command over others. Someone who may normally be a rational person becomes consumed with his own self-importance. The airlines were full of such captains. It's hard to remain humble when the airline has entrusted this ego to take two or three hundred passengers on a trip through the perilous skies, and bring them safely to their destination. It's a task that only a superman can do.

The Budworm Project

After the long, thirteen-hour trip right across Canada, we finally arrived at Newfoundland, the home of charming, incomprehensible Irish accents and inexpensive lobster. Considering what I had seen of Paul so far, I had wondered what I would do if I, as a highly intimidated F/O, was put into danger by my captain. Over the next six weeks I would find out. The worst fears that I had about someone else being in charge of my life were about to become a terrifying reality. Once the project began, Paul no longer ordered me to do things in a rational voice – he often shouted. He also did everything himself on every trip, including unfolding and trying to read a large map of the area we were working while we were flying. It filled his side of the cockpit completely and obscured his vision. Every trip was a nightmare. Instead of spraying from the 300 feet as was required, he did it from just above the tree tops. He couldn't concentrate on the lines he was supposed to fly and went wildly astray on numerous occasions. As often as I volunteered to take on part of the work load, he wouldn't delegate or ask me to do anything. It was his airplane. I wasn't to touch or do anything he didn't command me to do. Aside from doing crazy things that endangered our lives, he did poorly on the project.

In the time that we flew together, I took over the controls of the airplane on seven occasions. Each time I did so, he flew into a rage. I had dared to touch his airplane. As the commander in charge, he did his screaming in the airplane but when we landed I heard quiet words I found hard to comprehend. This bellowing inquisitor suddenly became rational again. He would take me aside and tell me that he wouldn't turn me in to the company for my indiscretions, if I promised not to talk about any of the events to anyone. The clear message was that for the protection of my own career, I was to remain silent. He knew that I was right each time that I took control of the airplane, but I suppose he thought that he could use my insecurity as a new F/O and concern for my career as blackmail to keep me quiet. For the entire project, I was never allowed to fly the airplane. The whole experience came as such a shock to me that I was firmly convinced that if I survived the trip home, I would never get into a DC-6 again. The six weeks that I flew with this man took a lifetime.

Glassy Water

Our spray flights were done immediately after daybreak when the air was calm and before the sun's heat caused convention currents to prevent the spray from descending. We were flying on one of our "blocks" when from a short distance away I could see that we were approaching a very large lake. The far horizon looked like it could be about fifteen or more miles away. The air was perfectly still so the water was dead calm. The lake had not yet awakened from its night of sleep. That kind of stillness is known as glassy water. Not a single wrinkle crossed its serene face; the lake was not yet ready to greet the day.

We were at our usual low altitude of about fifty feet above trees, themselves about fifty to sixty feet high. The lakeshore rose out of the water by about thirty to forty feet, so we were somewhere around 150 feet above the water just as we crossed the shoreline. For some unfathomable reason, Paul descended after we got over the water. I would guess we dropped about half our altitude. It is one thing to be at treetop-level – at least one can see the trees. But to be at no more than seventy or eighty feet above glassy water with no close shoreline for altitude reference is insanity.

On a normal sunny day with a little breeze, ripples give the water a well-defined surface, the very thing a pilot flying a floatplane needs to make a safe landing. But glassy water reflects the sky perfectly. Flying over that spellbinding, surreal place is like skating on crystal clear, very thin ice. No one should be there. On an approach for landing, there is absolutely no way for a pilot to know where he's going to find the water. It's like trying to land on the sky. When I started bush flying, the experienced boys gave me the word and they knew what they were talking about. I had thought that flying close to a shoreline would provide a perfect reference for altitude: watch the shore line when rounding out for landing and you've got it made. It turned out it was not quite as simple as that. The shoreline puts the pilot close to the water, but he can still round out twenty feet too high, or worse, fly into the water at the wrong attitude. It's a bush pilot's nightmare.

The correct, safe procedure calls for setting up the airplane into a slight nose-up attitude, a two-hundred-foot-per-minute descent, and to hold this descent until the airplane hits the water. The hot shots don't like this idea because the landing isn't a "greaser." Pilots don't come on with a gentle touch of the keel and let the v-bottom on the floats act as their shock absorber. The airplane unceremoniously arrives with a seat-flattening thump and may even bounce out of the water. But the idea is to hold the attitude, reduce power slightly and let it arrive, big splash and all. Not pretty, but safe.

The blackness of the night sky was just giving way to a soothing deep blue. The colour was breathtaking: the air was so perfect we knew we could fly to any altitude, to infinity, to anywhere in that still, all-encompassing blueness. We flew over the water and the world changed, the infinity above us had descended to the water. The Earth had vanished. Infinite space was everywhere, the fathomless blue in all directions was our universe. We were suspended in space and time. There was no sensation of speed or any motion at all. It was eerie and formless, an all-consuming beauty. I immediately went on to the instruments. We had to stay absolutely level and couldn't descend even a few feet.

Suddenly I couldn't believe what I was seeing. Paul started a steep turn to our left. My mind was racing. *I shouldn't be here, I should have pulled up right after we left the trees, but here I am, and I can't understand why he's doing a steep turn at low level over glassy water.* As much as we appeared to have infinite space everywhere, we were in extreme danger. It was a beauty that's instantly unforgiving of a mistake. We were in a formless void without knowing how far we were above the water and the horizon was too far away to provide a useful reference. Putting the wing down in a steep turn would have our left wing clear the water by little more than a dozen feet, if that.

With no horizon, a perfectly level turn must be done on instruments, and I had already seen his proficiency in that regard. One little slip; just let the nose drop an imperceptible fraction and the left wing would hit the water. I was watching the instruments in fixed terror when I saw the needle on the vertical speed indicator take a dive for the bottom of the instrument.

We couldn't have been more than a fraction of a second from the wing digging into the hard water. At 150 knots, the immense water drag on the wing would have pulled us over into a cartwheel. The cockpit would hit next and be crushed by the impact. As the needle on the vertical speed indicator needle plunged downward, my protective consciousness instantly presented my position to me with perfect clarity:

> *You have no time to consider alternatives or to wait to see what happens, Linc. In the next infinitesimal tick of time, an irreversible chain of events will occur that will cause your death. But it is not written that it is time for you to go. I am granting you only this fleeting moment of the present to take the necessary action to assure your future.*

It was obvious that Paul didn't know about the deadly hazards of glassy water. He was looking around and was completely unaware that the airplane had taken on a sudden descent. I didn't wait for him to come to that realization. I knew it wouldn't happen. The vertical speed indicator needle had plunged to a thousand-foot-a-minute descent at the same instant that I pulled back hard on the control column. We went from absolute stillness to a sudden, nose-up 2 g climb.

There was no time to think about any other action than what I did, and it needed to be immediate. I would argue about taking control in this situation once we were at a safer altitude. Paul seemed suddenly to wake up to the deadly place we were in only after I pulled us out of it. He didn't argue about my actions, which was completely out of character to the other times I took control. Amazingly, he didn't say a word. I let go of the control column, we finished the turn at higher altitude, and headed for land.

For a few moments, I thought about the words of the Air Marshall: In flying, there is no room for carelessness, incapacity or neglect. Paul and I shared the guilt of committing all three. Paul showed complete ignorance about the hazards of glassy water. He showed carelessness and incapacity for good judgment by even starting a steep turn when he didn't know how high we were. If he was going to do a turn here, he neglected to go on to the instruments immediately. I showed ignorance and neglect for even allowing us to get into that situation.

At the end of the project, I wrote out a nineteen-page report on our relationship during the project, detailing what happened each time I took control of the airplane, and submitted it to the company. After I had made my submission, I was still very much under the impression that the captains were the exalted gods of our training and that I would either be fired for my insolence or sent back to the A-26. I told the company that I would never again fly with this man and if this demand was unacceptable to the company, I would rather be fired than have someone like him kill me. The company did something that I least expected: they took him off the DC-6 immediately and sent him back to the Tracker he had been flying. Paul later landed the Tracker wheels up, giving the company the reason they were seeking to terminate his employment.

My Fire Bombing Captains

Now I was now back in the land of big trees and the wonderful British Columbia pubs. But I did miss the friendly "Newfies" and their incomprehensible language. I was assigned my Fire Bombing captain.

Ralph Boulton was a rough diamond: his manners would make the Queen wilt at a dining table and his language would send a convent full of nuns into a flurry of prayer for his soul. I already knew Ralph by reputation. Ralph was about six feet tall with brown hair and blue eyes. He had a tough, athletic build and could match any man drink for drink at a pub. He was a solid friend and would back you up in any circumstance. A single man, his title of "Rotten Ralph" came about from his less-than-refined approach to women. Nevertheless, after learning that his unpolished manners were quite harmless, he was a very likeable man. He was a superb pilot and one of the company's best at Fire Bombing.

Nevertheless, I came to our relationship totally spooked from my Newfoundland experience. Six weeks of white-knuckle flying with Paul and the fact that I had to take over control of the airplane on so many occasions had honed my survival skills to hysterical levels. From the first minute I started to fly with Ralph, I was watching his every move and was fully prepared to take over the airplane if Ralph was bent on suicide.

The differences between the two men began to show immediately. I was assigned my duties as the F/O and allowed to carry them out. On bombing runs, Ralph asked for the airplane parameters he wanted from me and carried on with his own job of bombing. By contrast, my behaviour couldn't have been more obvious: I was "minding the store" (looking after the airplane by setting the pitch control, keeping engine temperatures in the safe range, and so on) and trying to keep track of his bombing activities at the same time. I promised myself I would do that to make sure that I caught a disastrous move in the making. On our third bombing action he commented on what I was doing. Ralph didn't mince words; he came to the point when he wanted to say something:

"You can't do your job and mine at the same time, Linc. You look after the airplane and I'll do the bombing. Do that and we'll get along just fine."

I understood what he said and accepted it only conditionally. I would have to be convinced of his mastery of the airplane and bombing procedures before I would even remotely let my guard down. With each trip it became very apparent that I could not have asked for a better teacher, or felt safer in an airplane than with Ralph. He had a no-nonsense approach to flying and was the consummate professional at his job. He knew and flew the airplane expertly. He was precise and "spot on" in Fire Bombing.

He was right: in the bombing role, the F/O is relegated to keeping his head inside the cockpit and looking after the workings of the airplane. The captain will call for the flap and the power settings he wants and the F/O makes sure that these requests are carried out promptly and accurately. The F/O is kept extremely busy through each climb, descent and bombing run. He can't be looking outside to monitor the fire situation, and do his own job at the same time; the situation is too fluid and too much is happening. Bombing is the captain's job, and it takes all of his attention. Looking after the airplane is the F/O's job, and that takes all of his attention. As much as the F/O may not like it, his head must be inside. If the captain makes a mistake and leads them into a crash, it's not likely that the F/O will spot what's happening.

I soon learned that I was with a safe and competent pilot. I did my job without fear that he would do something stupid. I completed a summer with Ralph and learned how an expert handled the DC-6 as a Fire Bomber.

Ralph shared the concern of many of us about the need for a union and was among the trusted inside group that was first on board. I looked forward to a long friendship, but the fates would deny it.

A couple of seasons later he was killed in France while checking out a French pilot on one of Conair's newly converted Fokker F-27s as a Fire Bomber. I never imagined that it could happen to Ralph, for he was so very good. But it wouldn't be the last time that a superb pilot would fall victim to this business. Fatalities were becoming a regular occurrence.

My next captain, Al Mehlhaff, was an equal delight, a man that knew what to do with an airplane and the load of retardant that it carried. We got along famously. He flew by the book, we each did our job and we had a great, stress-free season. The next year I would get a captain's seat.

Chapter Nineteen
Inevitable Change Becomes Win-Win

A superior pilot is one who uses his superior judgment to stay out of situations that might require the use of his superior skill. Anonymous

One hot August Sunday in 1978 when our bomber group crew was on standby at the Abbotsford Air Show, we got into a discussion about pay with our Forest Service Birddog Officer. He was a government employee and we, of course, worked for Conair Aviation, which contracted to the Forest Service. We had known for many years that we were grossly underpaid, but a conversation with him rubbed salt into the wounds. He related his many perks: paid flights from his isolation at a bomber base to back home to see his family on regular occasions, free telephone calls to stay in touch with family, triple-time pay to stand by on Sundays that were statutory holidays, generous pay and equally generous retirement pay. On this particular day of stand-by, he was getting paid four times as much as I was. He pointed out that he was entitled to this generous package because, after all, his job was considered a dangerous occupation. Government is exceedingly generous to itself with taxpayer money. It was distressing in the extreme to compare equally dangerous jobs and see the differences in how we were paid compared to a Government Employee. We were like starving kids watching a fat man eat. That disturbing conversation on that day was the best thing that could have happened: it triggered an irreversible chain of events that was long overdue.

Forming the Union

I enjoyed living in British Columbia and would never consider living anywhere else. I flew with the company because of the well-maintained equipment they were flying and because I could remain in the place I loved.

299

When we go to work for a company fully aware of the poor attitude that management has for the employees, those of us who care about fair treatment for ourselves and our fellow man are immediately saddled on the horns of a dilemma. I've heard the argument countless times:

"You knew what the conditions were like before you joined, so why all the griping? If you didn't like what you saw, why did you come and work here?"

I suppose it can be said that there is some validity to this argument. If you don't like what you see, go work for someone else. As happened to be the case in British Columbia, there wasn't another company that flew TBMs – there was no "someone else." If I wanted to fly a land-based bomber in British Columbia using world-beating bombing techniques, my choice was to fly for this company or not at all. Each pilot had a choice to make: take the conditions as they were, or not work there.

For many years, I searched my own soul for answers to my dilemma. I loved the flying, I wanted to stay in British Columbia, but we prostrated our human dignity each day that we allowed the company to exploit us shamelessly. How could I resolve the fact that I worked there of my own free will and yet would not leave when I suffered the humiliation of our pay and working conditions? We were being used, yet we stayed. We were like the children of many Third World countries. They have a choice to make, too: take pennies a day to work in a sweat shop or not work at all.

Skyway, the company that I worked for in the early TBM days, had changed hands and received a new name – Conair. The name was new but the management wasn't, so the same mentality was in charge: pay a pittance for a wage and hire pilots who will work for it and stay quiet. The pay was poor with scant regard given for years of service or experience. Company "yes men" rather than experienced pilots were assigned the bases that offered the most flying. Discontent was rampant among the pilots who constantly complained about the pay and working conditions. I was no different than anyone else; I stayed because I loved flying. We all liked the job and we wanted to fly in British Columbia. The company had us and they knew it.

When I rejoined the company in 1973, the pay was still poor but I accepted it. The biggest unresolved issue which preyed on my mind for so long was whether it was a betrayal of my principles to want to change what I had voluntarily accepted. The words "You knew what the conditions were like before you joined..." rang in my ears for too long.

I had reached a point of making a decision. Do real men accept the status quo and complain, do they leave or do they do something about it? I realized that if no one ever got angry enough to rise up against oppressive governments or decided to change the working conditions of the 1800s sweat shops, we would not be the progressive society we are today. In the Third World countries of unrestrained capitalism, the rich and greedy exploit the poor with no twinge of conscience. Many businessmen are no different here. Minimum wage laws, government-legislated work conditions, business competition and the power of unions are the compelling influences that force change.

In 1979, I had made my decision. I was no longer going to take the situation as it was. We had to have better working conditions and pay. Twelve years earlier I had failed to get better pay when I asked for it on my own, but now the conditions were different. There were many more pilots in the employ of the company and they were not the least bit happy. If we took our organizing steps quietly and kept our progress secret among some trusted individuals, there were enough discontented people among us to organize into a union. I would talk to people that I could trust about forming a union, or joining an existing union that would give us strength in bargaining. If we wanted a better deal, we would have to fight for it.

Tom Wilson was a trusted friend who had, in confidence, spoken to me about organizing. He shared my agony and wanted what I wanted: a better deal for everybody. I approached Tom to talk about a plan of action. In secret, we had agreed about which unions each of us would approach to see if they would accept us. We agreed that we had no power as an association on our own. We needed the power of a big union if we wanted muscle in negotiating.

We compared notes as we talked to different union representatives and decided which ones we didn't want to represent us. Every union that we visited would accept us except one, the Canadian Airline Pilots Association. A very important-looking pilot at their Vancouver office told me that they only worked with the Big Airlines. Anyone else who flew an airplane didn't exist in their books. They were not the least bit interested in taking us in, or (and I found this hard to believe) in giving us guidance when putting together our first contract. It was made quite apparent to me (importance gushed out of the four stripes on his shirt epaulettes) that we bomber pilots were not the equal of Airline Pilots. I had the impression that we had shown an appalling, disrespectful impudence in even asking for their help.

We finally found the union that was most happy to represent us: The International Union of Operating Engineers. The next and most critical step was to sign up nineteen of the company's twenty-five pilots. Tom and I agonized in a big way over that one – whom to trust that would not spill anything to the company before we signed up the required numbers.

I have never forgotten the day of the initial sign-up. Tom and I were still intimidated by the idea that the company could fire us. The union representative continued to reassure us that they couldn't do that because we were protected. We continued to ask questions. We still had doubts that we were doing the right thing. Did we have any power? After all, the company had had total control over us for so many years. Could we really change anything now? We vacillated about the moment of decision because once we signed up, the clock would start ticking. We were into serious business.

Finally, after considerable torment, Tom and I signed the first two cards and took the rest of the cards we needed with us. There was no turning back. We had to get the rest of the sign-ups, or this attempt at improving our conditions would be gone. Getting the rest of the signatures became a race for time. To be certified as a union, we first had to post a notice with the company that we had the required membership. Once we had done that, the company could not stop the process. We launched the sign-up blitz when we knew that company management was in Europe for a conference. We thought they might be out of easy reach from any informants.

Tom and I each knew of a few trustworthy individuals who would quickly come on board but they wouldn't be enough for the needed numbers. We had to gamble that we could quickly get enough people at widely-spaced bomber bases to sign up once the process got under way. Time was of the essence and we had to work fast. People volunteered their time and money to fly out to the bases for signatures. We were desperate for four more sign-ups when George Plawski assured us that he could get them. The word would quickly get out about what was going on and the company could still intimidate people and stop us. George got four out of five to sign up as his base and success was assured. In the space of four interminable days we had the necessary cards. Our certification was posted on the company hangar door on a Sunday.

But the company had already gotten the word, even in Europe. That very day, the management had urgently flown home from their conference and I watched them rush up to the office door. But the notice was there and they could do nothing. Thankfully, legislation also provided that neither Tom, nor I, nor anybody else could be fired for our organizing activities.

We never found out who informed the company of what was happening. It would be hard to imagine that it was someone who signed a card. Some people that were approached didn't sign and perhaps it was one of those who had unswerving loyalty to the company. It didn't matter. We now had the power to improve our lot.

We formed a negotiating committee of Tom, me, George, a fellow pilot by the name of John Truran and two other pilots who are now deceased. We decided to do our own negotiating.

Where were we to start? We turned to the Airline Flight Attendants. Help in formulating our first contract would come from the charming ladies of CALFA, the Canadian Airline Flight Attendants. We secured a copy of their agreement with their airline (Pacific Western Airlines) and over the course of several meetings drafted our own first agreement. It was a hefty document that included virtually every clause that every pilots union had won over many years of negotiation.

We presented this to the company and were met with a stone wall. How preposterous of us to ask for some reasonable perks, a pension plan and much better pay. It was a huge package and, in hindsight, too huge. We were asking too much for the first contract. After several meetings, we were nowhere.

We took the next step to show just how determined we were. We organized a pilots' meeting and asked for a strike vote. It received overwhelming approval. We now had real power. We could stop the company's operations and a picket line would prevent fuel delivery and other services from getting to the company. We had another ace-in-the-hole: the forest service was unionized. If we went on strike, the Birddog officers would not cross our picket line.

All we wanted was a better deal for the pilots, but we were later to discover that the company feared we were seeking the power to call the shots about running the company. We were both intransient in our positions so we finally both agreed that we should go to binding arbitration.

Both the company and the union had agreed on an arbitrator by the name of Vince Ready who was not only well known in British Columbia, but all of Canada. Vince was an extremely well-groomed, stocky man somewhere in his forties. His alert mannerism and soft voice reassured us that Vince was the perfect man for the job. He was a former labour leader and had seen the deleterious effects of strikes on the economy. He quickly and confidently informed us that an agreement suitable to both parties would be reached without the need for a strike. We were dubious; we had long experience with the company's condescending attitude toward the pilots. Vince was very well prepared for these negotiations: he understood and respected both our and the company's positions.

We had several meetings spaced at various intervals with our viewpoints narrowing somewhat, but we weren't close to an agreement. The time had come for Vince to resort to a well-known and very effective tactic. Both our negotiating committee and Conair management were literally sealed in a room in a hotel and negotiations would continue non-stop until an agreement was reached. Being in the same room didn't work: there being too much anger and mistrust from both parties. We were separated, and Vince carried the agreement back and forth between our two rooms as he coached both sides into becoming more reasonable.

This process went on and on. It seemed to take forever. Finally, at 3 A.M. we reached an agreement. Reaching this agreement settled more than just the matter of our treatment and remuneration. When we re-entered the company's room and finally shook hands, there were tears in the eyes of hard-nosed company people as well as ourselves. We ended up actually hugging each other. A new respect was born in each of us. We had no intention of wanting to run the company as they had suspected. They were free to do as they had always done — run the company. They were immensely relieved. We had won the company's respect because they understood that we were dead serious about our position for getting better pay for the work we were doing.

I was head of the negotiating committee for the first two of our two-year contracts. As pilots, we had structured our first contract and continued to do our own negotiating. In hindsight, it was a mistake. We weren't intimidated by the company since they couldn't fire us, but we were our own worst enemies. As was explained to us by the negotiators from the International Union of Operating Engineers, because we loved flying, it coloured our perspective as to how much we should earn in a highly dangerous occupation. We undervalued ourselves. City firemen and Safeway truck drivers were still earning more than we did.

It wasn't until many years later that the pilots finally decided that professional negotiators from the parent union should negotiate for them. And they got a much better deal. The pay, perks and pensions finally became adequate enough for the pilots to make Fire Bombing with Conair their lifetime flying career.

A few years after our first contract, I was completely taken aback one day when the president of the company, Barry Marsden, made an admission to me. He said that getting the pilots' union was the best thing that had happened to the company. I could hardly believe what I was hearing. He said it cut out the constant complaining about who went to what base, and how promotions to new airplanes would be awarded. It was simple: seniority decided.

But his most telling admission, and of course the one that mattered most to the company, was that they saved an enormous amount of money in training costs. The pilots were at last making this company their lifetime career. They were staying on, year after year. Previously, numerous pilots would leave the company after one season of flying. It meant a huge training expense for a lot of new hires every spring. Recurrency training was far cheaper than long courses involving ground school and full type ratings along with instrument rides.

The pilots were never a militant group intent on revenge against the company; there was no ill feeling on our part. All we wanted was to be treated as respected human beings who were being paid for what the job was worth. We knew we had power. We could strike to back up our demands, but we never did. We decided to put grievances aside during the flying months to be resolved after the flying season was over. We wanted the company to function smoothly and earn a profit.

The entire atmosphere between the company and the pilots was to take on an amazing transformation. The company got dedicated, reliable pilots who were in for the long term and responded in kind. To have a balanced view toward company-pilot relationships, the company always selected aircrew management from the ranks of the union. A solid relationship worked to make the company and the pilots prosperous. We all came out winners.

Finally, in 2003 the pilots stopped doing their own negotiating and had the union negotiators do their contract for them. Pay scales have improved considerably, but there is still a vital step to take in how the pilot gets paid. The pilot's earnings must not be conditional upon the number of hours he flies during the season. I played a dangerous game with my fuel loading on the DC-6 in order not to miss a minute of flying time. We have all done it, and some have paid the price. The pay scale must be generous enough to reflect the hazards of the occupation, and pay should be for all hours on standby or worked with no separate category for flying time.

**DC-6 in a flight to the edges. How is the target found? How does the pilot make a hit? How does he find his way out?
Photo courtesy Conair Aviation**

Chapter Twenty
The Wonderful DC-6

Pilot's "Squawk": Dead bugs on windshield.
Maintenance fix: Live bugs on order.
Quantas Airlines

The Spiralling Climb

As an F/O, I hadn't spent enough time in the airplane to have any emergencies other than man-made, practice ones. However, it was over the sixteen years I spent as captain of the airplane that some interesting events took place. Hard service near the limits of engine performance made engine failures inevitable. Other humourous and not so humourous events made life interesting. The longer I flew the airplane, the more respect I had for it; that marvelous bird always performed true to her design and always brought me home.

Barry Marsden made it a point to take new captains up in the DC-6 to reveal a rather jaw-dropping maneuver. We were using the DC-6 as a Fire Bomber and we had to know how to get the most out of the airplane. We spent our time down low, and often in tight valleys. Before showing me this amazing performance, Barry said:

"The maneuver I'm going to show you will get you out of trouble if you're ever in a tight valley in bad weather and have nowhere to go. You can do a really tight climbing turn and I'll show you how it works."

He told me to reduce speed to 125 knots, put the RPMs up to 2600 and drop fifteen degrees of flap. As soon as I did that, I was to put on full dry power and do a maximum climbing turn. I did as he said; I went into a steep turn to the left and pulled up on the control column. As I was climbing Barry said: "Pull the control column all the way back, into your stomach."

I pulled it back as far as I thought it would go, or should go, because the airplane was shaking on the edge of a stall.

"You haven't got the control column as far back as it will go," said Barry. "I mean right back, until you can't bring it back any more."

"Okay, Barry."

I hauled it back even more until the airplane was violently shaking on the edge of the stall.

"We're on the edge of the stall, Barry."

"It won't stall, Linc. Get the nose higher."

I was now witnessing the DC-6 in a tight climbing turn, on the verge of a stall, shaking like a rattlesnake's tail and, hard to believe, climbing at a ridiculous angle. He was right. It didn't stall. We climbed for awhile and then Barry told me to get the airplane back into cruise and head home. Barry had shown me a life-saving maneuver that I couldn't have imagined with that airplane, should I ever need it. As it turned out, I never did.

Crew Resource Management

In the TBM, the F7F or the B-26, the pilot handled the controls of the airplane while also assimilating the bombing scene and the Birddog's instructions. We worked the airplane and did the bombing all by ourselves. I did it for so many years that it became easy and natural.

When I transferred to the DC-6, I had a great deal of difficulty being in the F/O's seat. I was no longer in charge. Relieved of understanding the bombing plan and of doing the actual bombing, I had a secondary role: just look after the workings of the airplane.

Now, as captain, I would be flying the airplane and doing the bombing again, but didn't have to look after power settings, flap and the engine parameters anymore. I wouldn't be manipulating the controls by myself; the F/O would be doing what I asked for. It was a delegation of crew responsibility and was something that took me a while to get used to. It didn't take long, however, before I found that working in a crew environment was much more enjoyable than flying alone. When we weren't busy, we could talk about important things like the possibilities of the new Hadron Collider in Switzerland discovering how women think.

New flight safety procedures were evolving with the airlines. It was decreed that the captain was no longer God and he would be required to work with the crew as if he were merely their equal. While he did have the responsibility for the safety of the airplane, the entire crew were to be involved in the safe flying of the airplane. It's called "Crew Resource Management."

I made it very plain to every F/O that I flew with that we were not in a "one man" airplane. I wanted to hear from him when he had some input about our trip. Our duties would be shared as per the check lists, and I most certainly wanted to be told if he thought I was endangering the flight in any way. I made it understood that if he thought he needed to take some action for the safety of the flight that he should do what he thought necessary, and we would talk about it later. As it happened, such a situation never arose. I always had an excellent relationship with every pilot with whom I flew.

DC-6 with a twelve-door dropping system. Photo courtesy Conair Aviation

The Split Cylinder

The DC-6s that Conair had acquired primarily came from the airlines, and, as passenger-carrying aircraft, the engines had a pretty good life. Full power for takeoff lasted a minute or less, there was a short time at METO (Maximum Except Take Off) power to get up to climb speed and then the power was reduced for a steady climb to altitude. Once at altitude, the power was reduced again for the long cruise to destination, which could be anywhere from a few hours to twelve or more. The power was then gradually reduced for descent and, with no sudden changes, the crew had adequate time to keep all the engine parameters within limits. Our use with bombing on level ground was not too great a departure from airline use, so we could be fairly gentle with the engines.

Conversely, it was when we were bombing in the higher levels of the mountains that we introduced engine-abuse into the equation. To begin with, we were usually operating in hot mid-summer temperatures, so we would already have a built-in cooling problem. The eighteen-cylinder Pratt and Whitney R-2800 radial, air-cooled engine has two radial rows of cylinders. The back row of nine cylinders are spaced in the open areas between the front row of nine. While the front row received adequate cooling, the back row tended to get more "cooking" than the front row and ran hotter.

For takeoff, we generally could stay within the two minute limit for full power, but the climb was a lot tougher. In hot weather and unpredictable winds, it was often a real grind to get to our orbiting altitude above the fire, which could be anywhere from a couple of thousand feet to eight thousand feet or more.

We would orbit for a few minutes until we were given our run. If it was to be downhill, we would cut the power to idle and dive down the mountain. The engines were then rapidly cooling and the cylinders were shrinking.

At the end of the run, full-climb power was applied to get back up to altitude in preparation for the next run. The engines were

LINC W. ALEXANDER

unceremoniously rammed into rapid heating and the cylinders were expanding. If another dive down the mountain was requested, the hot engines would be pulled back to idle, and the engines go through the rapid cooling and shrinking again.

We would pull out of the dive and again apply power to full climb or even METO power, initiating rapid heating and cylinder expansion. This could happen several times while getting rid of a single load. The engines would be taking an unmerciful beating.

With this kind of punishment, they couldn't last long, and they didn't. This abuse, combined with the fact that many-times-overhauled cylinders were used for engine rebuilds, resulted in many engine failures, which explains why we all had more than the proportional share of engine failures compared to a single-engine airplane.

The most common failure was the split cylinder. Its symptoms were consistent and classic. The engine started to backfire and, at about the same time, the engine fire warning light and bell came on. The RPM gauge would be fluctuating and the BMEP gauge, which tells how much power the engine is delivering, would be going wild. The cylinders generally split right down the middle, between the intake and exhaust ports. This split allowed the exhaust gases to exit right onto the fire detector.

With additional air now coming into the intake manifold, the backfiring began. The split cylinder no longer contained the piston within its tight walls to have it run smoothly up and down. The piston would slap around and how severe this was depended on how wide the cylinder had split open. If it was wide split (up to an inch or more), this wild thrashing would quickly disintegrate the piston and the pieces would fall into the crankcase. Now the much-harder connecting rod and piston rings would have their way with tearing into the more tender parts of the engine

The trick that would hopefully save the engine was to feather it after no more than about two backfires. If we could be that fast, the piston might stay together and no more damage would result.

312

When it happened the F/O and I almost simultaneously called "Fire on engine number_" (whatever engine it was). And practically in the same breath, I called for "Feather engine number _." He confirmed, "Feather number_." The propeller feathers and stops. We check for a fire visually. If nothing is visible and the warning signals are out, we generally don't have to proceed with the fire emergency. From memory, I called the engine "clean-up" for the F/O to execute: "Mixture to idle cut-off." The F/O repeats each command after he carries it out, "mixture to idle cut-off. "Fuel selector off." F/O "fuel selector off." "Pull oil shut-off." F/O "oil shut-off pulled." I call "engine secured." And our little emergency is over.

It happened so often it was almost routine. We immediately recognized the symptoms and took action. These failures often happened during a climb while on a fire action, but I also had quite a few occurrences while in cruise.

With all the expanding and shrinking during the bombing runs, the cylinder finally says that it's had enough and calls it quits. If we're working a fire, our mission is over.

A landing with an engine out is supposed to be reported to the MOT (Ministry of Transport) as an incident. If I dutifully submitted a report each time I had a three-engine landing, I would have requested the same pay as the Ministries Inspectors for spending full-time filling out volumes of paper. A failure during a bombing session meant dropping the rest of the load and going home. We did not attempt to bomb on three engines.

The gentle lady, Flying the DC-6 with Conair

As the engines went through more and more overhauls and more and more used cylinders were installed, my last several years of flying the DC-6 really became a betting game as to which engine would crap out and when it would do it. If I didn't come back to the airport each week with one engine feathered, there was no excitement in the air. I once had three such failures in one week. In looking at the number of engine failures I've had compared to my flying hours, I found that I was averaging an engine shut-down for about every fifty hours of flying. This is a rather mind-boggling statistic considering that many airline pilots will go through a thirty or forty year flying career without ever having a single engine failure.

After we landed, my wounded bird would be sent off to the parking area where the engineers (Americans call them mechanics) checked for the extent of engine damage. There she would ashamedly sit with downcast eyes while waiting for the repair that would make her well again. The first thing they did was pull the magnetic oil screens to check for metal and particularly hard metal like the piston rings. If they found hard metal, it was time for an engine change. If there was no metal or only the bits of soft aluminum as is often the case, it simply meant a cylinder change.

These dedicated individuals would immediately start to work on an unservicability and, if necessary, work all during the mosquito-infested night to have us flying the next day. I lost very little flying time due to maintenance. I could not have given the engineers assigned to us higher praise for the incredible work they did. For them, it was a matter of pride to keep the airplanes flying, and they did an exemplary job.

The Potty

One of the conveniences that was much appreciated after I started flying the DC-6 was the fact that we pilots could get up and relieve ourselves when the occasion demanded. We often did long flights with the DC-6 such as taking a load of firefighting equipment to Quebec from British Columbia, a flight that took about twelve hours. Needing to do a number one, specifically having to pee, was no problem. Someone had discovered that when one of the rear windows was unlocked, it floated open with a space of about three to four inches. The venturi effect that it created was quite entertaining; one simply aimed the stream at the opening and the terrific suction did the rest. Nothing touched the aircraft or the window; the stream went out dead centre. It soon became apparent that some experimenting could be done with the strength of the suction. One could back up to about the middle of the fuselage and watch a jet straight stream go unerringly out the gap. That was all well and good for us pee'ers, but there were complaints that there was no provision for number two. The company had ripped out everything they could to make the airplane lighter for Fire Bombing.

One day I noticed that a little squat, cream-coloured, square, box-like THING appeared in the back of the airplane. I went over to inspect it. It was about two feet high, two feet square and had nicely rounded corners. It looked like it was built for comfort. It sat there and didn't move. The lid was shut but I still had the distinct feeling that this THING knew of my presence and was watching me. I looked sternly at it to prove I was boss but it just sat and scrutinized me. The piercing stares went back and forth and back and forth. Who would crack first? I finally had to break the stand-off and head for the cockpit so I could get on with my flight. I had a strong suspicion that this was no innocent potty. Something was fishy; there was something sinister about it. I couldn't help but see it every day that I came up the rear entrance ladder. It just sat there, watching and waiting.

A time or two, I'd thought about raising the lid to see if I'd find the cause of my unease about this THING, but I thought it would look stupid if I raised the lid of a toilet just to look inside. When people raise the lid of a toilet, they're serious about making a deposit. The feeling persisted day after day as I continued flying the airplane. Someone had put the THING there and I knew that it was always watching me. I don't know why I felt this strange feeling. It was a potty placed there for emergency purposes when we really needed it. It was supposed to be good, but in my heart, I knew that it had anything but benign intent. It was evil.

I did my best to keep it out of my mind. What were these stupid thoughts I was having? I must be losing it to think that this THING was alive and had some malevolent intent. I ignored it. Our flights went on day after day and anytime I needed a pee, I simply shot over the top of its head. It didn't intimidate me, I was the master here, and I didn't need it anyway. Our flights are only a few hours at best. I did my potty stuff at the base.

One day the call arrived for some cargo to be transported to Quebec. As luck would have it, I had the only airplane with cargo doors, so I got the dispatch to carry a load of firefighting equipment. Great stuff, I thought, Kamloops to Matagami – about twelve hours down and thirteen to fourteen hours back, really easy flying and more than I'd get in the next few days' Fire Bombing. We loaded the airplane in the afternoon so we could have an early takeoff the next morning. I filed GPS direct, which would take us on a great circle route for a trip of about eleven and one half hours.

It was a comfortable flight. The air was smooth and visibility great. GPS gave us a great-circle route and I was surprised at how far north it took us, far different than following the usual southern chain of radio aids. Four hours into the flight, I got the unmistakable urge. Peeing over the top of the THING wouldn't do it. The time had finally come when I had to confront that THING. I was going to have to face whatever that evil little box had on its mind. I held for a while, thinking that perhaps I could hold out till we got to Matagami, but that was hours away.

Explosive gas pressure was building in my inner plumbing and the bowels were screaming for relief. I was in pain as I held out and with each minute the agony increased. There was temporary relief as I surreptitiously released some of the gas pressure. Volcanologists have discovered that the high-frequency seismograph rumblings of a volcano switch to low-frequency rumblings just before the volcano erupts. Unmistakably, mine had just switched to low frequency. The F/Os face became more contorted as each one of my silent bombshells assaulted his nose. He suddenly broke the nicety protocol between captain and F/O and said:

"It's about time you stopped dropping those fetid farts, Linc. Don't shit in here, go back there and have a shit."

There was no stopping the call. I had to go back and finally face the box. I was desperate; I tip-toed up to it and bravely opened the lid. I had expected Pandora's wrath, but I couldn't have been more surprised. It looked as if it was designed for the tender attentions of a lady. There were no medieval torture devices inside with which to attack my family jewels. The bowl had graceful curved lines, was perfectly smooth, and had a flush hole that looked to be about six inches in diameter. There were no hidden traps and certainly nothing could get stuck in there. All would easily flush down. Why all these morbid feelings about this beautiful potty? It was there to save my life. I settled onto the comfortable but slightly cold seat. It was not a discomfort that could stop my mission. A roll of toilet paper sat conveniently nearby.

Little needs to be said about the relief that comes to body and soul when the deed is finally done. Life became livable again, the intense abdominal pains were gone and I basked in the glory of a healthy body that quit farting. The clean up functions were done, the pants came up and I faced the box.

I left the lid open so I could see the working of what looked like a very functional and clean design. The flush handle was on one side so I leaned that way slightly so I could press down on the handle. Suddenly an emphatic, full-mouthed WHOOSSH sent the contents ripping into and by me. Fortunately, I had leaned to one side to flush; otherwise I would have worn the entire package. One edge of the blast caught my right side and out of the corner of my eye I could see the shredded fragments flying past my right shoulder. The entire load was blown out of the bowl and what didn't hit me sprayed out into the fuselage. The back of the airplane smelled like a Russian airliner.

I now had the job of cleaning myself as best I could, and I used copious amounts of toilet paper to mop up the floor of the airplane.

Finally I went back up front, bringing the fragrance with me, and related the inexplicable behavior of the potty to my F/O. That insidious little monster had me pegged from the day it got there; it knew that I didn't know its dirty little secret. It was only a matter of time before it would get me.

In response to our requests for a potty, someone in the company had obviously spotted this cute, lightweight, functional little box in a camping or construction equipment catalogue and ordered it for the airplanes. The potty was well-built. Nose assuagement demanded that there be a tight seal between the deposit bowl and the storage compartment. The dome that was pressed into the flush hole had a tight seal to prevent the deadly odours from coming up out of that noxious box. In use on the ground, the air pressure top and bottom would be the same. No problem with flushing.

But this little potty was not meant to go flying. The seal on the dome was tight enough to not leak any air out as we climbed to altitude. Hence the pressure in the storage compartment remained at the airport of departure pressure as the air pressure in the airplane decreased with altitude. At an altitude of 9,500 feet there was a substantial difference in the two pressures, with the storage compartment pressure being substantially higher than the open bowl pressure. All that was needed to spring that diabolical little beast's trap was to press the flush handle. I swear I heard "Aha, gotcha" as the air blasted out with great conviction and hurled the bowl of detritus with it.

Every day that I got into the airplane I saw the little cream-coloured box demurely sitting there. I now knew its dirty little secret and so did my F/O. But next season someone else would be flying this airplane and the little box would be sitting there, waiting.

The Fall

Low-level flying meant that we daily collected a swallow's ransom of bugs on the windshield. And we, the fellows that like to see outside (the captain and the F/O), had the duty to clean the windshields. We didn't impose on our mechanics to do it. They had their hands full doing the aircraft maintenance. The safest way to get at the main big panels in front of our face was to slide the side windows wide open, sit on the window ledge and lean out far enough, squeegee in hand, to do the job. It involved a bit of contortion on our part, but the procedure was safe.

Another way of getting at the windows very conveniently was to prop the loading ladder which we used to climb into the back door of the airplane, just under the front windshield. To reach the windshield with a short squeegee, it was necessary to stand on the very top platform of the twelve foot ladder. I got into the habit of cleaning the windshield this way because it was easy to reach the glass without having to go through the convolution of hanging out of the side window.

I had been doing this for a good part of the summer and although it was hazardous, it was easy. I knew better because I had to lean both ways from the very top of the ladder to reach the side and front windshields adequately. The ladder was simply leaning against the fuselage; there was nothing to stop it from shooting out from under me if I got the centre of gravity away from dead centre.

One day, it happened. At Manning, Alberta in 1986 I leaned too far to my right and the ladder shot out from under me to my left. The ladder was on its way down and I was falling with my back to the concrete right behind it. Instinctively, I held my head forward so it wouldn't hit along with my body. From a height of twelve feet, I landed flat on my back on concrete with my left hip landing on the edge of the ladder. It knocked the wind out of me and for a few minutes, I didn't feel any pain. In fact I thought that if I just rested there for a few minutes, I could get up and get on with my day.

Flat on my back after a twelve foot fall. Photo by Jim Simpson

Several people as well as the Birddog, Jim*, who was also a paramedic, saw me there and came rushing to see if they could help me. I found it odd that the first thing Jim said was: "Linc, do you have an erection?"

"Wasn't exactly in the mood, Jim."

"Tell me Linc, do you have an erection? Please say no."

"I don't have an erection, Jim. Why do you ask?"

"If you had an erection, your back would be broken. You say you don't have one. That's good."

"God, I'm sure glad to hear that. If you just let me lie here for a couple of minutes, I'll be fine and I can get up and finish cleaning the window."

The easy way in for a cripple. Forward a bit and slightly lower, please. Photo by Bernie Holmquist

"You're not going anywhere, Linc. An ambulance will be here in a couple of minutes."

Jim was one of the most compassionate people I have ever met. Before he became a Birddog, he was a fireman and got badly burned while going back into a burning mobile home to see if a missing person

322

was inside. No one was inside, but that attempted rescue resulted in severe burns for Jim. He still wore bandages on his legs that wept blood daily. Jim was suffering every day, but he always remained cheerful and positive. Humanity needs more people like him.

We had hardly finished these few words when the entire universe turned into agonizing pain. So far my body had protected me from reality by putting me into shock. I felt nothing. But when the initial shock was over, every inch of my entire body felt as if it had been severely beaten with baseball bats several times over. I was utterly and completely helpless, suffering an excruciating, all-consuming pain.

In a very short time, the Manning Hospital ambulance arrived. It was time to get me off the concrete and on to a stretcher. Several people held me and tried to move me as little as possible while they were making the transfer, but the slightest movements amplified the mind-shattering pain.

When I arrived at the hospital, there was worse to come. For some reason, the attending doctor would not allow my pain shot until after the X-rays were finished. Every inch of my body was to be X-rayed and this involved turning me on to each side, on to my stomach and back to lying on my back. The slightest movement was agony, but I was told it had to be done. These are moments one never forgets. The odd thing about our memory is that we can recapture a fragrance, or a taste, or the feel of something, but the memory does not allow us to recall physical pain. We can only remember the experience of it and we have to be thankful for that.

The rolling over of my body and the pictures took forever, but they finally finished and I got my shot. I could never have imagined that I could go from terrible, unbearable pain to instant euphoria. But there it was: in mere seconds, the wonderful world came back. All was well.

"I feel great," I sang, "lemee out of here. I can go flying now."

I was transferred to my room on my back to spend a couple of days in that position. I was to get a shot every three hours and by the end of the second hour, I was begging for it. If I was being given morphine, it's not hard to see how easily people can get addicted to it. The euphoria is so high that one never wants to leave that state.

By the third day I could sit up and the pain was subsiding somewhat.

But there was some difficulty with sitting; there was a football-sized swelling where my hip hit the ladder. Much to my dismay, the shots were discontinued. I could have stayed on that stuff forever. The boys were allowed to come and visit and, of course, they brought a few refreshments along. We drew the curtains around the bed and had a party. The head nurse came by and said:

"No drinking is allowed in the room, boys, I hope you're not having anything to drink."

"No we're not — just having a few laughs."

"That's good, boys. We have to follow the rules."

She knew that we were having a few beers, but she played along with the game. The X-rays showed no injury to anything whatsoever. No broken bones anywhere and no internal injury to anything else. Each day I felt better, but on my release on the fifth day, I could walk only with the aid of crutches. So it was back to base I went as a limping, mobile tripod.

The check pilot had been covering my airplane for the time I was in hospital, but as soon as I could fly, he was needed elsewhere.

Being crutch-bound, it was impossible for me to climb the boarding ladder to get up into the airplane. Easy solution there — the mechanics put a pallet on the forklift forks and lifted me up.

It was time for a little test. I sat in the pilot's seat and while the F/O and check pilot looked on, I proved I could handle the control column and move my legs and operate the rudders with no problems. Okay — I was back on duty. So, on the seventh day after a fall that could have killed me or left me paralyzed from the neck down, I was back to flying the airplane.

Getting into an airplane with the assistance of a forklift was nothing new. In 1964, while flying at a Budworm project in New Brunswick, I collapsed one day shortly after getting up in the morning.

I lay in a heap at the bottom of the stairs of our mobile trailer. I was in agonizing pain and was rushed off to the hospital. It turned out that I had an appendix that was ready to burst and it had to come out. I gave my approval. The thing was extracted and I was released two days later. As anyone who has had the experience knows, a cough or sneeze was a stab in the gut with a pitchfork. (I involuntarily tried it a few times and it was no fun.)

At that project, all of our earnings came from flying and I didn't want to miss a minute. I headed for the base walking with the aid of crutches and I was ready to fly. But the pilot who was brought in to relieve me wouldn't give up the airplane after only two days. He browbeat management into giving him two more days while my stitches healed and I agonized over the loss of flying pay.

Finally I was ready to fly on the fifth day after my appendectomy. I couldn't climb up into the airplane in the usual manner since I could have ripped the stitches out. So, the boys lifted me up tenderly with a forklift and then helped me into the cockpit. I couldn't walk without crutches, but I could sit just fine and fly the airplane.

My "little" fall at Manning in Alberta was not too different from the time I crashed a hang-glider. The crash was severe enough to have killed me, but it seems that I'm gifted with an iron constitution. I incurred no injuries that time either. I'm one of those people who regards a non-fatal event as just an inconvenience to getting on with life. Not dead or crippled? Carry on, Linc.

Of course, being hospitalized in Manning was never mentioned to the Department of Transport. I wonder what would have gone on some inspector's report about a guy flying an airplane who couldn't walk without crutches. And not only that, he had to be forklifted up into the airplane. Perhaps a prohibition about flying while using crutches should be written into the air regulations. Perhaps not. These minor little details are best forgotten.

The Flat Nose Wheel Tire

It must be difficult to grasp what a pilot is talking about when he describes nose wheel shimmy. After all, what's shimmy? My only exposure to what I would call shimmy were the shapely Hawaiian dancers at a luau. The word shimmy is so inadequate to describe a shaking so violent that it gives every indication that the airplane is being torn to pieces. One terrified Conair pilot came close when he talked about what happened to him in one of Conair's A-26s on landing. When the vibration and noise suddenly hit, the control of the airplane was ripped out of his hands and he put his arms up in front of his face to shield himself from the expected flying debris. He said the noise was like being in a giant coffee grinder that was ripping the entire airplane apart. And all he had was a flat nose wheel tire.

In Arizona, I saw the twisted fuselage of an A-26 that experienced nose wheel shimmy from undone scissors during an attempted takeoff. The airplane was a write-off. But more disturbing was the pilot's story of how the airplane shook so hard as almost to defeat his attempt to cut the throttles to stop the airplane. He said that the vibration was so severe and so violent that it took his hands right off the throttles. He had an extremely difficult time to grab and hold on to them firmly enough to pull them back.

These stories were tucked into my mind with the half-belief that the boys must have been exaggerating. Surely an entire airplane can't vibrate the way it was described. My DC-6 vibrated when the engines weren't synchronized and that buzz traveled through the entire airplane. I offered this as the possible feeling. Nothing like it, I was told. The buzz was just a friendly reminder to synchronize. Anyway, nose wheel shimmy is like crashing. It happens to someone else. I never had a concern that it might happen to me.

One calm day, a routine landing turned the stories into a terrifying reality. I had taken off from La Ronge, Saskachewan to bomb a fire. When that drop was finished, I was directed to go to Slave Lake,

Alberta for a reload. Everything was normal on the approach and for the landing.

Shortly after touching down, just as I was getting ready to reverse, the airplane suddenly began to shake so violently that I thought an engine had thrown a propeller or some other catastrophic event was taking place. The noise was mind-shattering and every part of the airplane was shrieking in agony from the incredible vibration. The magnitude of the sideways oscillation must have been at least a foot wide and with a frequency so fast that I couldn't image that this was happening to the entire airplane. The instruments and the throttle quadrant became a blur. Shimmy or vibration doesn't describe it. A giant metal shredder had attacked my airplane. A minute of this would surely have torn the airplane to shreds. Pieces had to be flying off the airplane.

I was already on the throttles for reverse, so in a death grip, I pulled back hard to apply as much power for reversing as the engines could handle. At the same time I was standing on the brakes. While this was happening, I was not aware of the fact that the airplane had turned about twenty degrees to the left and was heading off the runway. Full power in reverse, and the frantic application of brake stopped the airplane just short of the edge. Slowing down seemed to take forever. The violence of the shaking and the incomprehensible noise didn't quit until the airplane came to a complete stop.

As soon as we stopped, I shut the engines down and the F/O and I abandoned the airplane with the speed or two gophers diving down a hole to escape a hawk. We were certain of devastating damage somewhere and possibly a fire. We had no idea what happened. As soon as we were out of the airplane we could see the nose tire smoking so I asked the F/O to get the fire extinguisher to deal with a possible fire. We shot a little CO_2 at it and the heat and smoke subsided. We now had the time for a closer examination of the tire: it was contorted all around the wheel rim and partly shredded. How was it possible that something as inoffensive as a flat tire could propagate into such a devastating, full-airplane mauling?

Having just experienced the incomprehensible thrashing from a flat tire, I could readily understand how unfastened scissors could destroy an airplane. I had flown only a few trips with this reluctant F/O and he was now uttering words to the effect that I would lead us to certain destruction.

The runway at Slave Lake has a housing development paralleling the runway not more than 150 feet away. It just so happened that a couple of fellows were sitting outside on their patio having a beer and cooking on their barbeque. They had watched the whole event. We were right beside their house where we stopped on the runway and they were ready with their comments:

"Glad you guys stopped. We thought you were coming over for a beer."

Comedians everywhere.

"Hi fellas."

"Your airplane sure was shaking. It's amazing that no pieces came off, and it made one hell of a noise — never seen anything like that."

"Yeah, it was like that inside."

"No wonder you guys got out so fast. You must have crapped yourselves."

"We didn't know what was wrong so we thought we'd better get out."

"Want to join us for a beer?"

"Thanks for the offer, fellas. Sure could use one, but not today."

"Hope your airplane's okay."

My extremely shaken up F/O and I remained at the airplane while we waited for the engineers to arrive with another nose wheel. As they were gathering up their kit, the air radio operator informed the engineers that a disabled airplane on the runway was cause for an investigation of an "incident." The airplane would have to stay put until a Department of Transport (DOT) inspector came to investigate.

So much shaking in so little time.

They immediately called the Edmonton DOT office to summon whoever had to make his report. Within about three hours, a tall gentleman wearing a dark suit appeared and began to survey the scene.

It didn't take him very long before he looked at me and said:

"Did the shaking start when you let the nose wheel down or did it start a bit later?"

"The nose was down for a while and I was getting ready for reverse."

"I think I know what caused the tire to go flat. Let's go for a walk."

I wasn't sure what he meant by that remark, but we started to back track the path where we landed.

After walking for awhile he bent over and picked up the valve stem from the tire.

"Right here is where this valve stem broke off and the tire went flat." It was about 500 feet from where we came to a stop.

"How did you know what to look for?"

"I've seen it before — the tires and tubes still used on these airplanes are old and quite brittle. The valve stems break off every now and then. You guys were lucky you stopped so fast. It could have been worse."

I don't know how much worse it could have been. As far as I was concerned, the airplane was severely damaged and was no longer flyable after such an incredible thrashing. It just didn't seem logical that a wobbling tire going straight ahead could cause such an extreme horizontal amplitude in the shaking. I was trying to construct a picture in my mind of what the tire was doing. Perhaps the loose tire alternately rode on each side wall in rapid succession pulling the entire gear support mechanism rapidly sideways to both limits — or beyond. There had to be broken pieces inside the nose compartment, if not all over the airplane.

I took the trouble to look up inside the nose wheel well to check all the attachments that the nose gear had to the fuselage. Surely the nose gear assembly had to be torn away from its mounts. Something had to be broken. I even had visions of the fuselage being torn away from the wings. A suspicion completely out of proportion? Not after that ride. I did a very thorough search, because it wouldn't be long before I'd be expected to fly the airplane that I considered to have just become a piece of junk.

I couldn't find anything wrong, but I'm not a mechanic, so I asked our maintenance crew to check the airplane over with a fine-toothed comb. There must be damage somewhere. They took the rest of the day and the next to give it a real going-over. They found absolutely no damage. I couldn't believe that an airplane could be shaken with such violence that the cockpit became a blur. And yet there was no damage.

The engineers informed us that the airplane was in good shape, and it was okay to fly it. I and the nervous F/O, now more firmly convinced than ever that I was going to kill him, talked it over and agreed that if the engineers said it was okay then it must be okay, so we very reluctantly accepted it as flyable. We were both extremely nervous for the next several trips. I imagined that pieces of the airplane were just waiting to fly off. But the airplane carried on as if nothing had happened. I had learned something more about my amazing DC-6: it's not only a forgiving bird in flight, but it's one incredibly strong airplane. We flew it for the rest of the season with no problems.

Chapter Twenty One
Flying in the Great Canadian North

Good judgment comes from experience.
Unfortunately, experience comes from bad judgment. Anonymous

Canada's Yukon and Northwest Territories is a land so vast that it's almost a fifth the size of the United States. The McKenzie River valley and its Arctic Delta is a fertile land suitable for any kind of agriculture. The Territories contain vast reserves of oil, minerals, forests, diamonds and gold and its lakes are teeming with a variety of freshwater fish. It could be the home of millions of people, except for one harsh reality: It has the Arctic winter. It's Canada's Siberia. Surviving the cold means taking exceptional measures to avoid prolonged exposure. Travel in wind-blasted cold temperatures that drop to -50 °F (-46 °C) or more will bring death quickly to the unprepared. And it indeed takes a special kind of person to endure six months of total winter darkness.

This bitter harshness engenders something in people that we southerners don't understand. If a person were to fall on the street of a heart attack in New York or Toronto, people might simply step over the body. We suffer from a cold impartiality toward our fellow man in the big city. The cold of an uncaring society can be worse than physical cold. It's different in a northern community. People know their neighbours and if someone is in trouble, help comes quickly and willingly. People who live in the North find gratification and self-worth in supporting each other's survival. Perhaps it's like the military; everyone looks out for everyone else. People also help others because there may come a time when they themselves need help and in the uncompromising bitterness of an Arctic winter, it's essential to know support is there. There's security in that kind of interdependency. We call these people "bushed," but many would never trade their close-knit Arctic community for any other life-style. Only a few thousand devoted, masochistic people call this boundless land their home.

Canada's forest wilderness begins outside the back doors of people in Vancouver, Winnipeg, Toronto and Ottawa and extends to the edge of the tree line far to the north. Watered by the McKenzie River and nourished by the rich soil, large forests grow on the McKenzie River Delta all the way to the Arctic Ocean. Elsewhere, the trees gradually become smaller until they melt into the grassy tundra a short distance above sixty degrees north. Still, there is an expansive area of valuable forest which is harvested for building timber and pulpwood. Like the forests farther south, these areas are protected in the event of fire. Bomber bases are situated across the top of all the provinces and in the Yukon and Northwest Territories all the way to the Beaufort Sea in the Arctic.

I had always thought that the frigid Arctic air stunted the growth of trees and as one went further north, the trees became progressively smaller and finally petered out because of the severe weather. I got a huge surprise the first time I went up to our tanker base at Inuvik which is only about sixty miles south of the Arctic Beaufort Sea. Two vastly different floras were within a few feet of each other. The McKenzie River's edge separated the beautiful big trees on the McKenzie River Delta from the grasslands that extend for thousands of miles across the Arctic. A wide stance would place a foot on two different worlds. My thoughts about the severe weather only partially applied. The tree growth depended on the available moisture as well as the severe temperatures.

The company had bombing contracts in the Far North and some of us had the dubious privilege of a summer of standby in these remote northern bases. Hay River and Norman Wells were just such bases.

Hay River

Being sent "Up North" meant anything north of Edmonton and the farther north we were, the more impoverished the social scene became. The northern bases were nothing like being in Penticton where a continuous deluge of ladies from Vancouver sought to enhance their tans on the beaches of the sunny Okanagan. In the evenings, they would frequent the many night clubs and pubs, so the southern bases were the place to be. If seniority got a pilot into the Territories, then he was destined to spend time in some very remote places.

A less-than-desirable base, socially speaking, was Hay River. It sits at the southwest corner of Great Slave Lake and is the headquarters and supply depot for the company that ships bulk supplies to the Arctic. Huge barges are assembled in train and are pushed or pulled by giant tugboats all the way down the McKenzie River to villages on the Beaufort Sea and the Arctic Ocean. The barges and the tugboats are shallow-draft to assure easy travelling down the many shallow areas of the river. The tugboats have downward-pointing propellers on each side both fore and aft. If they get stuck on a sandbar, powerful downward jets of water sweep away the river sand and allow the train to continue. While hundreds of men work at this terminal, very few single ladies find this northern town to be an appealing place to live. It had to be the climate; it certainly wouldn't be the lack of attention from a bullpen full of lonely, eager men. I'm surprised that there isn't a stampede of women flocking to these northern towns. Whatever ladies were available, the local boys had long since claimed before the arrival of our bombing crew.

Hay River was already a revelation of how desolate life could be in the North. Its premier night club, winning the title handily because it was the only night club, was the Back Eddy. We spent our evenings there in preference to relaxing with the boys in one of our rooms. There we could watch the lineup of men waiting their turn to dance with the three queens of the North. I had actually never seen men form themselves into a line and wait their turn for a dance. These ladies were the only fair-sex diversion at the club and were the nighttime hit of Hay River. Men were at their feet.

One evening, I decided to do a count of the club attendance. What were the odds in favour of these three? I counted a total of ninety-three men ready and willing to indulge the resident ladies' every wish. What was it about these social butterflies that made them so popular?

334

In about six weeks' time, I knew the answer. Weeks of isolation, a dark club and several beers revealed feminine charms in these ladies that were hitherto extremely well hidden. As the evening wore on and more beer improved my judgment, they became more and more beautiful. In fact, they became nothing short of stunning. It wasn't surprising that men who had been there much longer than our bombing crew eagerly awaited those few moments they had to shout their endearments to their partner over the numbing volume of the band. The North does strange things to men, quickly making them find the bottom of the barrel in female pulchritude attractive. That night I had enough beers to not have stood up long enough to get in a dance, so I left the sweet things to the attentions of more worthy men.

So the summer went in Hay River. I did my flying and came home to an evening with the boys. Going to the Back Eddy was simply a diversion to get out of the hotel room.

Hay River did have one amenity; it had an excellent set of tennis courts that were never used. The Birddog pilot played tennis and we were fairly evenly matched. It was easy to get a court any time, so being the tennis buffs that we were, it was a great diversion.

Norman Wells

Getting Hay River as a base was bad enough. Norman Wells was even more remote. It was a mere sixty miles south of the Arctic Circle. Above that imaginary line, the sun doesn't set all summer long. Oil was discovered in the 1930s at "The Wells" and, as history would have it, oil in this northern location would precipitate an urgent series of ventures during the Second World War. After the Japanese invaded the Aleutian Islands, it was thought that an invasion of Alaska wouldn't be too far behind. To meet this threat, two important projects were undertaken. One was the building of the Alaska Highway, and the other was the building of the Canol pipeline from Norman Wells to Whitehorse. Oil would be pumped one thousand kilometers from Norman Wells to newly built refineries in Whitehorse to supply the American military for the coming fight in Alaska. Huge amounts of money were spent on the Canol project, but the refining of oil never really got underway. The Japanese deserted the Aleutians, the threat ended and there was no need for this oil to be sent to Whitehorse. It was abandoned and the overgrown construction road and bits of the pipeline are still visible today. Camp Canol, just across the McKenzie River from Norman Wells, was demolished and all the military equipment at this huge base, which housed ten thousand men, was buried.

Spending a summer at "The Wells" with hundreds of oil workers and a few dedicated forestry personnel was hardly a place to provide pleasant social diversions at the day's end.

When I was destined for a summer at Norman Wells, I resigned myself to hoping for a great season of flying. It would be the only entertainment. My social life would be as barren as the northern tundra. I had been to "The Wells" before and it didn't have a Hay River resident three; there was nothing. As I approached for landing, I surveyed this little town on the edge of the McKenzie River and realized that it would be a bleak summer. I called for the airport advisory:

"Norman Wells radio, this is Tanker Four Seven — five minutes south, landing Norman Wells, request your advisory."

A honeyed voice came over the air that would melt the rock-hard permafrost that began a couple of feet below the surface.

"Tanker Four Seven, winds are light and variable, runway two seven is in use and the altimeter is 29.46. Cleared to land."

I could hardly believe my ears. What angelic creature gave those instructions? Only a vision of outstanding beauty had a voice like that. It was sweet, appealing, oozed with feminine charm and it filled the northern ether with music. Instantly, my head was racing. How old is she? Is she married? Is she taken?

I had visions of a delicate beauty who would appreciate the attentions of a captain of a DC-6. I would call her my beloved and she would call me Mon Capitan. What a different summer this would be. There would be romantic evenings sitting on the banks of the

McKenzie River swatting mosquitoes. We would watch the washed-out trees from up river, complete with the torn out roots, slowly drift by. In the twilight of the evening, we could lay on the muddy banks and count satellites as they made their spy flights over an axis of evil. My head was spinning, but the fantasy was broken when my F/O suggested we get on with the landing check.

On the trip up from Vancouver we had a perfectly clear sky and I was able to survey the grandeur of the North for what seemed like a thousand miles. "The Wells" was also clear and the horizon was unlimited. The weather map showed the entire North to be clear with unlimited visibility. Nevertheless, on landing, it was necessary for me to do a weather check. The voice of the siren came from the weather and flight advisory office.

Immediately after landing, with nowhere else to fly, I needed to know about the weather. I tried to conceal my hurried pace as I rushed to the weather office. Inside I approached a woman who appeared to be in her wrinkled late 50s or early 60s. She was about five foot six inches, had dark, straight hair and wore baggy pants topped with a brown, safari shirt that hung loosely from her rather bony, slim build. I breathlessly panted:

"I'd like to speak to flight advisory for a weather check."

"Hello, I'm the flight advisory."

Something went instantly wrong. It was the same voice that sent me on a wild fantasy instead of concentrating on my landing. For a stunned minute, I didn't quite grasp that I was three feet away from the voice that caused a thousand trips to the weather office. Then I went into expectation-shock. This heavenly voice sounded like it should have come from a gorgeous, voluptuous, blonde lady devoid of any encumbrances that looked like wedding rings. But alas, it came from this plain woman who flashed a diamond the size of a walnut on the appropriate hand.

She sighed:

"Did you just land in the DC-6? Would you like a weather briefing?"

"Uh...no, I just wanted to find where the office was for later on."

She was friendly and helpful, but my fantasy of sitting on the banks of the McKenzie swatting mosquitoes and counting spy satellites was shattered. The summer at Norman Wells would be as every summer was in "The Wells."

The Spectacular North

For a few short summer months, the Yukon and the Northwest Territories display scenes of breathtaking beauty. Some features were particularly stunning. Flying from Norman Wells to Yellowknife took me across Lac Le Martre, a large lake easily found on any atlas that has a map of the Northwest Territories. In the full bloom of summer the lake is a setting out of the Caribbean Sea or the South Pacific. I could not resist descending to about 100 feet of altitude to take in this spectacular sight. The water is incredibly clear and the lake hosts several islands completely surrounded by wide, sandy beaches. In flying over, I had no idea of how deep the lake was, as the water was so clear that I could see the bottom everywhere. Out in the middle reaches of the lake, large boulders carried there by the glaciers littered the unknown depths of the bottom.

The south end of the lake had a special beauty. Shallow water, perhaps no more than ten feet deep, revealed an extensive beach that extended out from the shore for at least a half mile, making it a perfect place to swim or water ski. It appeared that a few hundred natives who had their homes just off the beach made their living fishing its clear waters. The lake flowed out into a vast shallows of clear water and emerald-green grass which gently swayed in the current as if blown by a gentle breeze. The grass reminded me of the ocean kelp seaweed. Thick stems grew from the bottom supporting long blades of grass about four or five inches wide and several feet long that floated on the surface. I didn't know that this type of seaweed, if that was even a proper term for it, existed in fresh water lakes. The sun gave a brilliant sparkle to the clear water and the iridescent flowing green. This could not be the frigid North. It had to be the Everglades or one of the many clear springs in Florida. This alive spectacle would eventually narrow down to a river that flowed into the silted water of the West Arm of Great Slave Lake.

Great Slave Lake offers two very different panoramas of scenery. The western half lies in the rocky, low-lying hills of the Canadian Shield while the eastern half has a terrain of high hills and deep water carved out by departed glaciers. An almost perfectly straight line defines the clear water of the East Arm of Great Slave Lake from the silted and muddy West Arm of Great Slave Lake.

The "East Arm," as it's called, has recently been made a National Park because of its grand and spectacular beauty. It's the deepest lake in North America at 2010 feet and red granite cliffs rise vertically for a thousand feet out of the incredibly clear water. Fishing boats look like they're virtually suspended in space.

The Action at Butte Inlet and the Homathko Ice field

One of our operational bases was Campbell River on Vancouver Island. It was an excellent location because we could cover the northern part of the island and be available to bomb fires to the north and east. Great pubs and friendly ladies completed the day. All that was necessary to enjoy the best salmon fishing in the world was to put a boat in the water and hang out our lines. It was a pleasure our crew enjoyed on occasion. Not too far away was a fisherman's paradise called River's Inlet, where catching fifty to sixty pound salmon was a daily occurrence. The world knew about Campbell River salmon fishing. One would often see a Saudi Prince's coat of arms on the tail of a DC-8 or the lion of an African dictator on the tail of a 727 parked at the airport.

On April 5, 1958, the largest planned non-nuclear explosion occurred in Seymour Narrows, only a few miles from Campbell River, removed Ripple Rock. Ripple Rock consisted of two underwater peaks that were a hazard to ships travelling the "Inside Passage" on the way to or from Alaska. The explosion blasted away enough rock to deepen the low tide clearance for ships from 2.7 meters to fourteen meters (about forty-five feet). It removed the hazard which would eventually make travel safe for the many cruise ships that take the Inside Passage on the Alaska cruise.

One day a dispatch sent me to a fire on the east side of Butte Inlet. I received the approximate location and was told that I should contact the Birddog when ten minutes out from the location. Apparently, I was going to need special instructions about how to get to the fire.

Sure, sure, I knew what special instructions meant: the Birddog had an impossible place for a DC-6 to get into and out of. In all seriousness, there would be some special instructions about how to do a dive to a fire at the bottom of a sheer mountain face. The only approach would be a dive starting over the top of the mountain about three thousand feet above the fire. It would take a five g pull out to clear the ground below the fire. But the Birddog would cheerfully announce that it shouldn't be a problem. They liked to spring a good one on us occasionally.

Butte Inlet is one of the picturesque "fjords" of the west coast. It's an inlet like many others that offers spectacular vistas of steep mountain slopes that rise out of the clear, blue water. I had not flown up Butte Inlet before, so this day's experience would be new to me. As I was flying up the Inlet, I was over top of a solid layer of cloud with no gaps anywhere. It was dazzlingly clear up top, and the view of the mountain tops was breathtaking. I didn't see any smoke above the cloud. *Where's the fire?* I wondered. *What little trick does Birddog have up his sleeve?*

"Birddog, this is Tanker Four Five, I'm about ten minutes from my X on the map but I don't see a fire."

"Tanker Four Five, the fire is under the overcast and I'm going to give you some instructions on how to get here."

"Roger, Birddog, go ahead."

"Tanker Four Five, you fly to the end of the Inlet and you'll see a glacier that slopes down to the water. You're going to need to descend just above the glacier as you'll be in a space between the glacier and the cloud. The gap is only about a hundred feet wide, but once you go down through, there's 700 feet of clearance between the ocean and the bottom of the cloud. The fire is about five miles farther up and I'll give you your target as you go by the fire. You'll get a better view out of your side. After you get the target, you'll have to fly about another three or four miles further up where there's a spot wide enough to turn around. You'll be doing your first bombing run on the way back. There's enough room to turn around again at the bottom of the glacier."

"Got that, Birddog."

"The visibility in here is bad, but it's good enough that you should be able to get your target and make your runs okay. Get fairly close to the edge of the mountain on the way by. I'll explain what we're doing the first time you go by."

"Okay, Birddog, I'll let you know when I'm over the water and ready for my instructions."

I arrived over the Homathko Ice field to a scene that was glaringly white and stunningly beautiful. From up above I could look down into deep crevasses that seem to be lit up from below with a pale, blue luminescence. I set up for bombing and slowed down for what Birddog said would be a gentle ride down the slope of the glacier. The Inlet had a cloud cover that was around two thousand feet thick, and while the cloud covered the Inlet, it stopped short of the glacier and nestled itself about 100 feet from the surface of the ice.

I started the descent just above the ice. Just like Birddog said, a just-wide-enough opening showed up between the cloud and the glacier, and I slid underneath the cloud. The blinding white now began to darken, and as I descended into this narrow, cave-like opening, I could see that it looked dark and foreboding down below. It was almost like flying between two layers of cloud except that this bottom layer was solid. I had to stay just above the ice to keep the cockpit clear of the cloud. It felt like I wasn't clearing either by more than about twenty feet. It was a gentle, serene ride down the slope of the glacier in perfectly still air.

It was rather unsettling as it got darker and I was just hoping that the rest of his instructions about the 700 feet of space between the ocean and the cloud were right. I broke out below the cloud and what I saw fit his description. The still air below the cloud had held the smoke in the Inlet and visibility was at best, about half a mile. It was dark and smoky but still good enough for safe runs.

"I'm approaching the fire, Birddog. Go ahead with your instructions."

"Tanker Four Five, you'll see that there's a line of retardant put above the head on top of this fire and some loads down the flanks. I want you to place your loads downhill on each flank. You can drop one door each time you go by, one on the right flank on your first run, turn around at the glacier and the next one on the left flank. Work your way down 'til you've dropped all your doors. You should have enough retardant to finish the job."

"Got that, Birddog."

It was going to be one door at a time. I got the plan of attack and now I moved over to the other side of the Inlet and headed about four miles farther along to the spot he said was wide enough for a turn. There it was, and there was adequate room for the turn — provided that I laid on forty-five degrees of bank and cranked the airplane hard in a tight turn. I did a left turn and headed back for the drop. I picked up my target okay and one door went out. I had eleven more. I flew back to the glacier and turned around to come back for the next drop on the left flank.

"Good shot, Four Five. Work your way down just the way you're doing it."

"Roger, Birddog."

Coming down the glacier and getting everything right on the first run had some pucker factor. There was much to trust about Birddog's judgment: a clear slot in the cloud next to the glacier, low ceiling, marginal visibility and Birddog getting the turnaround spots right. But I had a very experienced Birddog. He called everything right. The next eleven runs were like flying in a three-sided box with a lid, where I was just able to see the sides. I could not have climbed up the glacier with a load, so I had to turn when I got back there. The Inlet boxed me in on two sides and the overcast closed the lid. If Birddog hadn't been right about the turnaround spot farther up, my only recourse would have been to fly down the Inlet until I got over the ocean, climb up to the top of the overcast and start all over again at the glacier.

All twelve drops demanded total concentration. It was a twilight zone of limited visibility in smoke, it was partially dark and there were shadowy walls all around. Because it was so smoky, the targets could only be seen at the last second, so I tried to adjust the height above the water to line up for the next drop well back from the fire. It was a menacing hour and a half, but all the drops were on target and there was sufficient retardant to finish both lines.

When the action was over, it was indeed a relief to climb out of that dark, smoky hole and into the brilliant sunshine. All above was immaculate; there was no smoke to contaminate the scene. The brilliantly blue sky and the pearly white top of the overcast highlighted the magnificent mountain peaks. The Homathko Ice field was a radiant white. There was no sign of a fire and no trace of human activity. It was hard to leave a place of such dazzling beauty.

TYPICAL ACTION DOWN A VERY STEEP MOUNTAIN

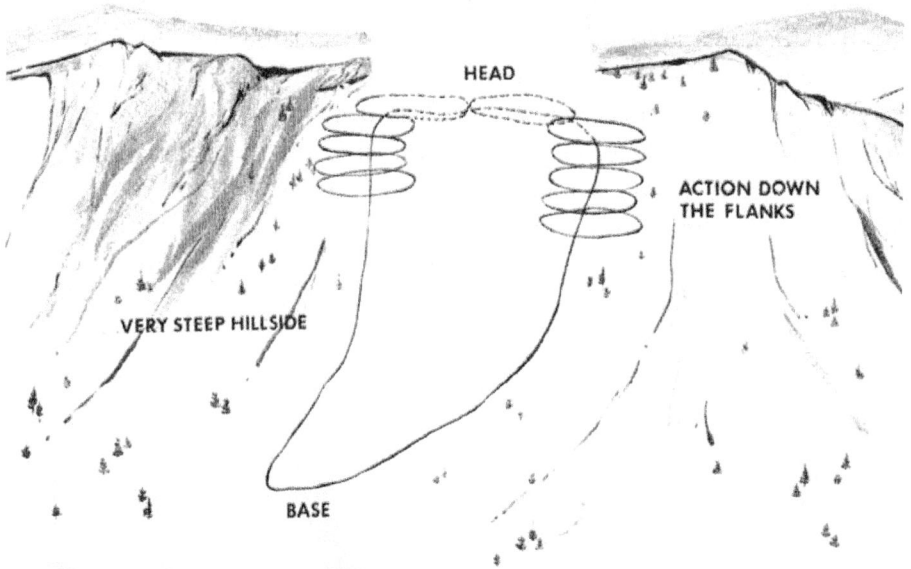

HEAD

ACTION DOWN
THE FLANKS

VERY STEEP HILLSIDE

BASE

STRAIGHT DOWNHILL DROPS DOWN THE FLANKS NOT POSSIBLE

Rainbow Lake

Rainbow Lake lies at the edge of the foothills of the Rocky Mountains in northern Alberta. Other than the main street, the rest of the town is hard to find. Narrow streets and large building lots were judiciously carved out of the forest. Strips of dark evergreen trees, not fences separated neighbours. Open space is scarce. The town's residents and bears could have co-existed without either knowing they were there. The little town of approximately 1200 transient people owes its existence entirely to oil. The country is criss-crossed by countless seismograph lines and oil pumping heads are everywhere. The airport was built to take the smaller, corporate airplanes used by oil companies. It was less than suitable for a slug of an airplane like a loaded DC-6. Nevertheless, we did a fair bit of flying there because of the frequency of the fires.

Alberta is home to a weather phenomenon called the Alberta Cold Front. Daytime heating at the eastern foothills of the mountains causes powerful updrafts that create some spectacular thunderstorms. In the hot summer months, a line of such storms is practically a daily event. These sometimes particularly nasty pillars begin their stately march eastward across the prairies, manifesting all the characteristics of a cold front.

The field elevation is 1700 feet and the runway is 4500 feet long. The problem with the runway is that it has a fairly steep gradient to it which made uphill runs extremely tight for the DC-6. It didn't matter which way I took off, uphill or downhill, the nose was rotated right at the end of the runway. On the grind uphill, I've often had the feeling that even with the nose of the airplane well up in the air, the main gear lifted off the runway only in the last couple of feet.

Ironically, the luck of my seniority number caused me to spend a few years in Alberta with the DC-6. One particular event in Rainbow Lake made me famous with the company and pilots but much less popular with the Alberta Forest Service.

The Birddog and I were dispatched to a fire to support other bombers working on a fire to the north of the base. I was parked in the loading pit directly behind the Birddog on a narrow concrete strip just barely wide enough for the wheels of the DC-6. I had loaded with retardant while waiting for Birddog to leave but he wasn't moving. Birddog had burned out a starter on one side and was out of service for the day, so I was stuck behind him and was impatient to get on my way to work with the other Birddog already at the fire.

I should have waited for enough people to arrive to push the Birddog out of the way, but my impatience to get airborne took over:

"Rainbow Dispatch, Tanker Five Zero."

"Go ahead, Five Zero."

"Birddog is unserviceable. I would like to turn around and go out the other way. Is the graveled area on my left hard enough for me to turn on?"

"No problem, Five Zero, it's hard-packed gravel."

"Roger, Dispatch, I'll turn around and head out."

I accepted his word as assurance that I could turn around from where I was because there was a solid surface where I wanted to make my turn. The concrete and the graveled area would have given me plenty of room to turn around and I could leave by the route we normally used to come in to the loading pit. I could get on with the dispatch.

What I didn't know about the nicely "hard-packed gravel" was that all of the many clean-ups of the loading pad were washed off across the concrete into the graveled area. Unknown to me, just below what looked like hard-packed gravel were years of washed off retardant and the thousands of gallons of water used to put it there. It was, in fact, a mud hole, deceptively topped with a coat of crushed gravel, yet it looked so perfect to support the weight of the airplane.

I didn't waste any time in the turn. I used a fair bit of power so I could turn quickly and get off the gravel as soon as possible, but this haste only got me farther across this supposedly secure surface. Part way through the turn, I had a sinking feeling. It's the fear of all fears in a heavy airplane. The main gear sank down into the mud with that terrible certainty of permanence. An overly desperate blast of power didn't move me an inch. I shut down the airplane and submissively crawled out to see what folly I had committed.

A thought crossed my mind about Robert's* punishment of me if I didn't get out. Robert was the chief pilot who had a sadistically inordinate need to punish everybody for everything. He was the type who, in his search for pilot indiscretions, would actually dip the tanks on a DC-6 after a pilot brought it back to home base at Abbotsford to see if there was a fuel imbalance prior to landing. Discovery of this "grievous mismanagement" of fuel distribution meant a trip to his office for suitable admonitions. Now I had committed something really worthy of Robert's wrath. Would it be bread and chains?

Gary* my F/O was an airline pilot who was flying for Conair in between the periodic lay-offs common with airlines. He was F/O on a DC-10 and irreverently referred to my DC-6 as a steam-powered ornithopter. He had been struck by lightning three times while in a DC-10, which may have accounted for his unappreciative view about the glories of Fire Bombing.

As we stooped to go under the wing, we were joined by everyone on the base. The main gears were surrounded by awed onlookers pointing and staring at the wheels as if they had never seen a DC-6 almost down to the axles in mud before. One of the loaders was caressing a main wheel and actually bent down close to the ground to verify that part of the tire was actually out of sight. Everyone had the same look and the same question: "Whatcha gonna do, Linc?" Gary always kept a straight face, so sometimes it was hard to tell if a sliver of humour was showing. Gary's brain carefully assessed our situation; he looked at me very gravely and said:

"You picked a good spot to park. We'll always be first in the pit."

"How are you on a shovel, Gary?"

"Is that to bury you when Robert finds out?"

"There's no sweat, Gary. Flapping the wings will get us out."

The permanence of where we were sitting was sinking in. I was stuck in mud: genuine, first-class Alberta clay gumbo. Just the right amount of water in Alberta clay makes a sticky, thick putty that adheres to everything so tightly that it takes a stream of high-pressure steam to get it off. We were in a Venus Fly Trap. This stuff just didn't stick; it held with a powerful suction. But something more ominous was happening as I watched: the wheels were almost down to the axles and the airplane was slowly sinking. It didn't escape the onlookers, either. They had come to watch the Titanic go down. The propellers cleared the ground only by about four inches. It would not be too many more minutes and the propeller blades would no longer clear the ground. The clock was ticking.

At the pace things were happening, I realized it would only take a short time before not just the wheels would be stuck. The airplane would continue to sink until it sat on the retardant tank. My thoughts about flying were also sinking along with the airplane. I could be out of action for days while an armada of heavy-lift cranes would be attempting to get me out.

Even sitting where I was, getting out would be a long and labour-intensive undertaking. It would mean digging trenches out front of each set of main gear and laying a ramp of heavy planks down to support the weight of the airplane as it was pulled through the mud. Trying to shovel out a trench in this kind of gum would frustrate the most ardent gravedigger. The clay would stick to every attempted shovelful. The caterpillar or mule (the name given to the low-slung, wheeled vehicle specially designed to move airplanes) used for pulling would exert a tremendous pull on the nose gear, perhaps too much and other pulling arrangements on the main gear would have to be considered. The situation was bad and getting worse by the minute.

I had a thought about getting unstuck but had to have my try in a matter of the next few minutes. First, I asked the base manager for permission to drop the load of retardant. He said he'd call headquarters and try to get it. He said try, because we were both of the same opinion: they may refuse. It seemed to take forever before he finally got the okay from head office. I was immensely relieved, as at least I did get it. I was cleared to drop the load.

I told Gary my plan of action:

"We'll start up and lower thirty degrees of flap. Then we'll go to dry power to give the wings maximum lift. I'll select "all" on the drop selector and when we're up to dry power, I want you to hit the drop button. I'll be on the nose wheel steering and be ready to haul off the throttles as we'll probably get up to speed real quick."

"I don't think it will work, Linc, but if you want to try it..."

"Jump in. We have to get on with it now."

I have to admit that I did have an inspiration for this plan. One day at the DeHavilland Aircraft factory in Toronto, I watched a Buffalo short-takeoff-and-landing aircraft with full flap down do a run-up at full throttle against the brakes. As he applied power, the airplane lifted up to the full extension of the gear oleo legs. It had so much lift, it was close to coming clear off the ground, and it didn't take much of a run before it did. It was a remarkable demonstration of just how much lift is generated by the propeller slipstream as it passes over the wings.

I was going to do this trick with the DC-6. At full dry power and flap at thirty degrees, the wings would be developing considerable lift. Letting the load go at that point would suddenly make the airplane thirty thousand pounds lighter. I thought the instant change of weight should give us the bounce that hopefully, would clear us out of the mud. At least that was my theory.

We anxiously got back into our seats, started up and proceeded with the plan. We dropped thirty degrees of flap and applied fifty-three inches of power.

"Drop!"

Gary hit the drop button and I felt a sudden, euphoric jump. The engineers watching from the outside said it looked like the airplane jumped at least three feet and clean out of the holes. With all that power, we must have skated across that fictional hard-packed gravel because I had to pull the throttles back immediately to stop from going off the other side of the concrete. We were cleanly out of the mud.

Our crew and everybody on the base cheered. Unfortunately the forest service then had the unpleasant job of washing away thirty thousand pounds of slippery, sticky retardant from the loading area. They were none too pleased. And it would all be washed under the nice, "hard-packed" gravel.

I presume Conair was charged for the load of retardant, but management, including Robert, never mentioned a word to me about the incident. My greatest satisfaction came afterwards: Robert didn't have his shot at punishing me.

DC-6 laying line down the flank of the fire.
Photo courtesy British Columbia Forest Service

Chapter Twenty Two
Confronting the Dragon

The probability of survival is inversely proportional to the angle of arrival.
Anonymous

On support actions, we would often make several runs to the same fire. And it would be just as likely that other airplanes would be there as well. On this day, the action was far enough to the east of Kamloops to be out of the desert and into heavy forest. I was dispatched to a fire burning inside a tight ravine on a steep mountainside. Ground crews were working the fire by hand and wanted their hand-lines reinforced with retardant. The fire had reached the top of the ravine, and another DC-6 had laid a line of retardant along the top which was actually the head. I made the usual call:

"Birddog, this is Tanker Four Seven. I'm five minutes out."

"Roger, Four Seven. I'll have your drop as soon as you're over the fire."

"Four Seven — overhead."

"Okay, Four Seven, do you see that line of retardant across the head on top of the ridge?"

"Roger."

"I want you to lay a string drop at half-second intervals down the left flank with all twelve doors."

"Got that, Birddog. A string drop down the left flank at half second with twelve doors. What kind of winds are you getting there, Birddog?"

"A bit bumpy, Four Seven, but it doesn't look like your run should have any problems."

There is consolation and assurance about a safe run because Birddogs make the run ahead of the bombers to check for turbulence and downdrafts and for the best entry and escape route. They make all of their turns at the same bank angle as the bomber, thereby simulating bomber performance. If all went well, our exit would be the same as his. But if there was a sudden downdraft, he was in a light airplane with great turn and climb capability while I was in a missile that's pointed in my chosen direction and doesn't want to do anything but go straight ahead. It's dubious assurance.

A thunderstorm was not too far away and was slowly moving in the direction of the fire. The winds were already quite variable and I would have to be popping overtop of the ridge to go steeply down one side. It didn't look good. I had no idea what to expect for winds when it came time to go over the top. At least I had the comfort of starting to drop the load at the very top and would quickly have a light airplane. I noticed that Birddog hadn't mentioned the storm heading our way; I guess he felt that it wouldn't cause us any problems.

Birddog said it was safe: the smoke was fragmented and so far the winds didn't look too strong. I elected to arrive at the top of the ridge at normal drop speed, no slower. If I fell, I'd have an open ridge below me for escape. The load started out and I was pushing the nose down to stay with the contour of the mountain. The "light looking" air was anything but – I was getting badly shaken. I was hanging on, but the airplane was being battered into wild pitching, wallowing and skidding. It was a most unpleasant ride. I was not gaining a lot of airspeed like I thought I would, but then I wasn't exactly sure of what the airspeed indicator was telling me, since the needle was bouncing all over the instrument. The load was finally out and I could get out of there. The air was bad.

"How was your run, Four Seven?"

I gave the usual euphemistic answer: "A bit rough... but safe enough."

Fear of the Dragon's Leg

"Reload and return. Tanker Five One will be going down the other side of the flank up top. On your next run I'll be wanting you to join on to your existing load and lay a string to the bottom of the fire."

"Roger, Birddog" said I, hoping to disguise the apprehension in my voice. I didn't like what I heard one bit. The next drop would be starting way down the mountain at the end of my last drop. That could be one bloody awful ride. I thought that by the time I got back, the storm would either be close or on us. I hoped that it would be on the fire, for then I wouldn't have to make the drop.

Worrying about air behaviour prior to a drop that was coming up was something that I never did. There was no point in it; neither I nor the Birddog would know what the air would be doing until I arrived at the drop scene. And even that wasn't a problem. At this stage of my bombing experience, I could readily deal with whatever the situation presented.

But now thoughts were entering my mind that hadn't been there before. It was certainly true that I loved the bombing business. I thoroughly enjoyed the airplane I was flying, but at this late stage of my flying career, should I be taking unnecessary chances? I was only a few years from retirement. What odd thoughts these were. *Unnecessary chances? This whole business was about taking unnecessary chances.* Was I now becoming afraid of the flying that I loved so much? *Are you starting to chicken-out in your old age, Linc? You've always been very good at what you're doing. You can handle any situation.* But the thought came back: *The unexpected does happen.* I'd had an airplane fall out from under me twice – and now superstition was grabbing at my emotions. *The third time could be out.*

The airplane had been reloaded and I was about half down on my fuel load. That was good: it was where I wanted it. Full fuel along with a full retardant load makes for a heavy airplane that slides downhill a bit too fast.

Janson Kirk* was in the right seat. He looked as unperturbed as usual. We worked together extremely well. Checks were always precisely and professionally done. When it was his turn to fly the airplane, he flew it with consummate precision. We lined up on the runway. I did the final briefing and we were on our way.

Forty minutes to the fire...

The upcoming drop was preying on my mind. A thunderstorm was tossing some very unpleasant and dangerous air into where we were working. It was about to make things unpleasantly worse and I'd be back in time for a horrific ride. *I thought that if it's bad enough or I think it's unsafe, I can always refuse the run. I've done it before.*

One day I was asked to do a drop on a small fire at the edge of Garibaldi Lake, located close to the famous ski resort of Whistler Mountain. The deep lake about five thousand feet above sea level radiates a deep blue colour and sits in a depression surrounded by slate-gray mountains. A "plug" of glacial silt contains the lake on the east side. Previous resort residences in this area have been removed as a precaution against this wall shaking loose from even a mild earthquake. If this dam were to fail, a wall of water and mud would rush the thirty miles downstream to sweep the town of Squamish into the ocean.

From above, I could see the wind lanes on the water showing gusts blowing in all directions. There was only one way in and one way out. The Birddog demonstrated the run and the escape as a steep turn along the edges of mountain tops on the east side of the lake. It would be a tight turn, but the Birddog gave assurances there would be no problem.

On circling above, I came to the conclusion that while he could do his escape turn with his light airplane, it would be somewhat of a squeaker to try it with the DC-6. To test my assessment, I did a turn above the lake simulating my escape route. Nope — too tight — too big a risk. And I wouldn't get a chance to come back and try it again if it didn't work the first time. I told Birddog I wouldn't do it, that it was just too tight quarters with the variable winds inside the bowl of the lake. He accepted my decision and called off the action on the fire. That was the one and only time I refused a run.

Janson and I are now up to altitude and have the airplane trimmed for level flight.

Thirty minutes...

The Tunnel

My mind went back to a previous fire I did with Janson. As I was dispatched I was informed that I was going to a fire that has escaped the fire line, and the ground crew wanted immediate help to lay a line of retardant across the head of the fire. Having a large load of retardant on an airplane like the DC-6 is not only an excellent load size to work a spot fire, but its best use on a moving fire is to lay a line out in front of the head where no Fire Boss would dare put men or equipment. An awesome experience was waiting for me, an encounter I've had only a few times in my entire thirty-seven years of Fire Bombing. It's a situation that sets itself up for a few minutes and is gone. If the pilot has some luck he'll see and live the fury of a raging fire in a way never seen by others. It's the adrenalin-charged moment that one lives for in this business.

I reported a few minutes out and the Birddog began his briefing about what he wanted.

"Tanker Four Three, I want to place a line of retardant just in front of the head. It's obscured in smoke but the ground is level, there are no snags and if you stay a bit high you won't have any problems. I've checked the route when I've had a few breaks in the smoke and the run is clear."

"Roger, Birddog, I'll have a look in a minute as soon as I'm overhead."

I got into position for a look at the line.

"Okay, Birddog, I can't see the head, so have you got some markers for my line?"

Markers to indicate a line in smoke are chosen outside the fire in clear air. The Birddog may pick the edge of pond or lake at one end of the line, and some prominent landmark on the other side of the fire. If the smoke is too high to pick out a landmark on the other side of the fire, he may pick two landmarks to line up on one side of the fire and tell you that if you continue on that line, you'll be where you should be to get an accurate drop.

This kind of attack in smoke across the head with a bomber is common practice. A bomber can fly along the fire front and lay a line of retardant on unburned fuel just outside the fire head. It's the perfect attack in a zone where ground firefighters or equipment would never venture.

"Roger, Tanker Four Three, I'll fly the line for you and show you the markers for lining up."

"Go ahead, Birddog."

"I'm just over the south edge of this clearing and heading for the light-coloured patch of poplar trees. If you line those two points up, that will set you up for where the load should go. Got that, Four Three?"

I'm overhead and I could see his line perfectly.

"Got it, Birddog!"

"I want a string drop at one half second for the entire load."

"Roger."

I asked Janson to do the bombing check and he ran off the items out loud. I was lucky I was doing a left turn to pick up my line. I could see the landmarks continuously as I was turning and descending. Watching the target or the line-up landmarks during the turn to final was extremely important for me to pick them up when I was down low. There is a vast difference in perspective from seeing the target or run from above the fire and seeing it on the final run at low level. If the pilot doesn't have the picture firmly in mind, and especially if he's not able to see what he's aiming at during the descent and turn, it may be difficult or, in obscured conditions, impossible to pick it up on final.

"That line will put your retardant about two hundred feet out from the head. Start your drop right at the edge of the smoke."

"Roger."

It looked like the run would be about a quarter mile long. I turned far enough out that I could line up the landmarks to establish my line.

"I'm on final, Birddog, and armed for a string drop for the entire load."

"Roger, Four Three, that should take the line all the way across. Your line looks good."

The doors were set to open one half second apart. This door timing is perfect to have the beginning pattern of the next drop exactly join the tail end of the last drop. There are no gaps for the fire to burn through and the load is extended to give maximum coverage. There are twelve doors on the DC-6 and a string drop will make a line at least a quarter mile long.

While I was on final the fire head changed; the smoke lifted and there was a tunnel of clear air along the head. The trees were one hundred to one hundred fifty feet high and the flames looked like they were going up at least two to three hundred feet above the tree tops. The heat was so intense that the flames went straight up even though there was a fairly strong wind of fifteen to twenty miles per hour driving the fire. At about two hundred feet above the flames, the wind won out and sent the smoke curling down to meet the tree tops a few hundred feet downwind from the fire head. Natural forces had conspired to create a tunnel of clear air along the head of the fire and there it was – in front of me – at the perfect moment.

My run tactics then changed. I had originally planned to be a bit high, but that became unnecessary. I could stay in the clear air. We would be at normal drop height, putting us about halfway up the wall of fire. I would still be in front of the fire head, but maybe a little closer than I would have liked. Still, it was a chance for a good, accurate shot.

I had encountered this phenomenon which I call "the tunnel" a few times before. It can happen with moving fires on flat ground. It generally doesn't occur with a fire moving uphill as the fire and smoke tend to lie on the side of the mountain.

"I've got clear air right now, Birddog, so maybe I can finish this before the smoke moves back in."

"Roger, Four Three. Go for it."

As I entered the tunnel, I was completely mesmerized by the sight. A wall of fire much higher than our altitude was a brilliant orange-red and the flaming trees emitted an eerie, hissing roar. The sound became surreal as it was superimposed on the throbbing rumble of the engines. My adrenalin built up as we were enveloped in the otherworldly colour of the flames, the dome of fire and black smoke that enveloped us, and the intense radiant heat. The right wingtip wasn't really touching the fire, but it felt as if we were that close. Janson was closer to the fire than I. I wondered if he was any hotter than I was. There was no time for words. We were awed by the spectacle. The tremendous heat of this wall of fire had deflected the wind and turbulence overhead to give our airplane a tunnel of smooth air. We were flying down a death zone; animals, insects and birds had fled or they perished. Nothing could survive this intense heat and we felt it rapidly building up inside the cockpit. The only other noise I heard above this indescribable sound was the slamming of the retardant tank doors as they open and shut. I knew that each door was dropping the weight of a baby orca whale as we flew along the fire line.

We approached the end of the tunnel, and suddenly it was over. I had reluctantly come out the other side. I wasn't ready. This surreal adventure had to be lived again and again. I wanted reruns instead of the memory. We were among the privileged few. There are no fireworks, complete with the roll of a thousand kettle drums, that could match what we had just experienced. I wondered if this was a preview of Hell for the believers. I looked over to my F/O to see how he felt about it.

"How'd you like that, Janson?"

"I've never seen anything like it."

Janson Kirk had faith in me. I had never placed us into any bad situations before, and his demeanor said that he knew we'd be okay. Janson was cool and professional and I've never seen him get rattled about anything. He just went about his duties with cool, matter-of-fact precision. He would later become a Captain of a 747, flying charter work all over the world.

The noise that a crown fire makes while burning the green needles on the top foliage of pine trees is a difficult one to describe. It changes as the fire progresses. As a boy brought up in the woods of Northern Ontario, I had lit many a campfire and would often place pine branches on the fire to watch the fireworks. I had done it many times and the sound was familiar. All I had to do was light a single bough and the needles would go up with a spattering crackling sound not too unlike the spatter of heavy rain landing on rain-soaked pavement. When an entire tree goes up, as I was later to observe, the sound becomes an eerie, crackling hiss. A wall of fire turns the hiss into a frightening roar.

While we made a spectacular drop, the action did nothing to stop the spread of the fire. The fire wall had so much lifting convection that it carried a million burning embers high above the fire. From there, the prevailing wind carried them far out in front of the head to start new fires. The fire was out of control and it was time for everyone to back off.

Twenty minutes ...

Janson and I are now talking about the drop coming up. He's of the same mind as I am. We're both hoping that the thunderstorm moves right over the fire before we get there so we won't have to drop. Long downhill runs are part of the job, but conditions have to be very much in our favour if we want to stay within the operating limits of the airplane. The thunderstorm is giving us both cause for concern.

"Birddog, this is tanker Four Seven, about twenty minutes out. How close is the thunderstorm?"

"Four Seven, it's getting close, but I think we'll be okay to work the fire."

It was not what I wanted to hear. Thunderstorms have horrific updrafts and downdrafts that have smashed into the ground jet airliners with far better climb performance than we have.

The Dragon's Leg

I knew about thunderstorms; one day I experienced the full force of a downburst next to one. A thunderstorm gives plenty of reason to stay well enough away from it. It happened near one of the towering storms that frequent Rainbow Lake.

We had been on a fire just to the north of the airport for a good part of the afternoon and were keeping watch on a giant thunderstorm, which was getting bigger all the time, about ten miles north of the fire. This storm was a rapidly-growing, super-sized monster that suddenly seemed to encompass the entire area, including the airport. I had just dropped my load and was returning to base when a hurricane wind smashed into the airport. The base is surrounded by deciduous trees, mostly poplar and aspen. The underside of the leaves is a chalky, light green, almost white colour which shows when they are exposed to a stiff wind. The entire airport area became a deranged field of pale white as the trees were bent over to the point of breaking.

We were at circuit altitude when we started to descend. We were going down rapidly. The fire-breathing dragon's leg was stepping on us. I called for climb power on the way down and tried to climb, but it didn't make any difference. We kept on rapidly descending. The wind was directly across the runway so we couldn't land. I was now beating a cowardly retreat southbound away from the vicinity of the airport and the fire. It seemed to be the best direction to escape the gale that was raging at the airport. We were still descending, and at about 200 feet above the trees, I called for dry power. We were already slowed down to about 125 knots and all that power just barely held us above the trees.

A powerful downburst from the storm had reached out for us. We must have been near the edges of the downdraft and were escaping its full force. So far we had been lucky. If we lost any more airspeed, we'd have to take the last recourse: wet power. I hoped that we didn't have to as we only had a few minutes of water injection left. The only thing I could think of that kept us off the trees may have been our riding a ground cushion the storm had conveniently compressed for us. I couldn't believe how far away we had to fly from this storm to finally escape the dragon's wrath: about twenty miles.

That outsized storm looked to be at least thirty to forty miles across. We later learned that it created its own large, low-pressure area like a tropical hurricane. We stayed out of its way for a few hours until it passed and then came back to land.

Fifteen minutes...

We're now about fifteen minutes out and my mind is racing. I can see the storm but can't quite tell how close it is to the fire.

As bomber pilots, what causes us deliberately to seek an occupation where we not only immerse ourselves in the most dangerous part of the atmosphere, but where we will be routinely expected to fly into dangerous conditions? In answer to this question, I can only search the depths of my own soul to ask myself why I chose this career. I really loved to fly and it's not hard for pilots to become fanatics about it. We'll do anything, and for any price, if it means flying some impressive airplanes. Flying is a passion only to be understood by those who have it. Fire Bombing takes a special breed. Yes, we love to fly, but there has to be some spice in it. Going from point A to point B in level flight at altitude doesn't carry much excitement. Flying next to the edges charges up far more adrenalin. I had enough confidence in my own flying to know that it wouldn't hurt me. All I had to do was stay awake and follow the rules. No flight is ever the same, no drop is ever the same, the challenges to do a good job were always there and I eagerly looked forward to it. Flying a Fire Bomber was like the sports I loved: scuba diving, ski racing and hang gliding. I enjoyed doing things that challenged my abilities to the fullest. I never worked a day all the while that I flew Fire Bombers; I was ready to fly from the moment I woke up until it was dark. While on fires, we worked seven days a week and needed to be available from dawn till dark. The pay wasn't great, so why would anyone in their right mind do this?

Author at the bottom of a downhill run. Photo courtesy Dave Ralston

The trouble is we like flying, and we enjoy flying on the edge. Operators take advantage of this kind of devotion. We'll work for far less than the job deserves, and we take the inadequate pay we get because we love what we're doing so much. Furthermore, we don't believe there are dangers to this job. It's true, people were getting killed at it, but it was all their fault. They got killed for stupid reasons. They didn't have to be killed. That's what we say to ourselves to rationalize the dangers away.

This was still the way I spoke to myself until the first time the bottom dropped out from under my airplane. *Hey – this isn't in the job description – there should be no surprises.* Then it happened again – twice now. I'm not so smug anymore about why pilots get killed. Surprises when you're next to the edges can kill people, even highly-competent pilots. The reality is I'm not immune from it happening again.

362

I think back to the occasion when I refused even to enter a fire area. I had been dispatched to a fire in the McKenzie River Valley just to the south of Norman Wells. I wasn't sure why I was even sent. The visibility in smoke was so bad, even the birds were walking. There had been fires burning in the area for over a month, exacerbated by the fact that the North has a caribou moss which carries a fire quickly and burns with a smoke that's thick and acrid. There were several fires covering tens of thousands of acres, which filled the air with this foul-smelling smoke that burned the lungs.

I found out just how bad the visibility was after getting airborne. I could only climb to 800 feet of altitude. Above that, I couldn't see the trees below. The Birddog was at the fire and I asked him about the visibility. He told me it wasn't good but he had the fire in sight and said the visibility was good enough to work the fire. I told him I was at 800 feet, which must also be my forward visibility. He agreed, but felt we could work the fire. I was also hearing other traffic on the radio of other airplanes coming up from the south to land at Norman Wells. There was just too much activity to suit me in a situation of extremely restricted visibility. There would be another problem with the way the DC-6 performs: I'd lose sight of the fire on every turn trying to come back to the target.

When I put it all together, visibility at 800 feet, more flying traffic entering the area and the fact that this amount of visibility just didn't give me a fair chance to see a possible mid-air collision in time or even to work the fire, I asked Birddog to reconsider the action. If he had insisted we continue, I would have refused. He agreed that it would not be wise and we both returned to base.

Ten minutes...

We're ten minutes out and it looks like the storm is almost on top of the fire.

"Birddog, Four Seven — ten minutes out."

"Tanker, Four Seven this is Birddog."

"Roger, Birddog, go ahead."

"The storm is just off to the west of the fire, but I think we can get your drop in before it gets here."

This is the first time that Birddog has mentioned the thunderstorm. It must be giving him a pretty good shaking. Birddog pilots have something in common with bomber pilots: we're masters of understatement, and no one will say that they're getting tossed all over the sky. If it's rough, it's rough. There's nothing unusual about rough air. We're in it most of the time. I've never heard a Birddog say it's too rough for a bombing run. If a stranger were to tap the Birddog pilot on the shoulder and ask how rough the ride is, the most likely answer would be, "A bit bumpy, but no problem."

Know Your Own Limits

My mind kept working. Sure, I could refuse a run if I think it's too dangerous. Other than that thought, it never occurred to me that any situation was beyond my flying ability. I sweated bad visibility for instrument landings on occasion, but my proficiency was adequate. Now I think about how difficult it might be to place the load accurately if the turbulence is severe or I get a downdraft. Making accurate drops was always a source of pride with me; I didn't like to misplace a load. A twinge of thought registered that the conditions might be beyond my ability, rather odd thoughts for a guy with my cockiness and ego. I had always performed when I needed it, and that included the countless flight tests and instrument rides over the years. *Put the doubts aside, Linc. You've got what it takes.* For a moment, my mind went back to coming through with skill that I wasn't sure I even had.

The Air Force pushed us hard in training, through a learning curve we were expected to meet. We kept up the pace or we would no longer be pilots in the RCAF. They couldn't spend forever training the incompetents. One day at Jet School I was up solo in a T-33 practicing various maneuvers when a snowstorm moved in to the airport, producing heavy snow. Visibility was next to zero. This was the type of occasion when all aircraft were recalled to base. Needless to say, I was concerned about getting down. Zero visibility at my home base did not sound like the place I wanted to land.

I didn't have much instrument time in the T-33 and had only done a few GCAs (Ground Controlled Approaches). This system of radar on the ground creates a couple of beams: one is a localizer that aims the pilot at the center of the runway, and the other is a glide slope that gives him an easy-to-fly descent angle to the threshold of the runway. Nowadays it's called Precision Approach Radar (PAR). The operator on the ground watches the aircraft's radar return on his screen and directs the pilot by voice to fly on these beams.

"Portage tower, Flight Eight Two five minutes out. Request landing instructions."

With the visibility being as it was, and being the green student that I was, I expected a diversion. There was no such luck.

"Eight Two, you're cleared for a GCA," said the control tower operator in a very matter-of-fact voice, perhaps not realizing that he was talking to an inexperienced student.

"You're cleared from your present position to Bravo beacon to descend to 2,500 feet. At Bravo, switch to __ frequency for a GCA approach"

He didn't seem to realize who I was and that the visibility was zero.

"Roger cleared to Bravo to descend to 2,500 feet."

Did I just say that? Am I in possession of my senses? *Hey tower man, the visibility is zero. Nobody lands in zero visibility.* Maybe it would get better when I got there. But I came back to reality and realized that getting there would only be a matter of minutes. I couldn't back out; I was committed. I had done it under the bag (the hood we pull over the inside of the canopy for instrument practice in the back seat) a few times before and the operator had talked me down on a perfect approach. At the precise time, he told me to round out as I was now over the runway. But that was practice; I had an instructor up front who would save us from oblivion if I did anything wrong.

This time it was for real. It was all white outside. The visibility was zero. *Time to ignore the reality. Pretend it's practice. You've done it before, just do the same thing again, Linc.* I told myself that it's actually no different than being under the hood. I hoped I would get the same operator who had a calm, confident reassuring voice – a man you'd follow anywhere. He could sell ice to an Eskimo. I called at the beacon and just the man I was hoping for came on.

"Flight Eight Two, you are cleared for a GCA. You do not have to acknowledge my instructions. If you do not receive instructions for a period of ten seconds please execute a missed approach."

"Roger," said I with faked bravado.

He started his instructions in the full confidence of having done a million of these approaches without ever having driven someone into the ground. *But I'm a green student, I could be the first.*

"You're four feet high on the glide path; increase your rate of descent slightly. You're three feet left of the localizer. Steer right a bit."

And so the instructions went and I realized that I could follow his soothing commands. I had enough experience on the airplane to feel its every mood and I could make minute adjustments as the controller commanded. I continued to obey his comforting words. Correct a bit this way and a bit that way. Then I heard some very reassuring words:

"You are on the glide slope and on the localizer, one mile from touchdown."

I had nailed the approach. A few seconds later I heard it again.

"You are on the glide slope and on the localizer."

Even when no corrections were necessary, he continued his transmissions; it was reassuring to know he was there and watching over me every second. I was a half mile, then a quarter mile from touchdown. I was concentrating so hard, I hardly heard the words I was waiting for.

"You're twenty feet over the button of the runway. Reduce your power and begin your round-out."

I slowly reduced the power and started to raise the nose of the aircraft. As I did this, I could just make out the passing of one white centre line after another as I went down the runway. I felt the wheels touch. I was down. I had enough visibility to taxi down the runway and to the parking area. It all fit so nicely into place: I simply followed instructions and it worked. I landed in a condition I had considered dangerous and impossible, but I was just a newbie student. I didn't know how much would be expected of us. Radar approaches to touchdown even in zero visibility was obviously routine for Air Force pilots. It wouldn't be long before I was to learn more "impossible" flying — like formation aerobatics in cloud.

Five minutes...

"Roger, Birddog. I'm now about five minutes out"

As I enter the area to size up my drop, part of my turn is in rain. Then I'm out of it and the fire area is clear. The entire circuit is in fierce turbulence. We're getting a real shaking.

"Tanker Four Seven, your run will be the same as I had told you about earlier. You tag on to the bottom of your last load, and do a string drop at half-second with all twelve doors down to the bottom."

"Roger. Got that, Birddog."

"The storm shouldn't bother your run. I did it a few minutes ago and there was no problem."

Birddog just had a safe run, but it doesn't mean it will be safe for me even one minute later. Delta Airlines Flight 191 was slammed into the ground in a thunderstorm when the pilot attempted to land at Dallas-Fort Worth airport only two minutes behind an aircraft that had landed safely. Wind conditions change fast in the raging air around a thunderstorm. A reality that sets in very soon after one gets into this business is that Fire Bombing actions are not called off for turbulence. And yet it's the major cause for wing failures. Even though downbursts have driven airliners into the ground, we ignore the hazards around thunderstorms. Why am I thinking about this now? I've been in this environment for years and never really worried about being thoroughly shaken up. It is just part of the job.

367

My inner voice is speaking to me:

You've pushed it this far, Linc, and you've gotten away with it. Don't take unnecessary chances now.

I know within myself that I won't. Janson and I work the airplane together for our mutual survival, but when it comes to that actual flying of the aircraft, he has to rely on me. He's got enough confidence in me to know that I won't do anything stupid. Even though I liked the excitement of Fire Bombing, I had always taken every precaution.

Also, if I don't like what I see, I can always refuse the run. That's an option that I only exercised the one time at Garibaldi Lake. It's not something we do on a daily basis. When the Birddog makes a run for the bomber, he and the Fire Control Officer make a mutual judgment that the run is safe. They don't expect to be regularly challenged; they expect the Fire Bomber pilots to accept their decision. And we always do.

Do I waste enough time circling over the fire to allow the storm to get here — then chicken out? No, it's not the way I do things. I ask Janson for the bombing check and get set up to do the run. The Birddog has declared the run safe. I'll now make my own assessment as to when I'll start the run. I've got a little time. As I survey my side of the storm, I see the smoke making radical shifts of direction. With luck, it may turn and blow up the mountain.

The Dive

I don't have to circle long before it happens: the tortured trails of smoke make a turn in my favour. There is a rapidly rising column curling up the mountain, all the way to the top. The dulcet voice of my Fairy Siren speaks to me:

I have sprinkled green pixie dust along the path of your entire run. You are safe for now, my love, but remember that the air can become dangerous in a few seconds and I may not have time to warn you. Make your run quickly.

That column of rising air was as permanent as any other column of twisted air that rages around any thunderstorm. There is no time to waste. Regardless of my varying airspeed and the turbulence I feel as I'm lining up on final, I should have a headwind as I cross over the ridge and for the rest of the way down. I'm set up to drop and the tanks are selected on "auto" for the entire load. To make a long run down hill, it's absolutely essential that I cross over the top of the ridge at the slowest possible speed. We just clear the ridge at 115 knots with full flap. I've bet on my knowledge of the smoke to make an irreversible commitment. A tailwind or downdraft at that speed would send us into the mountain.

We're over the top. Now it takes a big push down with the nose to follow the contour of the mountain – we have almost zero g. Everything is working as I thought it should: we aren't accelerating too quickly, our airspeed will be a little high to start the drop, but we'll stay below maximum flap down speed.

Just near the end of my last load, I hit the drop button and I hear the doors start to bang. I have to keep pushing the nose down. The airplane wants to climb as it picks up speed and gets lighter. The load is gone. It's been a rough ride but a perfect drop. It will be a relief to get away from this storm. I'm surprised that conditions weren't a lot worse and that I was actually able to make a timely, accurate drop.

Tanker Five One is called off a short time later because the storm covers the fire.

This is the everyday stuff of Fire Bombing. There is no routine run. There is a singular truth to our commitment each time. When we start our run there is no turning back. I must have the memory of what I will see on a low approach, the correct target, the approximate trigger point, and our escape alternative all in place. And there still is never a guarantee of how each run will unfold. The day turned out to be a good one and I was thankful for that.

Chapter Twenty Three
The Odyssey Ends

Pilot's "Squawk": Left inside main tire almost needs replacement.
Maintenance fix: Almost replaced left inside main tire.
Quantas Airlines

Bomber Pilots have chosen a career of flying near the edges, near the edges of our own ability, near the edges of the ground and near the edges of our airplane's performance. We must always get it right. Fortunately, calm days with fairly easy actions on a hill top or flat ground reward us for the day's work with breathtaking scenery on our journeys to and from the fire. We are awed at the grandeur of where we work the spectacular results that we achieve and realize how lucky we are.

I considered it to be my good fortune that I got involved with Fire Bombing in its infancy. I was party to watching and participating in the quantum leaps of initiative that took this whole business from chaos to One Strike. I flew beautiful airplanes with effective bombing systems. But technology moves along; new drop systems like the Constant Flow tank and turbo-prop airplanes like the Lockheed Electra, the Tracker and the Convair are displacing the older airplanes. I would love to have flown the newer turbine-powered aircraft. Indispensable instruments like the SMI/AOA are making the Fire Bombing profession safer.

A Matter of Philosophy

After observing aerial firefighting tactics over the years with various agencies, a glaringly obvious fact about Fire Bombing became apparent to me: the use of aircraft in Fire Bombing is highly political. The entire aerial firefighting industry as well as governmental agencies in charge of wildfire protection have no problem with understanding the effectiveness of Fire Bombing when used on small fires. The concept of One Strike was developed and adopted early by the pioneering agencies, The California Department of Forestry and the British Columbia Forest Service. They put two and two together at the same time and realized that the Fire Bomber gave them a huge advantage in the fire equation. It's something that every fire fighter instinctively knows: **In extreme hazards, with time, fires spread and become more intense.**

Strangely enough, even after Art Kirk and Denny McDonald developed and proved One Strike in British Columbia, old-timers at headquarters were writing assessment papers about the system and using words to the effect: "Not the panacea for fighting fires but another tool in the arsenal to help the Fire Boss." Entrenched bureaucracies are hard to dislodge from their old, established ways of doing things, and new ideas seem to bring terror to their organization. How will they possibly cope with something new and how many jobs will be displaced or lost to change? It was not an instant or easy political sell.

After One Strike had been used for a few years, there was a complete about-turn in this thinking. It was recognized that the real genius of Fire Bombing emerged with One Strike.

Enter the Fire Bomber and One Strike

Enter now the Fire Bomber as the initial attack weapon. We can recall that One Strike is the concept of sending enough retardant to every reported fire to finish the fire's containment in one continuous action without the need for the airplanes to make a return trip. How much retardant and how many aircraft needed to make the strike are determined by the dispatch office. It's an experienced dispatch borne of having considerable knowledge of the local forest and fire behavior in the dispatcher's district. Sufficient retardant for containment could be several hundred gallons of retardant or a few thousand. British Columbia found that 3,000 imperial gallons was enough in the vast majority of dispatches.

It must be said again that this method of dispatch and initial attack by aircraft is a far faster and safer way to achieve early containment of a fire than a ground attack.

An initial attack by aircraft carrying sufficient retardant to contain a small fire literally takes place in minutes. An additional benefit is that no one on the ground is exposed to the probability of the fire exploding as they often do in extreme hazards. In British Columbia, a huge change of who had control of the initial attack took place. When the bomber action is complete, a ground crew moves in to achieve control at a quiescent fire. There is nothing more complicated about the concept than that. It is fast and safe. This overpowering ability to contain fires immediately at discovery now takes the airplane out of the category of "just another tool to help the Fire Boss." It's a complete initial action in itself, completely out of the hands of the Fire Boss. In fact, most One Strike actions take place even before the ground crew arrives.

Accepting the highly effective and fast initial attack by aircraft has brought about a different mindset. The recognition is there that the airplane or airplanes have an overwhelming ability to contain the small fire very speedily. This advantage can be lost just as quickly, so it's essential to dispatch immediately to every reported fire when the hazard is up. In these conditions, initial attack is exclusively the domain of the airplane. This mindset deploys numerous airplanes strategically situated at dispersed bases for quick arrival at a fire. Huge airplanes aren't needed. Ideal aircraft are highly maneuverable airplanes capable of carrying 800 to 3,000 gallons of retardant.

The Birddog, the Fire Bombers and their supporting crew are an autonomous group, charged with the responsibility of implementing One Strike. This autonomous group operates in the same manner as any local fire department: instant response with adequate resources to every reported fire.

The Enlightened Dispatch

The forests of western Canada and the USA do have their wet summer seasons. Every fire fighter has sat out the misery of a season with little action. But it's also true that various regions will have hot, dry conditions where the burning hazards in the forest will go to high and extreme. California is the best example of the entire state going to extreme hazard every summer, a characteristic of the Mediterranean climate. Fire behaviour is predictable for the entire state for most of the summer, if not its entirety.

For other areas of the North American West, East and anywhere else in the world, the fire hazard will go to extreme after two or three weeks of hot, dry weather and fire behavior will become predictable. All the fire indices will clearly say to anyone who is paying close attention: bad news – hazard extreme – explosive situation – take no chances. The proper response is clear: hit everything with One Strike. Perhaps the forest services should work on a sprinkler-system mentality: when the temperature (forest conditions) hits a certain value, the dispatch system automatically flips to instant go. Can the criteria for dispatch be that simple? In truth it can. But does this really happen?

It ain't necessarily so.

When the absurdly simple philosophy of sending bombers on "One Strike" to every reported fire in high and extreme hazards is implemented, equally simple results follow. I have taken one trip to thousands of small fires and seen hot, dry seasons without a single Project Fire.

Mrs. Jones and the Fire Department

Once upon a time, all city fire departments were instantly dispatched to every call with firefighting resources sufficient to handle most anticipated emergencies in the area of their coverage. Fire fighters prided themselves on how quickly they could get dressed and be out the Fire Hall door and on their way to the fire. They arrived at the fires while they were still small and putting them out was swift and easy. The system worked extremely well.

But one day an evil bureaucratic Fairy Godmother came along and said: You silly firemen, why are you responding to every call from people who aren't qualified to report a fire? You could end up going to a house where there is no fire. And why do you dispatch a Big Truck each time? If you end up at a house with a little grease fire, a small utility truck with a hand-held extinguisher could put it out. You don't need to send big trucks. Your fire department is spending far too much money to put out small fires. We bureaucrats at the Fairy Godmother think-tank have a better fire fighting plan for you, and one which will save you vast amounts of money. It's called Escalation of Effort.

The city fire departments were all anxious to save money so they adopted Escalation of Effort as their new method to fight fires. How would fire control work on Mrs. Jones' house if your local fire department fought fires with Escalation of Effort?

Mrs. Jones calls the local fire department and says:

"Please get over to my place at 123 Park Street because some grease spilled off my stove and lit my curtains on fire."

"Okay, Mrs. Jones, we'll send someone over to look."

The fire department no longer considers Mrs. Jones to be a qualified observer and reliable enough to report a fire accurately. It is therefore necessary to send over a fire investigator who is qualified enough to know that Mrs. Jones' report of a fire is correct. The investigator arrives at Mrs. Jones' house in the station patrol car about fifteen minutes after the call, knocks at the door and asks Mrs. Jones if he can come in to verify the fire.

He enters the kitchen and observes that the curtains are on fire and are scorching the ceiling, so he calls the fire station on his radio:

"I'm here at Mrs. Jones' house and the curtains are on fire all right, but it's only the curtains. If you send the utility vehicle with a five-pound fire extinguisher along with the one-inch hose and the 200 gallon reservoir, it should be enough to do it."

Fifteen minutes later, which is now thirty minutes after the initial call, the utility vehicle arrives and the firemen reel out the hose, start the water pump and come inside to fight the fire. By then the entire kitchen is on fire and the one-inch hose and the limited supply of water is totally inadequate to fight a hot fire. The utility truck driver gets on his radio and calls the fire station:

"The kitchen is on fire at Mrs. Jones' house, but it's only the kitchen. If you send the small fire truck here and a couple more men, we should be able to knock it off okay."

Fifteen minutes later, which is now forty-five minutes after the initial call, the truck arrives with a 500 gallon reservoir of water and the men determinedly burst into the house to fight the fire. The reservoir is quickly running out and the Fire Captain finds that the fire has spread beyond the kitchen and is engulfing the living room. There is intense heat next to the ceiling and it looks like a flash-over could occur at any minute. He calls the fire station on his radio:

"We've got a fire that's spreading fast. It's in the living room and a flash-over could occur at any time. Send over the Big Truck so we can connect to a fire hydrant and get some action on this thing."

Fifteen minutes later, which is now one hour after the initial call (time seems to slide by so quickly during the Escalation of Effort) Big Truck finally arrives to a home that's totally engulfed in flames. It takes another five minutes to hook up to the hydrant and turn the hoses onto a house that is rapidly becoming a burnt-out skeleton. There is no saving the house, but the houses nearby are saved because there is plenty of water to keep their walls cool to prevent them from catching fire.

We can see the progression of action that occurs when there is an Escalation of Effort in fighting what begins as a small fire. The whole concept totally ignores the most important element in the progress of a fire: **with time, fires spread, get bigger and become more intense.**

We must examine the process of logic at work here: if the initial action with the utility truck had been successful, the taxpayer would have been saved substantial money. The fire could have been put out at the cheapest cost. Unfortunately it didn't turn out that way, but that's just the breaks with Escalation of Effort. Everyone is quite sorry that the whole process took too long, but at least it's only Mrs. Jones' house that burned. Too bad for Mrs. Jones. Fortunately, that's not the way that fire departments respond to fire calls.

This hypothetical sequence of events at Mrs. Jones' house is fighting fire with the same logic as sending a small force by helicopter to fight a forest fire in extreme hazard that has the potential to escalate rapidly into a major holocaust. (Small fire, small effort – and accelerate the effort as the fire gets larger.) If the crew "catches it," money will be saved. In both cases the only rationale for the Escalation of Effort is the claim that the initial attack can be done at the cheapest possible price. The overwhelming early initial attack with Fire Bombers would be more expensive and that expense has been saved.

The huge daily cost incurred when a Project Fire is underway is not backtracked to the inherent weaknesses of the Escalation of Effort concept of fighting a fire in extreme hazards. Whether it's with Mrs. Jones' house or with a forest fire, Escalation of Effort leaves the fire fighters just behind the speed of expansion of the fire.

The Media

But there is another extremely important element that is present when Mrs. Jones calls the fire department to report her house on fire but which is missing when a Mrs. Smith calls to report a forest fire. That element is the media. When the media arrives to photograph and report on Mrs. Jones' house fire, reporters may immediately question the behaviour of the fire department. They may ask pointed questions: "When did Mrs. Jones call? How soon did the fire department respond after she called?" Local fire departments are under media scrutiny.

The media responds very differently in event of a forest fire. No one sees or even thinks to ask what the forest firefighting agency did early in the progression of a newly reported fire. Furthermore, the media doesn't question the assumption that the Mrs. Smith who reported the forest fire can't be believed and the sequence of the Escalation of Effort sets in.

In my own experience, I have seen the first column of smoke coming out of a new fire from my standby base at the airport. A massive aerial initial attack on the fire was possible within minutes. But that's not what happened. The column continued to expand until the spot fire went to the crowns of the trees and exploded into a rapidly expanding fire. Several bureaucracies had to make a decision before the Escalation of Effort could even get started.

When the fires get big enough and threaten lives and property, and especially when homes start burning, the media finally finds a story worthy of reporting. Weeping homeowners are the stuff of good reporting. What the forest firefighting agency did from the start of the fire is not a story unless the fire turns into a raging firestorm that destroys many homes. Then the media may get interested.

It's catastrophic for Mrs. Jones to lose her home. Tears in front of the camera make for powerful drama. It's trivial when a fire escapes in the forest and no one is threatened. It's just another forest fire.

The Problem Child — The Project Fire

There is an inescapable truth about having an agency to deal with large fires. Sitting out a wet season with little action means sticking within a budget for the fiscal year. It's tough going. There is little if any money for new equipment and the shopping list that every agency has. However, when a Project Fire is burning, the government purse strings open and unlimited money flows to the district having the big fire or fires. Now the agency has the money to buy all the goodies they wanted but had to wait for their big fire to get.

So it also ain't necessarily so that a district doesn't want to see some big fires.

Furthermore, when large fires are a frequent occurrence, the Escalation of Effort mindset is to have bigger and bigger aircraft carrying bigger and bigger loads of retardant. As a result, the bureaucracy and expenses escalate.

Perhaps it's like the difference between a problem child and a problem adult. If a problem child at age five were to steal gum from the local corner store, proper handling at that stage could likely solve the problem of the child's stealing habit with minimal effort and without the expense of society's intervention. If the stealing habit were allowed to continue and the problem child becomes a problem adult that robs a bank for millions of dollars, society intervenes with big police forces and large expensive jails. It's a case of catching the problem when it's small or waiting for it to get big.

Huge airplanes, like the Boeing 747 that carries 20,000 gallons of retardant, and the DC-10 that carries 12,000 gallons, are coming into use. These airplanes, of course, are used in supporting roles on big fires. They are of a different genre to the nimble, smaller aircraft used in initial attack. It seems to me that this trend to gargantuan aircraft is extremely counterproductive, expensive and a step in the wrong direction. Big bureaucracies appear to be like ponderous freight trains fixed in their direction, seemingly unable to get off the tracks. Decision makers at the top may know how One Strike works, but protecting the empire's status quo is of higher priority. Refusing progress shouldn't be a great surprise; it afflicts much of humanity.

Fighting wildfires in California is the bellwether for fighting forest fires anywhere in the world. California has the variety of brush and forest conditions found virtually anywhere. It also has two firefighting agencies responsible for their respective forests, CALFIRE and the USFS. Each employs radically different tactics in the use of the Fire Bomber. California provides the observer with a perfect comparison between the effectiveness of the One Strike concept used by CALFIRE and the Escalation of Effort used by the USFS. I had watched the difference many times in the late 1960s and wondered if the use of aircraft in initial attack was any different in 2010. I asked a number of people in-the-know and discovered that in 2010 not much has changed.

Bob Fish describes the difference between CALFIRE and the USFS this way:

The CALFIRE and Federal forestry management organizations (USFS, BLM, etc) use a completely different philosophy of employing their aerial firefighting capabilities.

CALFIRE embraces the "initial attack" (One Strike) concept. When an incident is called in to one of the CALFIRE Air Tanker Bases, both air-attack (OV-10) and air tanker (S-2T) aircraft are dispatched and fly to the fire site together. Upon arriving at the scene, the air-attack pilot immediately orbits the scene at 1,000 feet. This allows the Air Tactical Group Supervisor in the back seat to reconnoiter the situation and communicate with any fire team on the ground. He decides how best to deploy the tanker payload in an attempt to contain the fire while it's small. The S-2T will make the appropriate drop and, a high percentage of the time, gets the fire under control or puts it out.

On the other hand, the Federal program embraces the concept of "managing" a fire. They deploy air tankers as part of an overall fire suppression operation on a large project fire, usually after it has grown beyond the capabilities of the ground strike teams. Fire Bombers are focused on placing retardant lines in areas where the ground terrain is too difficult or there is a high probability of losing homes or valuable property. Since they use more expensive, less maneuverable, higher-capacity (ergo, heavier) tankers than CALFIRE, their observation aircraft have the additional Birddog assignment of "flying the drop route" to get a feel for wind drift, hot spots, obstacles, and an exit path with minimum issues for the multi-engined tankers (wind shear, smoke, flying debris, etc).

What Don't We Understand?

Do we need to remind ourselves to understand what every child who has ever built a campfire instinctively knows? No fire starts at 10,000 acres, no fire starts at one acre and other than a lightning strike, which may ignite an entire tree, or the action of an arsonist where an accelerant is used, every fire begins with a single flame, the match. If we could start there, a breath of air or moistened fingers would put it out. Given adequate fuel and the right conditions, it's just not possible not to understand that with time a fire gets bigger, and often very quickly. There is no simpler, nor easier-to-understand progression: **fire plus time equals a bigger, more intense fire.**

So the logic of fighting a forest fire should be equally simple: arrive at a discovered fire at the earliest possible moment with more than enough retardant to finish the containment expeditiously. The entire emphasis is on speed of containment and is best achieved by instantly dispatching aircraft to every reported fire with the object of achieving One Strike.

Is it possible to miss something so simple and so glaringly obvious? Massive initial aerial attack has proven to be so successful in containing small fires that a logical progression of the system would be to try and find fires at an even smaller size (perhaps with more air patrol) and to create additional bomber bases to have more aircraft strategically located to allow faster initial attack. The responsible agencies should think about putting systems in place to fight even smaller fires instead of bigger ones. I have often asked myself if it's possible that anyone could miss this logic. It was extremely distressing for me to be flying on a big fire when I knew that if I had been there a few hours earlier, the attack would have achieved exceptional results. But my job was to fly the airplane and leave the logic to someone else.

A Duty Fulfilled

In my years of flying the Fire Bomber, I made a difference where I could. Over the years, there were so many fatalities through improper bombing practices, I felt compelled to write the manual that needed writing. It was always my hope that *Air Attack on Forest Fires* scattered enough gems of wisdom to enough pilots to keep more of them alive.

For so many years, I and my fellow pilots were shamelessly underpaid for the type of flying we were doing. But the time came when I could do something about it, not for the entire industry, but for the pilots of Conair, and I was instrumental in getting our group into a powerful union and permanently changing how we were treated by the company.

Spring training was a month of work and stress that came along every March and April like clockwork. I looked forward to it every year; it was just spring ritual: study the manual, write the exams, do the check ride, have a stress-relieving night at the pub with the boys and be ready for another season. It just went on year after year and I thought it would never end. I hoped it would never end.

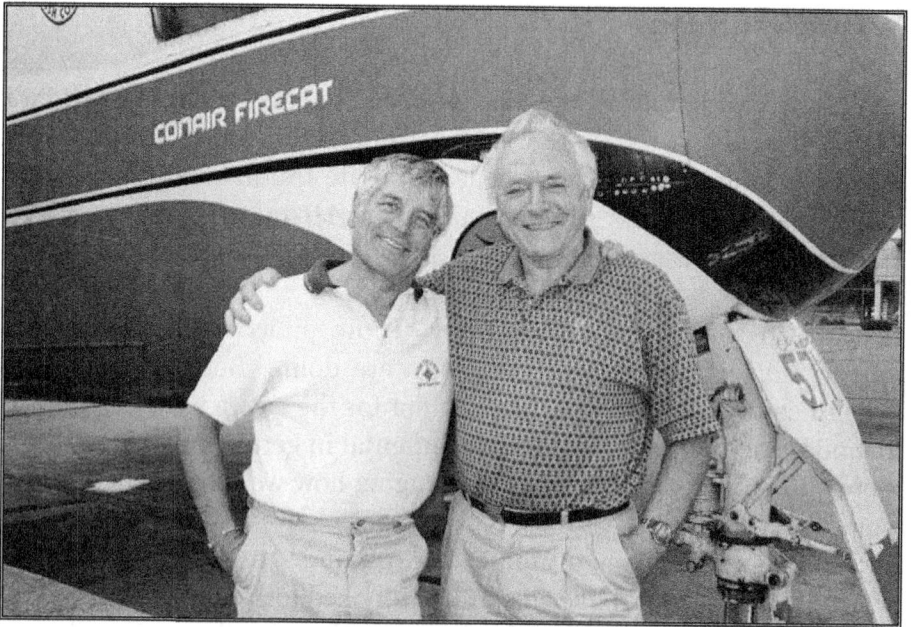

**George Plawski and I celebrating retirement
from the great adventure.**

But the year came along when the numbers on my birth certificate gave me away. *I have to quit. Why should I quit? Age is just a number. I'm still competent.* But I knew that my arguments about staying on with the company were futile. Retirement age with the company was written in stone and backed up by the Ministry of Transport. The season had arrived for the great adventure to end.

In 1996, we had been invited south after our season ended and I along with another DC-6 were standing by at Kalispell, Montana. When we were no longer needed, we were given orders to proceed back to Abbotsford. I knew that this was my last flight in the DC-6 and I had a terribly final feeling about it. I had been in that seat for eighteen years, and the lady had become a dear friend. Flying that gentle airplane and listening to the throb of the R-2800 engines was the way every summer was and the way I expected every summer to be. There would be no end.

382

It all began when at age six I hand flew my little Taylorcraft for a million miles. Little did I suspect the adventure that lay ahead. Now on my last flight, I had a few hours to recapture and relive the feeling, the sounds and the scents of Fire Bombing while I was still immersed in the envelope of my airplane. The lady was begging me to stay. "We are superbly matched partners in flight," she whispered, "why do we have to part?" I fought a barrage of sad emotions in the last half hour of the flight and was determined that my last landing would have the perfect, gentle touch. The tires gave that telltale little squeal when they gently caressed the pavement, and I slowly made our way to the parking area. My hands lingered on the controls, anxious to prolong each precious moment. Finally the time came to end the trip and a career. I lovingly fingered the throttles as I powered back and then pulled the mixture controls to "idle cut-off." The engines went silent for the last time. We did the shut-down check and the whine of the inverters tapered off to nothing. The departure was extremely difficult, and I was fighting back tears as I took one long, final look around the cockpit. I then left the airplane.

When I reviewed the panorama of my entire career, I realized that I had made all the mistakes that one can make in this business, and when my planning and precautions on a run weren't enough, nothing but pure chance stopped my unplanned dives in downdrafts from sending me into oblivion. The fates were on my side. When I began to fly a Fire Bomber, in my naïveté, I expected that the job would have its moments of excitement, but I never expected that it would turn out to be the deadly game that it is. Little did I know I would see the death of so many friends.

The newer bombers have far better performance than the marginally suitable airplanes that I flew (the F7F excepted). Better performing airplanes should be safer in the mountain environment, but the boundary layer of my time is still the deadly boundary layer of today. It lies in wait to spring its surprises.

I still have many friends who fly the bomber. My wish for you and all the pilots who put their lives on the line in the performance of this duty, is that your Guardian Angel graduated from the same Fire-Bomber Pilot Protection School as mine. Survive this business and live happily ever after.

Linc W. Alexander

In Recognition

Ron Thomas

Ron Thomas. Photo courtesy George Plawski

A very special camaraderie develops among people engaged in a dangerous occupation.

We make many fast friends with bonds that last for a lifetime. While I have sought to appreciate many of the individuals with whom I have worked, I cannot, in this short book, give written recognition to all the talented and devoted people that have contributed so much to this addicting business. But one individual commands respect for the marvelous work he has been doing for others outside of his own comfort zone. That individual is Ron Thomas, a man widely recognized both in CAL FIRE and among bomber pilots for his altruistic work on behalf of Fire Bomber pilot widows and orphans. His concerns touched my own feelings about a better deal for the pilots engaged in this business. Unfortunately Ron's work came to a premature end. I asked George Plawski, Ron's close friend to write a short biographical sketch:

Ron "Mouse" Thomas, 1939-2007

Ron grew up in Santa Rosa, Ca. After graduating from high school, he implanted his infectiously cheerful and optimistic disposition into the California Division of Forestry, now renamed CAL FIRE, becoming foreman at the Sonoma air attack base. In 1970 he retrained as an air attack officer, a position he held until his retirement in 1993.

In 1995 he co-invented a system which introduced aerial surveillance to the conduct of arson investigation. This required following suspected arsonists by a team composed of numerous vehicles controlled from an aircraft for the purpose of collecting the kind of conclusive evidence required by the courts.

From the aircraft, Ron followed the suspects' every move by the use of gyro-stabilised binoculars while directing his team on the ground via a discrete radio frequency.

Due to most arsonists' nocturnal habits, much of this exhausting surveillance had to be conducted at night, but the effort was well rewarded with numerous convictions.

Ron's most enduring legacy, however, springs not from the conduct of his work but from the content of his character which manifested itself in his unending desire to help others. All who knew him were aware of this bedrock of altruism which permeated his nature. Nowhere was this more apparent than in his organisation of the Widows and Orphans Fund. Unlike regular firefighters, air tanker pilots were not insured by the government in event of their deaths.

This prompted Ron to start a fund which disbursed moneys to families of pilots who lost their lives on the job. One of the ways in which he collected the cash was by staging an annual golf tournament for which he tirelessly canvassed contributions. He also organised fundraising dinners for which he not only provided much of the food, mostly in the form of viands from his hunts, but acted as chef as well.

Ron clearly understood that the gross unfairness of this situation required a change of legislation. With this in mind, he engaged the sympathetic ear of a congresswoman from Wyoming and made two trips to Washington in an attempt to have this issue reviewed by a congressional committee, but this initiative terminated in the summer of 2007 when Ron was diagnosed with cancer. He fought the disease with the same determination which defined his life, but succumbed on the 14 of February 2007.

The love and respect in which he was held was reflected in the celebration of his life which was attended by over 700 persons. He will continue to be missed by all who had the privilege to know him.

Glossary

Air attack: The containment or fireguard building done by aircraft at a forest fire.

Air Tactical Group Supervisor (ATCS): The CalFire "Air Attack Officer" in charge of air operations over a fire. Synonyms – Birddog, Lead plane.

Air Tanker: An aircraft equipped to drop water or retardants of forest fires as part of a planned containment or control action. Synonyms – Fire Bomber and Water Bomber.

Air Tanker base: An airport facility containing retardant mixing and loading facilities for Fire Bomber aircraft.

Angle of attack indicator (AOA): An instrument showing the pilot how close he is to the stall. Synonym – Stall Margin Indicator (SMI).

Arson fires: Forest fires/wildfires deliberately lit by arsonists.

Backfire: An extensive fire set along the inner edge of a control line, usually some distance from the main fire. The purpose is to consume the fuel between the main fire and the fire line.

Basic initial air attack: A Fire Bomber attack on a fire where the retardant is delivered on the fire head, flanks and base, in that order.

Birddog: In British Columbia, the Forest Service "Fire Control Officer" riding in the Birddog aircraft in charge of Fire Bombing operations.

Birddog aircraft: The aircraft flown by a contracted pilot carrying the Birddog.

Bomber base: An airport facility containing retardant mixing and loading facilities for Fire Bomber aircraft.

Bombing run: The path flown by the Fire Bomber during the approach, the pass over the target and the escape route.

Boundary layer: The atmosphere from the ground up to about five thousand feet.

Bull's eye: A load of retardant that has been accurately placed according to Birddog's request.

California Cannonball: Air breaking over mountain ridges creating the unexpected rotor winds, downdrafts, turbulence and instant tailwinds that are a hazard to Fire Bomber aircraft.

Cat line: A physical firebreak made by bulldozers.

Contained: A forest fire surrounded by a hand, retardant or equipment line.

Constant-flow, variable-quantity drop system: A retardant dropping system that allows for a selected flow at a constant rate from the Fire Bomber retardant tank. The drop door can be shut against the remaining quantity in the tank.

Crown fire: A fire that advances from top to top of shrubs or trees more or less independently of the surface fire.

Density altitude: Density altitude is the pressure altitude adjusted for non-standard temperature. Both an increase in temperature and humidity (to a much lesser degree) will cause a reduction in air density. Thus, in hot and humid conditions, the density altitude at a particular location may be significantly higher than the true altitude.

Downburst: A strong column of descending air associated with thunderstorms. Synonym – Microburst.

Downdraft: Rapidly descending air usually on the lee side of mountains.

Drop door: The door on the bottom of a retardant-tank compartment. Most Fire Bombing aircraft have two or more compartments on the retardant tank. Synonym – Tank door.

Dry lightning: A lightning storm with negligible precipitation reaching the ground.

Escalation of Effort: The philosophy of limited ground attack and upping the firefighting resources as needed when the fire continues to spread.

Extinguished: A forest fire that has had all traces of fire extinguished.

Fire Bomber: An aircraft carrying retardant for the purpose of laying fire line around a forest fire. Synonyms – Water Bomber, Retardant Bomber.

Fire boss: The man in charge of fire fighting activities on the ground (Canada). Synonym – Incident commander (USA).

Fire bust: The occurrence of a large number of forest fires in a relatively short time.

Fire front: A burning line of fire.

Fire line: A line scraped down to mineral soil by hand or mechanical equipment for the purpose of stopping the spread of a forest fire. Synonym — Fire guard.

Fire retardant: Water or chemicals that reduce the flammability of combustible fuels.

Forest fire: A fire burning forest values not part of a prescribed burn or part of forest management according to a pre-arranged plan (Canada). Synonym — Wildfire (USA).

Ground cushion: A cushion of air under a low- flying aircraft put there by the aircraft itself.

Ground loop: The uncontrolled spinning of an aircraft on the ground around its main landing gear.

Hand line: A physical firebreak made by hand tools.

Helitack crew: The crew delivered to an initial attack on a fire by helicopter.

Hot spot: A small area flaring up along a less active fire front.

Initial attack: The first action on a forest fire whether by a ground crew or by Fire Bombers.

Jettison area: A selected area near a tanker base where retardant is jettisoned to lighten an aircraft in preparation for landing.

Lead plane: A Fire Control Officer who both flies the airplane and directs the air attack.

Long-term retardant: A chemical (ammonium sulfate) that when mixed with water attacks all sides of the fire triangle, which are heat, fuel and oxygen.

Maximum drop speed: The speed limit for dropping a load of retardant. It is normally the top desirable speed for effective load drop, or the flap limiting speed of the aircraft.

Microburst: A strong column of descending air associated with thunderstorms. Synonym – Downburst.

One Strike concept: The instant dispatch of enough retardant to every reported fire to contain it in a continuous action without the need for the aircraft to make an additional trip.

Orbit: The Birddog assigned area and altitude for aircraft waiting their turn to drop.

Pacific High: A high-pressure cell producing a predominantly westerly flow of maritime air over California. A strong, persistent vertical temperature inversion is another dominant feature of the Pacific high.

Parts of a fire:
Fingers – The long narrow tongues of a fire projecting from the main body.
Flanks – The edges of the fire between the Head and the Rear or Base.

Front – Synonymous with Head.
Head – The portion of the edge of a fire where the rate-of-spread is most rapid.
Rear – The edge of the fire with the slowest rate of spread.
Base – Synonymous with Rear.

Pattern: The shape, size and wetness level of retardant on the ground.

Pitch-up: The pitch up of the nose of an aircraft caused by the downward flow of air on the aft fuselage and horizontal stabilizer moving into the area of low pressure immediately behind a dropped load of retardant.

Recovery: The increase in fuel moisture as a result of increased relative humidity, usually occurring at night.

Retardant tank: The tank for carrying the retardant. The tanks are in the bomb bay on surplus military aircraft and are mounted externally on civil aircraft. Purpose-designed Fire Bombers like the CL-215 and the Russian Ilyshin-76 and AE 200 have internal tanks. Flying boat adaptations such as the Martin Mars, Beaver, Otter, PBY, and Twin Otter also carry the water internally.

Return and load: A directive from Birddog to the Fire Bomber to reload with retardant and return to the fire.

Return and stay: A directive from Birddog to the Fire Bomber to return to base and stay.

Rotor wind: A strong wind blowing over the top of a mountain or a mountain range that causes rotational vortices on the leeward side.

Short-term retardant: A chemical, clay or surfactant added to water to increase the water's effectiveness in containing a fire.

Smoke jumpers: Men trained and equipped to parachute into remote areas for the purpose of making an initial attack on a forest fire.

Snag: A tree that is higher than the surrounding canopy.

Squirrel fires: Fires inadvertently lit by squirrels set on fire by their shorting-out of power lines

Spot fire: A fire of such dimensions that it may be straddled by a dropped load of retardant from any direction. It's normally the fire size when first detected.

Stall margin indicator (SMI): An instrument showing the pilot how close he is to the stall. Synonym— Angle of attack indicator (AOA).

Support action: Tanker action in support of a ground crew working on a fire.

Surface fire: A fire burning the fuel on the forest floor.

Tank door: The door on the bottom of a retardant-tank compartment. Most Fire Bombing aircraft have two or more compartments on the retardant tank.

Terminal velocity: A load of air-dropped retardant in its state of free fall and drift.

Top of canopy: The surface with reference to bombing procedure. The top surface of the trees as it appears from the air.

Updraft: Columns of rising air caused either by orographic lift, daytime convection currents or thunderstorms.

Water Bomber fire action: An initial and supporting attack on a forest fire based on a fast and continuous delivery of water by Air Tankers until complete control of the fire is achieved by ground personnel.

Wildfire: A fire burning forest values not part of a prescribed burn or part of forest management according to a pre-arranged plan (USA). Synonym – Forest fire (Canada).

Wind shear: The turbulent zone in between winds flowing in different directions shearing off against each other. The shearing can occur between winds blowing horizontally or between updrafts and downdrafts

About the Author

Linc Alexander began his flying career in 1951. After getting his commercial license, his first employment was with Superior Airways based in Fort William, Ontario. Two years of bush flying in the Canadian North convinced Linc that man-handling forty-five gallon drums of gas in and out of airplanes during the mosquito-infested summer and the sub-zero blizzards of winter were not the stuff of a great flying career. To really learn about flying and to have the adventure and fun of flying high-powered jets, Linc joined the Royal Canadian Air Force in 1953 for the Short Service Commission program. He didn't fly the fighters of his choice but spent his entire term in Training Command becoming a highly competent instructor. Immediately after his discharge from his military service in 1959, Linc began his Fire Bombing career. It was the adventure that would last for the rest of his flying life. In 1972, Linc published *Air Attack on Forest Fires,* the definitive manual on the techniques of Fire Bombing that sold to fire fighting agencies and pilots world-wide. In 1980, Linc did a name change from his birth name of Alexander Linkewich to Linc W. Alexander. Linc lives in Vancouver, British Columbia, Canada.

CPSIA information can be obtained
at www.ICGtesting.com
Printed in the USA
BVOW11s2103280717

490492BV00017B/254/P

9 781609 104368